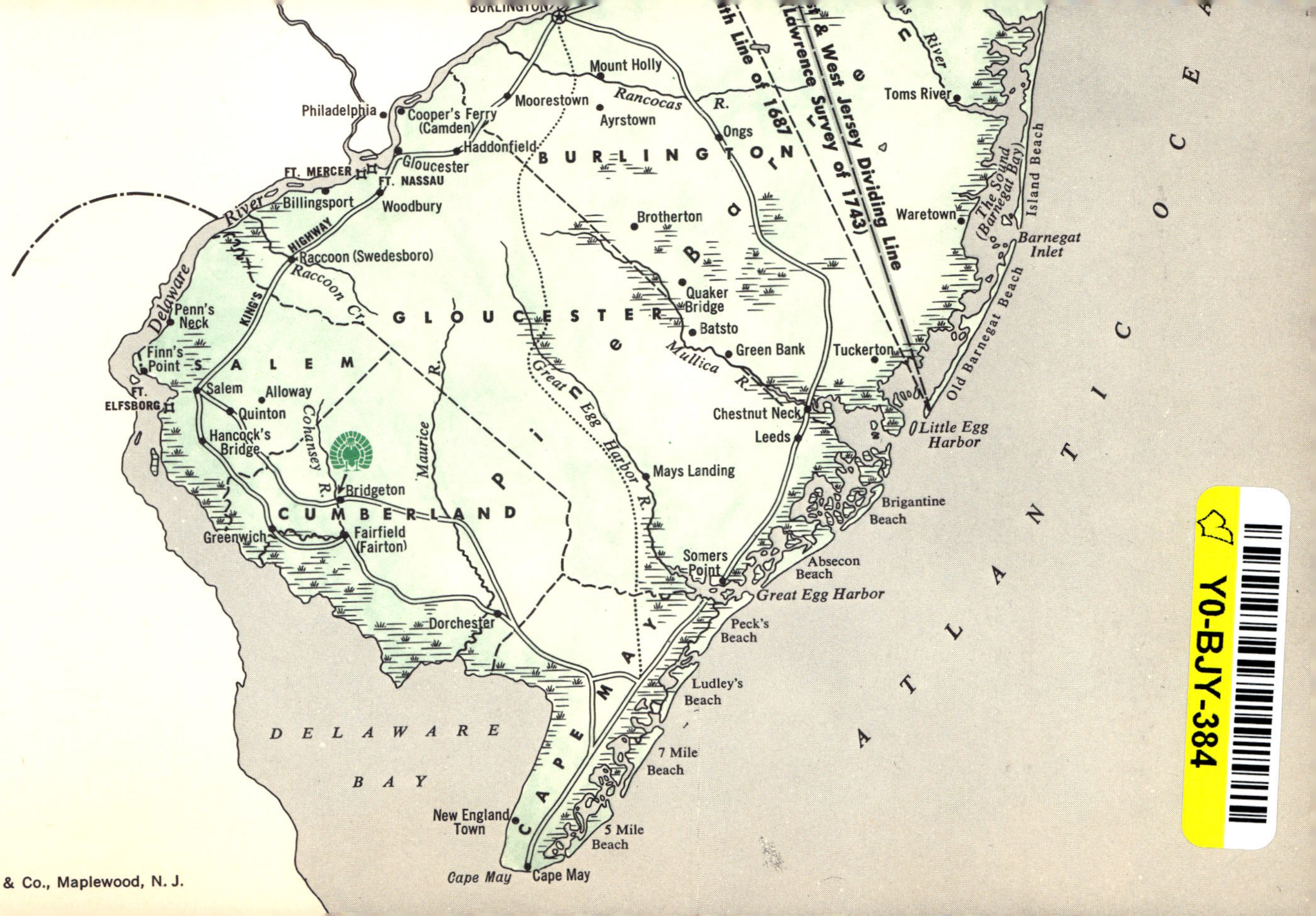

BURLINGTON
Mount Holly
Moorestown
Rancocas R.
Ayrstown
Philadelphia
Cooper's Ferry (Camden)
Ongs
Haddonfield
BURLINGTON
Gloucester
FT. MERCER
FT. NASSAU
Billingsport
Woodbury
Brotherton
River
HIGHWAY
Raccoon (Swedesboro)
Raccoon Cr.
Delaware
KING'S
Quaker Bridge
Penn's Neck
GLOUCESTER
Batsto
Finn's Point
SALEM
Green Bank
Tuckerton
Mullica R.
Salem
Alloway
FT. ELFSBORG
Quinton
Cohansey R.
Maurice R.
Great Egg Harbor R.
Chestnut Neck
Hancock's Bridge
Leeds
Mays Landing
Bridgeton
CUMBERLAND
Greenwich
Fairfield (Fairton)
Somers Point
Dorchester
CAPE MAY
DELAWARE BAY
New England Town
Cape May
Toms River
Waretown
The Sound (Barnegat Bay)
Island Beach
Barnegat Inlet
Old Barnegat Beach
Little Egg Harbor
Brigantine Beach
Absecon Beach
Great Egg Harbor
Peck's Beach
Ludley's Beach
7 Mile Beach
5 Mile Beach
ATLANTIC OCEA
East & West Jersey Dividing Line
(Lawrence Survey of 1743)
Keith Line of 1687

*Fundamental Laws and
Constitutions of New Jersey*

THE NEW JERSEY HISTORICAL SERIES

Edited by

RICHARD M. HUBER   WHEATON J. LANE

New Jersey from Colony to State—1609-1789	Richard P. McCormick
New Jersey and the Civil War	Earl Schenck Miers
New Jersey and the English Colonization of North America	Wesley Frank Craven
The Story of the Jersey Shore	Harold F. Wilson
Princeton and Rutgers: The Two Colonial Colleges of New Jersey	George P. Schmidt
Architecture in New Jersey	Alan Gowans
Elementary Education in New Jersey: A History	Roscoe L. West
The New Jersey High School: A History	Robert D. Bole and Laurence B. Johnson
The New Jersey Proprietors and Their Lands	John E. Pomfret
The Early Dutch and Swedish Settlers of New Jersey	Adrian C. Leiby
New Jersey and the Revolutionary War	Alfred Hoyt Bill
Fundamental Laws and Constitutions of New Jersey	Julian P. Boyd
Medicine and Health in New Jersey: A History	David L. Cowen
New Jersey in the Automobile Age: A History of Transportation	H. Jerome Cranmer
Religion in New Jersey: A Brief History	Wallace N. Jamison
The New Jersey Governor: A Study in Political Power	Duane Lockard
The Research State: A History of Science in New Jersey	John R. Pierce and Arthur G. Tressler
Radicals and Visionaries: A History of Dissent in New Jersey	Morris Schonbach
Historic New Jersey Through Visitors' Eyes	Miriam V. Studley
The Decorative Arts of Early New Jersey	Margaret E. White
Where Cities Meet: The Urbanization of New Jersey	John E. Bebout and Ronald J. Grele
A Narrative and Descriptive Bibliography of New Jersey	Nelson R. Burr
The Literary Heritage of New Jersey	Laurence B. Holland Nathaniel Burt and Arthur W. Litz
Painting and Sculpture in New Jersey	William H. Gerdts, Jr.
Life in Early New Jersey	Harry B. Weiss
The Geology and Geography of New Jersey	Kemble Widmer

SUPPLEMENTS

Woodrow Wilson, Reform Governor	David W. Hirst
Banking and Insurance in New Jersey: A History	Bruce H. French
Tours of Historic New Jersey	Adeline Pepper

Volume 17
The New Jersey Historical Series

Fundamental Laws and Constitutions of New Jersey

1664 - 1964

Edited with Introduction by
JULIAN P. BOYD

1964

D. VAN NOSTRAND COMPANY, INC.
Princeton, New Jersey
New York, N. Y. • Toronto, Canada • London, England

D. VAN NOSTRAND COMPANY, INC.
120 Alexander St., Princeton, New Jersey (*Principal office*)
24 West 40 Street, New York 18, New York

D. VAN NOSTRAND COMPANY, LTD.
358, Kensington High Street, London, W.14, England

D. VAN NOSTRAND COMPANY (*Canada*), LTD.
25 Hollinger Road, Toronto 16, Canada

COPYRIGHT © 1964, BY
THE NEW JERSEY TERCENTENARY COMMISSION

Published simultaneously in Canada by
D. VAN NOSTRAND COMPANY (Canada), LTD.

No reproduction in any form of this book, in whole or in part (except for brief quotation in critical articles or reviews), may be made without written authorization from the publishers.

PRINTED IN THE UNITED STATES OF AMERICA

To the Memory of
AARON LEAMING
and
JACOB SPICER

Compilers of *The Grants, Concessions, and Original Constitutions of the Province of New-Jersey* (Philadelphia, 1756), who understood well the nature of fundamental law and the responsibility placed upon editors of documents. Their work in protecting the foundation stones of New Jersey law should be regarded with pride and gratitude by all citizens of the State.

FOREWORD

Many tracks will be left by the New Jersey Tercentenary celebration, but few will be larger than those made by the New Jersey Historical Series. The Series is a monumenal publishing project—the product of a remarkable collaborative effort between public and private enterprise.

New Jersey has needed a series of books about itself. The 300th anniversary of the State is a fitting time to publish such a series. It is to the credit of the State's Tercentenary Commission that this series has been created.

In an enterprise of such scope, there must be many contributors. Each of these must give considerably of himself if the enterprise is to succeed. The New Jersey Historical Series, the most ambitious publishing venture ever undertaken about a state, was conceived by a committee of Jerseymen—Julian P. Boyd, Wesley Frank Craven, John T. Cunningham, David S. Davies, and Richard P. McCormick. Not only did these men outline the need for such an historic venture; they also aided in the selection of the editors of the series.

Both jobs were well done. The volumes speak for themselves. The devoted and scholarly services of Richard M. Huber and Wheaton J. Lane, the editors, are a part of every book in the series. The editors have been aided in their work by two fine assistants, Elizabeth Jackson Holland and Bertha DeGraw Miller.

To D. Van Nostrand Company, Inc. my special thanks for recognizing New Jersey's need and for bringing their skills and publishing wisdom to bear upon the printing and distributing of the New Jersey Historical Series.

My final and most heartfelt thanks must go to Julian P. Boyd, who accepted my invitation to edit *Fundamental Laws and Constitutions of New Jersey*, doing so at great personal sacrifice and without thought of material gain. We are richer by his scholarship. We welcome this important contribution to an understanding of our State.

January, 1964

RICHARD J. HUGHES
*Governor of the
State of New Jersey*

PREFACE

This is not a history of constitutional law in New Jersey but a selection of the fundamental instruments of government under which the people have lived during the past three centuries. These are presented in the belief that every citizen should know something of the origins of his own institutions, both because his public duty commands it and because his spirit, to be elevated, requires it. Other documents might well have been added, such as the judicial interpretations of the written law and the occasional acts of legislative construction. This selection is limited to those basic laws that could not by any standard of judgment be omitted. They are central to the record of constitutional experience in this state from 1664 to 1964. Among them is one—the Concessions and Agreements of 1677—so humane in purpose and so noble in dimension that it stands among the greatest of all monuments marking the course of government by consent. Others at times seem to point in various directions, even backward, as if in confusion and uncertainty. But all have in common one indispensable element. This is a seemingly fragile thread of gold—elusive, easily mistaken, sometimes forgotten, but unbroken and indeed indestructible—running through all of these fabrics of government and connecting the last with the first. The nature of that thread was identified by the first compilers of a collection of the fundamental laws of New Jersey, two centuries ago, as "Liberty, the great Legament."

When Aaron Leaming and Jacob Spicer published *The Grants, Concessions, and Original Constitutions of the Province of New-Jersey* in 1756, they declared that such a ligament had the strength to raise a kingdom, or, if broken, to "ruin the finest Constitution on Earth." They saw this as the true explanation for the progress and political stability of the people who in less than a century had transformed a wilderness into a civilized society. Civil and religious freedom were, they declared: not only essential for the speedy Settlement of a Colony, but also for the happy Government thereof; because the Prince by his Kingly Office not only protects the Subjects in the Enjoyment of their just Liberties, but they in like Manner defend him from foreign Injury, which creates a mutual Dependance on each other, accompanied with sincere Affection, and tempered with virtue and Morality, the social Blessings of human Life, and while this necessary Condition exists, the Frame of Government is inviolably preserved; break but the Chain and the whole Frame is dissolved, which is verifyed in those unconstitutional Revolutions . . . which happen at the Courts of arbitrary Princes, whose despotic Powers usurps the Peoples Priviledges, and they in their desperate Struggles dethrone the Tyrant.

The words seem awkward and unfamiliar today, but the men who wrote them and the fundamental laws they codified could only have emerged from a society having back of it centuries of experience in developing the concept of limited government. In the light of history the words also seem like an admonition, for within two short decades the connection between the kingly office and the subjects was broken. Yet in 1776 the people of New Jersey who disavowed their allegiance to George III did not think of themselves as engaging in one of "those unconstitutional Revolutions . . . which happen at the Courts of arbitrary Princes." They joined other Americans in declaring that allegiance and protection were reciprocal ties and "liable to be dissolved by the other's being refused or withdrawn." It was the monarch himself, they asserted, who had broken the compact by withdrawing his protection—just as Parliament had declared in 1689 that the King had invaded "the fundamental constitution of the kingdom, and altered it from a legal monarchy, to an arbitrary despotick power."

Thus the concept of limited government that had enabled England to plant a flourishing civilization where other empires had failed also furnished the rhetoric for revolution. When the time came, men in New Jersey and elsewhere proved that the idea of constitutional monarchy had prepared them well for the responsibility of self-government. One distinguished American jurist and historian who remained loyal to the Crown, William Smith, said that the dissolution of the ties had been made inevitable by those "chartered Republics of the Stuart Kings"—that is, by those documents of the seventeenth century such as the fundamental instruments of government in New Jersey that Leaming and Spicer, as if to prove him right, had called "popular Plans of Freedom." But the great ligament of liberty did not begin or end with kings. It ran unbroken through the upheaval of revolution that substituted democratic for kingly rule. Its existence was not dependent upon the concept of monarchy or indeed—as the Declaration of Independence itself implied—upon any particular form of government. Its origins lay deep in the human spirit and it would remain indissoluble only so long as it continued to be cherished there. Should men cease to value it, or begin to confuse the forms of government with the sovereign rights and duties that were theirs, no constitutions or laws could preserve it unbroken.

Like the constitutions of New Jersey themselves, this compilation owes much to the work of others, first of all to the two men to whom this volume is dedicated. To Mr. Bernard Bush, Historical Editor, Bureau of Archives and History, New Jersey State Library, I am indebted beyond my capacity to discharge. For his valuable assistance in locating and procuring copies of these basic laws and for equally important bibliographical aids, I wish to express my warm gratitude and at the same time to absolve him from any responsibility for errors of opinion or of textual presentation for which I alone should be held accountable. To the officers of The New Jersey Historical Society I wish to express my gratitude for permission to use their copy of the Concessions and Agreement of 1665. Efforts to discover a corresponding copy of that instrument in England proved fruitless, but for generous assistance to me in my quest I wish to thank Ambassador David K. E. Bruce, Mr. Francis L. Berkeley, Jr., Miss W. D. Coates and her associates in that remarkably useful institution, the National Register of Archives, Mr. Irvine Gray, Archivist of Gloucestershire, and of course the officials of the British Museum and the Public Record Office. To the Council of the Proprietors of the Western Division of New Jersey at Burlington I am particularly grateful for permission to use their magnificent original manuscript of the Concessions and Agreements of 1677. To my old friend and colleague, Professor Wesley Frank Craven, I am most grateful for encouragement and for protection against many pitfalls in the colonial period of New Jersey history. To Wheaton J. Lane and Richard M. Huber, who have included me within the sphere of their public-spirited endeavors, I am deeply obligated; they have been both patient and understanding. My gratitude to Mrs. Edwin C. Hutter, who compiled the index with her customary spirit of helpfulness and her equally habitual accuracy and thoroughness, is immense.

JULIAN P. BOYD

Princeton, New Jersey
April, 1964

CONTENTS

	Foreword	vii
	Preface	ix
	Introduction	2
I.	The Concessions and Agreement of the Lords Proprietors of the Province of New-Jersey, February 10, 1664/1665	51
II.	A Declaration of the True Intent and Meaning of the Concessions and Agreement, December 6, 1672	67
III.	The Concessions and Agreements of the Proprietors, Freeholders, and Inhabitants of the Province of West New-Jersey, March 3, 1676/1677	71
IV.	The Fundamental Agreements of the Governor, Proprietors, Freeholders, and Inhabitants of the Province of West New-Jersey, November 25, 1681	105
V.	The Fundamental Constitutions for the Province of East New-Jersey, 1683	109
VI.	The Instructions from the Queen to the Governor of New-Jersey, November 16, 1702	126
VII.	The Constitution of the State of New Jersey, July 2, 1776	155
VIII.	The Constitution of the State of New Jersey, June 29, 1844 (as amended)	164
IX.	The Constitution of the State of New Jersey, September 10, 1947 (as amended to November 1, 1961)	193
	Bibliographical Note	235
	Index	239

xiii

In every Government there must be Somewhat Fundamental, Somewhat like a Magna Charta, which should be standing, be unalterable.
—Oliver Cromwell

Had our former Constitution been unalterable (pardon the absurdity of the hypothesis), we must have gone to ruin with our eyes open.
—Thomas Jefferson

INTRODUCTION

Two cardinal and contradictory impulses have persisted, quite naturally, through three centuries of development of constitutional law in New Jersey. On the one hand there has been the insistent demand for an organic law establishing the form of government and placing the rights of the individual to his person, his liberty, and his property beyond the reach of arbitrary power or of legislative enactment. On the other hand there has been an equally insistent demand that the fundamental law itself be altered in order to meet the changing necessities of human society. These opposing impulses are characteristic of all limited government. They may indeed be said to reflect the two warring attitudes that Goethe, among others, thought had divided mankind since the world began: the spirit of stability and the spirit of innovation. Constitutions are therefore by nature born of conflict.

Hence it is not surprising that each of the four stages marking the major constitutional developments in New Jersey should have come at periods of crisis, of clashing ideas, interests, and aspirations. From the Concessions and Agreement of 1665 to the Constitution of 1947 no single instrument that could be described as fundamental law was created in a period of quiet and stability. All emerged in periods of agitation and controversy over issues that ran deep. Such was the age of William Penn in the seventeenth century when a new spirit of freedom, of toleration, of rational inquiry, and of religious diversity began to challenge the old absolutes of the royal prerogative, the alliance of church and state, and the hierarchical ordering of the social structure. Such was the age of the American Revolution when the germinating ideas of the seventeenth century caused a dismemberment of the British Empire and ushered in what the new nation described on its great seal as *Novus Ordo Seclorum* —a new order of the ages. Such was the second quarter of the nineteenth century when the equalitarianism of Jacksonian democracy collided with the dynamics of corporate finance and emerging industrialism. And such, above all, is our own age which stands at the beginning of a new era in history and in the midst of immense revolutions that tend both to fragment and to unify world society. It is almost axiomatic that the fundamental instruments of government between 1665 and 1702 and the constitutions of New Jersey of 1776, 1844, and 1947 should have come forth in a time of crisis.

It is equally so that, since change in the fundamental law is produced by contending forces, its various expressions should result in compromise. Only rarely in the progress of limited government have men been able to achieve out of conflict and suffering such enlightened views of human society as William Penn and his associates set forth in the Concessions and Agreements of 1677, placing there a beacon that would guide and influence those drafting constitutions a century later. Nor should it be surprising that the constitutions of this and other states harmonize and confirm attitudes belonging to the past more often than they introduce untried expedients. For the spirit that holds fast to the established order, that prefers what is known and certain to what is not drawn from experience, has almost always had the advantage in the struggle for constitutional revision. The fundamental law has the claim and the right to exist until arguments powerful and appealing enough to overcome its institutional inertia are brought to bear upon it. Not all basic laws are so explicit in affirming this as the Fundamental Agreements of West New Jersey of 1681, which declared "the prevention of innovacion" to be one of the reasons for its existence. But explicit or not, this is an inherent characteristic of such instruments of government.

Being compromises born of crisis and inherently conservative by nature, fundamental laws cannot avoid possessing from the moment of adoption many of the qualities of a strait jacket. These restrictive characteristics in the past three centuries have become progressively more dominant. The reasons for this are clear. The rate of social change in the twentieth century is far greater than in any previous age, and this force tending to increase the rate of obsolescence of the fundamental law has coincided with other factors having a similar effect. The first of these is the declining spirit of political experimentation. In the late eighteenth century—the greatest period of political innovation that the country has known—the people and their leaders, when confronted by a problem of unprecedented difficulty (such as that of devising a form of federalism applicable to a great extent of territory, something never before thought feasible), did not hesitate to hazard an ingenious and untried solution. Men of the twentieth century seem less daring in the realm of politics, though bold enough in scientific and other forms of exploration. Second, the outward forms of constitutional guarantees take on with increasing age the character of venerated stereotypes almost immune to challenge, yet lack the vibrant meaning imparted to them in an earlier day by the passionate convictions of those who first wrote them into law. Third, men of the twentieth century seem more readily disposed to embrace compromise and to avoid controversy than their predecessors were, thus magnifying the inherent dangers of constitutions as accommodations of competing aims and interests. Among other effects this has led to an increased blurring of the line between statutory enactments which belong properly to the legislative powers and fundamental principles which deserve the status of constitutional protection. All modern state constitutions reflect this tendency and it is therefore not surprising that the latest fundamental law of New Jersey should be the longest and most detailed in three centuries. There was even admitted to its declaration of Rights and Privileges, which theretofore had properly confined its guarantees to the rights of all persons, a measure applying to particular groups and therefore having some of the characteristics of special legislation.*

Such confusion over the nature of fundamental law foreshadows grave consequences for the idea of limited government as it has developed over the centuries. Paradoxically, the greatest danger may come in those areas that are the object of the greatest veneration, those guaranteeing civil rights. For, as the twentieth century has proved, these are unchallengeable as to the letter of the fundamental law, yet in its spirit they have suffered. When William Penn and his fellows declared in the Concessions and Agreements of 1677 that "No Men nor number of Men upon Earth hath power or Authority to rule over mens consciences in religious matters," they spoke out of bitter experience. This was not the first guarantee of religious freedom in American fundamental law, for Roger Williams had already won that honor for Rhode Island in the Charter of 1663. The New Jersey Concessions and Agreement of 1665 also took precedence over it, drawing its guarantee almost verbatim from the Rhode Island Charter. The Carolina Charter of 1665, William Penn's Frame of Government for Pennsylvania of 1682, the Fundamental Agreements of West New-Jersey of 1681, and the Fundamental Constitutions of East New-Jersey of 1683 all reflected the fact that the impulse toward full liberty of conscience had its roots in seventeenth-century England.

---

* Article I, Section 19, of the Constitution of 1947 recognizes the right of persons in private employment to organize and to bargain collectively, and the right of persons in public employment to organize and to make known their grievances. Even without legislative sanction this is a right almost universally conceded, but recognition through legislation would have been adequate and would have been the means by which, in any case, the terms defining and governing the exercise of the right would have to be stated. Excessive detail is particularly noticeable in Article XI, where provisions for putting the new system of courts into effect occupy as much space as Article VI providing for the judiciary itself.

But, in an age in which the civil and ecclesiastical authorities were everywhere united in the governments of Europe, the establishment of the doctrine of separation of church and state became distinctly an American achievement. Due in no small measure to the Society of Friends and to the fundamental instruments of government that they created or influenced, New Jersey was one of the four original states that never had an established or preferred religion. Nevertheless, while the doctrine of separation of church and state has back of it three full centuries of protection in the fundamental laws and constitutions of New Jersey, the ancient phrases have worn smooth with use. They echo but cannot convey the full meaning of authoritarian measures that brought them into being and caused them to be placed first among the fundamental guarantees of individual right. They cannot have the impact upon men in the twentieth century that they had upon their predecessors three centuries ago, for the heirs of those who first wrote the doctrine into fundamental law have never lived under any other, have never undergone the bitter trials over beliefs their ancestors experienced, and indeed have often failed to remember the hard-won lessons of that experience. Thus, while the letter of the law is hallowed and unassailable, its spirit has received increasing numbers of invasions in the decisions of elected representatives and officials and most of all in the attitudes and beliefs of men in an age in which controversy is avoided and compromise even on fundamental issues too readily embraced. On this issue with William Penn and his fellows, there was no compromise and no surrender, not even when the doors of prisons swung open before them.*

It is significant, therefore, that the noblest of the constitutions of New Jersey, while giving minute attention

---

* It has been estimated reliably that no less than twenty thousand Friends were fined or imprisoned during the Restoration period and that 450 died as a result of imprisonment. See W. C. Braithwaite, *The Second Period of Quakerism* (London, 1921), 88-176.

to the forms of government and to the protection of property rights, placed first among its concerns the fundamental principles of human rights. This great document, the Fundamental Concessions and Agreements of 1677, was not the work of men who avoided controversy involving civil rights. On such issues its authors met opposing convictions with unyielding loyalty to their own. Placing this early fundamental law of New Jersey beside the latest and bearing in mind the inherent characteristics of all constitutions, one cannot avoid noting a shift of emphasis over the centuries. Where concern for fundamental right once formed the impulse creating organic law and placing it beyond the reach of monarch or representative, the dominant emphasis now focuses upon the forms of government, the efficiency of administration, and the machinery of organized society. The shift of emphasis in constitutional revision from the rights of the individual to the efficiency of the governmental machine may point a useful lesson. It may also be symbolic of the greatest danger among all those confronting the idea of fundamental law. For as New Jersey enters her fourth century of constitutional experience, her people in common with all others enter an era in which the individual stands threatened from new directions by forces of an unprecedented character. The machines that promise freedom from age-old burdens and fears also threaten revolutionary new shackles for the human spirit. The future in its accelerating rush upon the present may prove, therefore, that the forms and machinery of government which received the greatest emphasis in the latest constitutional revision were given a disproportionate share of attention. The old guarantees of protection to the individual will remain fixed in the constitutional firmament. But, in a new epoch in human history that seems to threaten the individual in a manner inconceivable to the authors of the Concessions and Agreements of 1677, new concepts of individual right may have to be added to the old and hallowed propositions. If so, the new dangers can scarcely be met solely by repairing the machinery of government. The first need will be that of rescuing the idea of fundamental law itself from the confusions into which it has drifted. Once this is done the imbalanced emphasis may be redressed and the impulse to constitutional revision restored to something more nearly resembling that spirit which animated the beginnings of the idea of limited government many centuries ago.

"The American constitutions," wrote Thomas Paine, "were to liberty, what a grammar is to language: they define its parts of speech, and practically construct them into a syntax." But even the grammar of liberty is not immutable. "I am certainly not an advocate for frequent and untried changes in laws and constitutions . . . ," wrote Thomas Jefferson in 1816, "but I know also that laws and institutions must go hand in hand with the progress of the human mind. As that becomes more developed, more enlightened, as new discoveries are made, new truths disclosed, and manners and opinions change with the change of circumstances, institutions must advance also." A few years later this foremost American spokesman for human freedom stated the proposition that must be regarded as his single absolute: "nothing, then, is unchangeable but the inherent and unalienable rights of man."

Neither this concept of liberty nor the idea of fundamental law precludes a fresh assessment of the old guarantees or the possibility that new ones might be required to meet new dangers. Both, in fact, have always demanded this. In the beginning of constitutional law in New Jersey this insistent demand met with a ready response, animated by profound convictions that reason and justice should be made to prevail in the affairs of men. That is why the greatest of the beacons erected here still shines across three centuries with its assurance that this can best be achieved by fidelity to the ancient principles of limited government and also with its salutary warning that new guarantees in a later age might again become imperative.

The Fundamental Laws of New Jersey, 1665-1702

The grants of patents by Queen Elizabeth to Sir Walter Raleigh in 1584, by James I to the Virginia Company in 1606, and by Charles I to Sir Edmund Plowden in 1634 all embraced the area of what is now New Jersey. The grant to Plowden and his associates was, in fact, the first English colonizing grant in the disputed area occupied by Swedes and Dutch; but there was pressure from English settlements both north and south even before Charles II in 1664 simultaneously made a grant to his brother James, Duke of York, and mounted an expedition against New Netherland. The outcome was a foregone conclusion and the Duke of York, while the expedition was on the high seas, conveyed the better part of his grant of territory to John Lord Berkeley and Sir George Carteret, who had hatched up the scheme and had performed the not very difficult task of finding pretexts for this descent upon the Dutch. The following year Berkeley and Carteret issued over their signatures "The Concessions and Agreement of the Lords Proprietors of the Province of New Cæsarea or New-Jersey" as an encouragement to adventurers and settlers. With this document there began three centuries of fundamental law in New Jersey.

This instrument of government possessed the nature of a constitution even though, being handed down by a superior claiming both the right of territory and the right of government, it differs from the modern concept of an organic law as one created by the sovereign power residing in the people. It provided for a governor representing the proprietors, a council appointed by him and other officials designated by the proprietors or by him, and a general assembly consisting of the governor, members of the council, and elected representatives. The franchise was limited to freeholders and annual elections for the twelve representatives of the lower house were authorized. The legislature had authority to create courts of law, to levy taxes, to raise a militia, to establish local units of government, and to enact all other necessary laws provided they were "consonant to reason and, as neare as may be conveniently agreeable to the Lawes and Customes of his Majesties Kingdom of England" and not against the interest of the proprietors or their heirs. The proprietors reserved the right to give their assent or refusal to such legislation. Certain private rights were assured, among them the guarantee of liberty of conscience. No taxes were to be levied without the consent of the representatives. Possession of land for seven years operated as a proscription against review or resurvey.

Thus this first instrument establishing government in New Jersey was in the nature of an implied compact between the proprietors and the people, granting to the latter enjoyment of the stipulated "Freedoms and Imunities . . . untill the Lords see cause to the contrary." It was feudal in its underlying theory, but it did make a definite commitment to a government that was given a precise outline and was intended to operate within prescribed limits. It therefore possessed the essential element of fundamental law. It would be a mistake, however, to assume that the broad guarantees of freedom of religion represented genuine conviction on the part of the proprietors. The promise of limited government, the protection given to individual rights and immunities, and the assurance that the guarantees of religious freedom would never be revoked, along with the precise definition of property rights—all of these were intended to attract settlers to New Jersey and thus to promote the primary object of the proprietors, which was to increase the value of their estate. Added to this was the aim of drawing off from the realm the troublesome element whose radical dissent to the prevailing alliance of church and state found little sympathy in the breasts of the proprietors and of others who found the established order good. If this element so disturbing to the quiet of the realm could promote settlement, the proprietors found no reason for withholding from their Concessions and Agreement the religious guarantees that would serve as an inducement to colonization. Thus in one sense the underlying motive was not dissimilar to that colonizing policy of banishing felons, imprisoned debtors, and other undesirables to the colonies. Such a policy was regarded as a wholesome suppurative for the body politic.

That the objective of the proprietors was basically that of advancing their proprietary interest is shown by their "Declaration of the True Intent and Meaning, and Explanation of the Concessions" which they issued in 1672. This document was renewed in 1674, after the brief Dutch repossession of New Netherland and after the Duke of York's reconveyance of the eastern part of New Jersey to Sir George Carteret, Berkeley having disposed of his interest. The primary purpose of The Declaration of the True Intent was to increase the power of the governor and to restrict the liberties and privileges of the colonists. No person thenceforth could vote or hold office unless he held land under proprietary title. The rebellion of the inhabitants that had broken out in 1672 over this issue thus ended in an emphatic victory for the proprietors.

Berkeley sold his interest in New Jersey in 1674 to John Fenwick who was acting in behalf of Edward Byllynge. Both of these men were Quakers and the latter became a bankrupt whose affairs had to be placed under the management of trustees, one of whom was William Penn. In 1676 these trustees, who had decided to plant a free Quaker commonwealth in the new world, persuaded Carteret to permit a division of the province into East and West New Jersey. This was effected by the Quintipartite deed of that year signed by Carteret, Byllynge, and the three trustees, a division which lasted until New Jersey was reunited as a royal colony in 1702. William Penn and the other trustees were thus confronted with the task of preparing a form of government for the western division of the province and in 1677 they brought forth the Concessions and Agreements.

This notable document has long been considered to be primarily the work of William Penn—and with good reason. This great humanitarian had long contended that the rights and liberties of Englishmen were being threatened by increasing materialism and authoritarianism. In *The Peoples Ancient and Just Liberties Ass'rted* in 1670 and in other tracts he had repeatedly sounded this warning. On trial that same year for inciting to riot, Penn had suffered indignities and harrassment before an arbitrary court and had dared to challenge its abuse of the fundamental right of a jury to bring in a verdict, a challenge later upheld by the Court of King's Bench. This devout statesman, with his courageous liberalism, his insistent effort to harmonize the law and the Christian ethic, and his simple humanitarianism, was quite naturally regarded as the principal author of a document which included such eloquent affirmations of human rights as had never before been uttered in any American fundamental law. There, wrote the Trustees in 1675,

> we lay a foundation for after ages to understand their liberty as men and christians, that they may not be brought in bondage, but by their own consent; for we put the power in the people, that is to say, they to meet, and choose one honest man for each propriety, who hath subscribed to the concessions; all these men to meet in an assembly there, to make and repeal laws, to choose a governor, or a commissioner, and twelve assistants, to execute the laws during their pleasure; so every man is capable to choose or be chosen; No man to be arrested, condemned, imprisoned, or molested in his estate or liberty, but by twelve men of the neighbourhood. No man is to lie in prison for debt, but that his estate satisfy as far as it will go, and be set at liberty for work; No person to be called in question or molested for his conscience, or for worshipping according to his conscience; with many more things mentioned in the said concessions.*

One who possessed William Penn's profound convictions about civil and religious liberty might well have written

---

* Byllynge, Penn, and others to Richard Hartshorne, August 26, 1676, *New Jersey Archives*, 1st ser. (Newark, 1880), I, 228. This letter describes an early copy of the Concessions sent over to New Jersey.

these words. His influence undoubtedly was felt in the document. But recent discoveries suggest that Edward Byllynge should be accorded the greater share of the honor of having drafted this noble document.*

There is honor enough for all who may have had a hand in its preparation. The frame of government and guarantees of right in the Concessions stand in stark contrast to the Concessions and Agreement of 1665 and to the Fundamental Constitutions of Carolina of 1669. The plans of government prepared by John Locke and the Earl of Shaftesbury for Carolina had about them the smell of the closet, but this great application of principles of justice and reason to government was grounded in solid reality. It grew out of the actual experience of the Quakers as colonists on the Delaware and also out of the harsh realities of suffering they had known in England. The Concessions might indeed be said to be the first expression of fundamental law in the sense of the constitutions adopted by the American states a century later, for this document went as far toward placing sovereign power in the people as it was possible to go in an empire with a monarch at its head. It actually went further in giving reality to its expression of the idea of government by consent than did the Constitution of New Jersey of 1776, for its frame of government and its guarantees of right were not only submitted to the people— as the Constitution of 1776 was not—but was in fact a

* In John E. Pomfret's "The Problem of the West Jersey Concessions of 1676/7," *William and Mary Quarterly,* 3rd ser., V, 95-105, there is printed a petition of February 28, 1685, by Samuel Jennings and Thomas Budd—the former deputy-governor under Byllynge and the latter one of the original settlers and proprietors of West New Jersey—in which the Concessions is described as "of his [Byllynge's] preparing." Byllynge's later departure from the Concessions does not necessarily invalidate this suggestion. The Duke of York's award of sole right of government to him in 1680 may have awakened ambitions or excited instabilities that were held in check in 1677 by the influence of Penn and others. Pomfret has also given, in *The Province of West New Jersey* (Princeton, 1956), 95-96, the best appraisal of the Concessions as a document arising out of the reality of experience in America and in England.

solemn compact of proprietors, freeholders, and inhabitants in which no traces of the feudal concept of the Concessions and Agreement of 1665 could be found. By it the proprietors voluntarily surrendered their prerogative and gave to the inhabitants the right to elect men to represent their proprietary interest. The belief that all power resided as of right in the people found no more convincing expression than this until, a century later, the royal connection came to an end. Both the frame of government and the guarantees of right convey throughout, in letter and spirit, an unmistakable proof of the deep convictions in civil and religious matters out of which this monument to the progress of human liberty sprang. In every sense this was a true constitution. Its framers declared it to be the "foundation of the Government . . . not to be altered by the Legislative Authority." They forbade that authority to make any enactments "that in the least contradict differ or vary from the said fundamentalls under what pretence or allegation soever."

The General Assembly was granted extensive powers of legislation and representatives were to be paid a shilling a day for time actually served in order to remind them that they were servants of the people. Further, if any member of the assembly should wilfully move or incite any other to move anything whatever that was in contradiction or violation of the fundamental law, and if this should be proved by seven honest and reputable persons, he was to be proceeded against as a traitor—a drastic limitation on legislative construction that no other American constitution dared emulate. Fraud and corruption were also made punishable offenses. Cloture was forbidden, roll calls could be demanded, and the public could even question their representatives in the assembly. Executive powers were to be wielded by ten commissioners elected annually by the resident proprietors, freeholders, and inhabitants using a secret "ballating trunk" in casting their votes. The commissioners were also charged with important judicial duties. Only legislation contrary to the Concessions was subject to veto by the trustees of the proprietary interest.

This noble effort to establish a free commonwealth under humanitarian purposes suffered a disastrous blow when, in 1680, the Duke of York vested the right of government solely in the chief proprietor, Edward Byllynge. To the general astonishment of the people, Byllynge proclaimed himself governor, thus superseding the commissioners as executives and to that extent repudiating the Concessions. Under the influence of Penn and others, Byllynge appointed as his deputy Samuel Jennings, "a resolute and immoveable man," who until his death served as the undisputed leader of the province. Shortly after Jennings' arrival in West New Jersey the first General Assembly convened and as its first order of business adopted a series of resolutions intended as "Fundamentals to us and our posterity, to be held and kept inviolable." This, too, was a compact of the governor and proprietors, freeholders, and inhabitants. Its ten propositions forbade the governor to enact laws without the consent of the legislature, to prorogue or dissolve the assembly without its consent, and to declare war or create any militia in the absence of a legislative act. The overriding purpose of the Fundamental Agreements of 1681 was to reinforce and confirm the Concessions and Agreements of 1677, including its guarantees of religious freedom. Jennings by his signature—given without the knowledge of Byllynge, in whom the legal right of government rested—accepted the terms of this confirmation of the fundamental law of 1677. The first legislature adopted 36 laws based on the experience of the preceding four years of settlement, and many of these gave effect to various provisions of the Concessions and Agreements.

Byllynge was now apparently seized with ambition for power. By an award of eight of fourteen arbitrators chosen half by him (under threat of appeal to Whitehall) and half by representatives of the people, the frame of government under commissioners was determined to be invalid because the right of government had never been legally vested in the proprietors, since they held title by purchase from Berkeley. In 1686 Byllynge's "new charter and bills" were read to the assembly—these are not known to be extant—and a general committee reported after studying them that the governor had no right to make amendments to the fundamental laws. If Byllynge could depart from the Concessions made by him and other proprietors, they argued with irrefutable logic, he might the more easily nullify the provisions of his own. The committee's recommendations were unanimously adopted, and another committee was appointed to petition Byllynge asking him to instruct his deputy-governor to confirm such laws as the legislature might deem necessary. But with the death of Byllynge early in 1687 and the purchase of the right of government shortly thereafter by an ambitious colonizer and a court physician, Daniel Coxe, the disintegration of government under Quaker ideals began. Coxe not surprisingly took the position that the successors of Byllynge could not be bound by the Concessions and Agreements established before the Duke of York's grant of sole right of government in 1680. Legally his position was unassailable. Coxe did promise to confirm liberty of conscience, trial by jury, and other fundamental rights. He also was willing to confer upon the assembly "all powers consistent with the ends of good government." But the feudal element in government had been restored. These were promises handed down, not an unalterable compact entered into by proprietors, freeholders, and inhabitants. The way was thus being prepared in the western division of the province for the end of proprietary and the beginning of royal government in 1702.

Meanwhile, East New Jersey proceeded under its separate government with as much confusion, disorder, and conflict between popular and proprietary interests, but with no such majestic fundamental law as the proprietors and inhabitants of West New Jersey had brought forth in 1677. The dividing line separated not only two geographic and governmental areas but also two distinct societies, one predominantly Puritan in influence and the other under the sway of Quaker idealism. But the doctrine of government by consent was not the monopoly of either of the two groups—or even exclusively English in origin. Between 1665 and 1682 there were no less than four major upheavals in public affairs in East New Jersey. Philip Carteret, the deputy-governor, was dispossessed in 1680 by Sir Edmund Andros, who in 1674 had been appointed governor of all the territories between the Connecticut and Delaware rivers. But Andros' "usurpation" of the government of East New Jersey was disavowed by the Duke of York. Sir George Carteret died in 1680, and two years later his widow auctioned his estate in the eastern province to twelve purchasers, including William Penn. The Duke of York confirmed the transaction in 1683, and from then until the end of proprietary rule in 1702 the government under the Proprietors continued as before in a state of confusion and uncertainty.

After the unsuccessful attempt at government of East New Jersey by Andros the governor confirmed the Concessions and Agreement of 1665 as being still the foundation of government. But the lower house of assembly insisted that there had been various subversions of the privileges of the inhabitants, especially by the Declaration of Intent of 1672. In 1681 the deputies stigmatized that instrument as a breach of the Concessions and registered their desire—indeed their expectation—that it "be made voyd and of none effect." The governor and council, supported by law but bereft of common sense, replied to the representatives: "if you . . . had the benefitt of understanding, you would neither have desired nor expected the same to be made voyd." The house again registered its protest and then solemnly declared, in an act of open rebellion, that the people of the province were not obliged to conform to the Declaration. The point at issue was the denial of office and of the right of franchise to those settlers whose lands were not held under patent from the proprietors, but the exchange of insults and defiance between executive and legislature was over the nature of the constitution. The governor and council did not move from their position that the

Proprietors had reserved to themselves "absolute power" to issue instructions in accordance with the Declaration of 1672 and that there was therefore neither "incrochment upon the said Concessions nor infringement of the Liberties thereby Granted." From this legally defensible position they imprudently continued their devastating impeachment of the motives of the deputies, whom they declared to be holding forth the pearl of "nonsense and injustice to deceive the Kings Loving subjects and if posible to draw them into mutines and Rebellion against our Soveraigne Lord the King." Philip Carteret and his council had as completely lost the confidence of the people as did the royal governors who used similar language with provincial assemblies a century later.

The objective of the Proprietors was to make East New Jersey another Quaker province, despite its nucleus of Puritan settlers. After assuring the inhabitants that the rights set forth in the Concessions and Agreement of 1665 would be observed, the Proprietors produced the Fundamental Constitutions of 1683. This unrealistic and amazingly complex document was never put into effect, yet it exemplifies what its framers considered to be a good fundamental law. The executive powers were to be vested in a governor with life tenure, a resident deputy-governor, and a common council or upper house of the legislature made up of the governor, twelve proprietors, and twelve members chosen from the lower house. This unwieldy body of thirty-six was to exercise its powers through four committees dealing with public policy, trade and finance, plantations and general administration, and defense. The great council or general assembly was to exercise legislative powers and to consist of no less than 144 deputies chosen in annual elections with one-third rotating each year. A two-thirds vote was required for enactment of laws. Suffrage was restricted to freeholders owning 50 acres of land or leaseholders having personal property worth £50. Liberty of conscience was assured but not extended to atheists and a religious test for office was required. As if intending their fundamental law to conform to scruples of Puritan settlers in the province, the authors of the Fundamental Constitutions declared that nothing in this article was to be construed as giving sanction to "Atheism, Irreligiousness, . . . Cursing, Swearing, Drunkedness, prophaness, Whoring, Adultery, Murdering, or any kind of violence, or the indulgening themselves in Stage Plays, Masks, Revells or such like abuses." The amending process was cumbersome if not impossible. No alteration could be made unless approved by 22 of the 24 proprietors and by 66 of the initial 72 deputies. Whatever was deemed essential in the Concessions and Agreement of 1665 was to be regarded as incorporated in the Fundamental Constitutions. Late in 1683 this impractical model of government was approved by the requisite vote of 16 proprietors. It was not to be put into effect until adopted by the general assembly, and that body—joined even by the deputy-governor and the council—rejected it. The proprietors prudently decided to postpone any attempt to introduce it. A few of the provisions of the Fundamental Constitutions were cautiously inserted in instructions given by the proprietors to deputy-governors during the remainder of the period of government under their rule. But no matter how much the settlers from New England may have approved the Puritanical restrictions, they assuredly could have been expected to revolt against any attempt to superimpose so ill-conceived a government on their established system of local government. The Fundamental Constitutions merited its consignment to oblivion.

In the year in which this instrument was drawn up the legislature declared its adherence to the Concessions and Agreement of 1665. Under that aegis it enacted many laws dealing with fundamental matters. In 1698, for example, it declared in an act defining the rights and privileges of the inhabitants that Roman Catholics should be disqualified from holding office or sitting in the assembly —the first legislative enactment to violate the spirit of the Concessions. In another the legislature added to the structure of government such a unique establishment as the Court of Common Right—an institution far more adapted to the soil of New Jersey than anything that had been conceived abroad. The Proprietors produced neither a viable fundamental law nor a single settlement composed of members of the Society of Friends. In the last three years of their rule the province was almost without organized government.

By 1701 the proprietors of both divisions of New Jersey were ready to transfer all rights of government to the Crown. In October 1702 the Board of Trade declared that the proprietors had, in fact, surrendered their title to James II in 1688, that this had been accepted, and that no legally sufficient form of government had ever been established in the province. Both king and proprietors were ready for the change. Drafts of the commission and instructions to a royal governor were prepared and approved by the king in council on November 16, 1702. These were unanimously approved by the proprietors of the two divisions of the province, but the death of the king delayed actual execution of the Act of Surrender until April 15, 1703. Two days later Queen Anne gave her approval, and in July Edward Hyde, Viscount Cornbury received in New York his commission and instructions which, with their subsequent enlargements and renewals from time to time, constituted the basic law of the province until 1776. Thenceforth until that date united New Jersey was to be a royal province.

The proprietors' request for a general assembly to meet alternately at Perth Amboy and Burlington was granted, with six members of the council and twelve members of the lower house to be chosen from each division. Thus originated the principle of an equality of representation that has persisted so stubbornly in respect to the upper house that the Constitutional Convention and indeed the people themselves two and a half centuries later were, by an affront to the idea of fundamental law itself, not even permitted to consider its revision. The proprietors' request for the protection of liberty of conscience for all save Roman Catholics was also granted. Since church and state were allied in the realm, it was natural that the instructions to the governor should have included provisions tending to give preference to the Church of England. It is also natural that successive governors should have sought to advance its welfare in the province. An attempt was even made during the period of royal government to secure the enactment of legislation for the establishment of the Church in New Jersey. But this move was defeated and the province that had been founded in religious dissent, half Puritan in the east and half Quaker in the west, remained steadfast to its origins. Quakers were not only permitted to make an affirmation instead of an oath but were also eligible for office. Limited only by the discrimination against Roman Catholics, the guarantee of freedom of conscience set forth in New Jersey's first fundamental law of 1665 continued unimpaired from that time forward until at last in the nineteenth century all proscriptions based on religious belief were eliminated by the Constitution of 1844.

The progress and stability of the province that Leaming and Spicer noted at mid-century derived not merely from the concept of limited government expressed in the various grants and concessions of the seventeenth century and in the royal instructions and their modifications in the ensuing period. They derived also from the growing conviction of the people that theirs was a constitution in which the liberties and rights of Englishmen provided the great ligament. Despite the confusion, instability, and occasional failures of the early decades of the history of New Jersey, the concept of fundamental law that could not be violated by any authority but their own had been bred in the bone and marrow of the people. The structure of representative government created in the Concessions and Agreement of 1665 would endure in substantially the same broad outline not merely to the end of royal rule but for the next three centuries. So too would the system of local government begun in the seventeenth century. The deep conviction of the importance of a written fundamental law had been sustained by experience and, on the eve of the debate over the nature of the imperial connection, had been fortified by the appearance of Leaming and Spicer's *The Grants, Concessions, and Original Constitutions of the Province of New-Jersey*. This was a handbook of liberty that enabled the people in 1765 to base their protest against taxation without representation on the guarantees set forth in their first organic law. And when the pivotal year 1776 arrived, no one of the thirteen colonies emerging into statehood could look back to an expression of the idea of government by consent equaling in vibrant immediacy and in noble comprehension that to which the people of New Jersey, a century earlier, had pledged themselves.

The Constitution of 1776

The transition from provincial government to independent statehood in New Jersey followed the general pattern elsewhere. First there were public meetings of protest against parliamentary legislation, then the creation of local committees of correspondence, and finally the convocation of provincial congresses that would move gradually toward the establishment of a complete structure of government within the province, externally connected with that soon to emerge as a nation of confederated states. Because of her central position New Jeresy became a battleground in the realm of divided allegiances as well as in the area of armed conflicts, but, once the commitment to independence had been made, there was no warring over the idea of establishing a fundamental law. With New Jersey that commitment was by no means irrevocable even in her first constitution, for its terms held the door open by making its provisions inoperative if the colony and the king should compose their differences. The drift of events had already placed this eventuality beyond the realm of the possible.

The Provincial Congress of 1775, called immediately after news of the outbreak of hostilities at Lexington and Concord, created an elaborate militia system, levied taxes for its support, provided for annual elections, and established a system of committees of safety in all townships and counties. This was a provisional government paralleling the structure of the royal government in all save its executive and judicial branches. The regular legislature made its final adjournment late in 1775 and soon thereafter, as the "torrent of independence" loosed by Thomas Paine's *Common Sense* swept over the country, the Provincial Congress ordered an election to be held on May 28, 1776 to appoint delegates to the next Provincial Congress. Before that date the Continental Congress called upon all colonies that had not already done so to create constitutions for themselves. John Adams viewed this resolution of May 15, 1776 as the real act of independence, requiring only the additional formality of a declaration, and Thomas Jefferson thought that the task of drafting fundamental laws to bring them into harmony with republican principles was indeed "the whole object of the present controversy."

Thus the delegates who convened June 10 at Burlington were not authorized by the ordinance convoking them, or by the people who elected them, to adopt a constitution. But both the people and their representatives were prepared for the step. They were in the center of the line of communication stretching from New Hampshire to Georgia whose revolutionary impulses were recording the greatest era of constitution-making that had taken place up to that time. New Hampshire was the first, followed quickly by South Carolina. Virginia and New Jersey were next, both proclaiming their new fundamental laws as independent states before the Declaration of Independence was adopted. Six other colonies followed in rapid succession. None of the first ten state constitutions was submitted to the people for approval. Massachusetts convoked the first true constitutional convention in 1780 and placed the result before the electorate. Rhode Island and Connecticut continued under their colonial charters until well into the nineteenth century.

In this period of hasty drafting of organic laws New Jersey had only the examples of New Hampshire and South Carolina before her, neither of which influenced her own action. Early in 1776 Thomas Paine's *Common Sense* had proposed a democratic form of constitution that captured attention by being included in the author's stirring call for independence. John Adams, alarmed at seeing "so foolish a plan recommended to the people of the United States" and far more learned in the history and theory of government than Paine, put his ideas on paper. Soon multiple copies of Adams' concept of a proper fundamental law were circulating among members of the Continental Congress and he was prevailed upon to allow one of these to be printed as a pamphlet, entitled *Thoughts on Government*. In 1774, as he was journeying through Princeton to the first Continental Congress, Adams had met an able young lawyer, Jonathan Dickinson Sergeant, of whose abilities and zeal in the republican cause he at once formed a high opinion. In the spring of 1776, therefore, it was quite natural that the young Princeton lawyer—Sergeant was just thirty—should have asked the older and more famous man for a copy of his plan of government. Adams sent him a manuscript version that he regarded as "larger and more compleat, perhaps more correct"—correct, presumably, in the principles and structure of government recommended—than the one published.* Sergeant must have shared this with his fellow lawyers, Richard Stockton and William Paterson, both of whom were like himself graduates of the institution that one loyalist had called a "Seminary of Sedition," the College of New-Jersey. It can be reasonably assumed that, in addition to these, he also

* The best account of the present state of knowledge of the origin of Adams' *Thoughts on Government* is in L. H. Butterfield (ed.), *Diary and Autobiography of John Adams* (Cambridge, 1961), III, 331-342n.

shared Adams' thoughts with another zealous promoter of the patriot cause, John Witherspoon. That these Princeton friends were in close alliance in promoting that cause is beyond doubt. There are grounds for believing that an agreement had been reached among them by which Witherspoon and Stockton—both older and better known—would be named delegates to the Continental Congress, where the issue of independence hung in the balance. If such an understanding existed, it required that Sergeant leave his seat there and return to New Jersey to stand as a delegate to the Provincial Congress.

Sergeant was present in the Continental Congress in Philadelphia during the whole of the month of May. He was therefore in close association with John Adams and he may also have conversed with another delegate slightly older than he, Thomas Jefferson, who at this time was busily engaged in preparing drafts of a proposed constitution for Virginia. It is certain that Sergeant was in the Continental Congress when the decisive resolution of May 15 was adopted—the preamble of which, drawn by John Adams, so closely parallels the justifying argument for establishing an independent government as set forth in the New Jersey Constitution of 1776—and he was there when a Philadelphia newspaper printed George Mason's Declaration of Rights that, very soon thereafter, became a part of the Virginia Constitution. There can be little doubt that some delegate to the New Jersey Provincial Congress went there with a constitution already prepared, and, so far as credit can be assigned to anyone, the available evidence seems to indicate that Jonathan Dickinson Sergeant was the principal architect of the first fundamental law of the state.*

Neither he nor others of the Provincial Congress could have escaped influences permeating the consciousness of thoughtful men throughout the length and breadth of the

* The reasons for this conclusion were first set forth and cogently argued by C. R. Erdman, Jr., *The New Jersey Constitution of 1776* (Princeton, 1929), 34-37.

land. Nor could they have failed to know that in preparing a constitution they would be sustained by the people who had elected them. Many petitions from various local committees of correspondence urging the establishment of a new form of government had in fact been received by them. The sense of unity among the states and the desire to follow the prompting of the Continental Congress was proved by the overwhelming response of the states no less than by urgent necessity. Thus there was little debate and no delay. On May 30 the royal governor, William Franklin, issued a proclamation convoking the General Assembly. The Provincial Congress promptly resolved that this summons should not be obeyed and the next day declared the governor to be in contempt of the resolution of the Continental Congress of May 15, suspended his salary, and named him an enemy of the liberties of his country. Thus by implication what the Continental Congress had recommended—which in a legal sense was all that it could do—was regarded by the Provincial Congress as putting an effective end to royal government in New Jersey and elsewhere. Within a few years the recommendations of the government under the Articles of Confederation would meet with apathy and refusal, but in the beginning, on this great issue, its wish was given the force of law. The way was thus cleared for erecting a new system of government. No ordinance of New Jersey had stipulated this and no external law could compel it. The authority of the Provincial Congress as a constituent assembly derived from an overwhelming consensus born of rebellion and—as the Constitution itself declared—of absolute necessity.

The Provincial Congress appointed a committee of ten members to prepare the fundamental law and, indicative of the fact that one had in fact already been prepared, the committee reported back within forty-eight hours. The house, in committee of the whole, discussed its provisions for two and a half days, and then spent less than a day in debate on its final adoption. The debates were not recorded and could scarcely have been divisive. The reason for this is clear. The framers of the first Constitution of New Jersey introduced no novel or theoretical expedients. They adhered as closely as possible to the institutions that had brought stability and a remarkable degree of progress to the colony before the empire was rent with dissension. The document was simple, brief, and based on the realities of long experience. It is a tribute to the strength of the tradition inherited from the fundamental laws of the seventeenth century that the delegates felt no necessity to incorporate a Bill of Rights in the document and that the people made no protest over so conspicuous an omission. The Constitution did protect from legislative encroachment the old principle of annual elections, "the inestimable Right of Trial by Jury," and the guarantee of religious freedom. But the need to preface the constitution with an extended catalogue of natural rights must not have seemed so compelling to the delegates in New Jersey as to those in Virginia and other states. The Constitution of 1776 seemed to say by what it omitted that the protection of individual liberty lay rather in the tradition inherited from the past than in any precise definition of rights. The great ligament of liberty remained unbroken when all sovereignty was wrested from the Crown and resumed by the people. The imperative need was not to recapitulate the fundamental propositions of civil and religious liberty but to draft "some Form of Government . . . for the Preservation of good Order." The delegates sought that form in the same tradition in which they knew their liberties had originated.

In common with other states they reflected their old fears of abuse of executive powers by stripping the office of governor of almost all but the title to the "supreme executive power." The governor was elected by the legislature, he could not make an appointment to a single office, and he possessed no veto. He was given some legislative and judicial functions but his executive authority was shackled. The principal powers of government were concentrated in the legislative branch. There was indeed no limit upon the power of the legislature save the protection given to annual elections, trial by jury, and religious freedom. Its appointive powers were extensive. All officials of the state, including the governor, secretary of state, attorney general, treasurer, justices of the supreme court, county court judges, and justices of the peace as well as many county officers were appointed by the two houses sitting in joint session. The principle of equal representation in the upper house was continued by the allocation of one seat to each of the thirteen counties. That of annual elections—going back to the Concessions and Agreement of 1665 and to the fundamental law of West New Jersey of 1677 but not existing even in principle from 1702 to the Revolution—was reaffirmed and given the status of law untouchable by the legislature. The judiciary was not defined as a separate system, but was dependent on the legislature both in appointments to office and in the nature of the court system.

Since the Provincial Congress was not legally empowered to draft a constitution, since the terms of that document so clearly established a legislative power almost comparable in extent to the Blackstonian concept of parliamentary supremacy, and since the final result was not submitted to the people for ratification, its validity as fundamental law depended upon its being regarded as such by the people. The Provincial Congress recognized this necessity by ordering a thousand copies of the document to be printed and distributed. A century earlier the Concessions and Agreements of 1677 had required that its text be publicly recited, and in 1776 the first Constitution of New Jersey was read to excited throngs who also heard the words of the Declaration of Independence proclaimed. One speaker declared on such an occasion:

The plan of government established in most States and kingdoms of the world has been the effect of chance or necessity, ours of sober reason and cool deliberation. Our future happiness or misery therefore, as a people, will depend entirely upon ourselves. . . . If we are steady and zealous in putting the laws in strict execution; the spirit and principles of our new Constitution, which we have just now heard read, may be preserved for a long time.

Grand juries and members of the judiciary gave approbation to the "new and happy constitution." William Livingston, the first governor of the state, declared in his inaugural address that the constitution had "by tacit acquiescence and open approbation . . . received the assent and concurrence of the good people of this State." * For fourteen years the legislature re-elected Governor Livingston. So respected were the virtues of this distinguished patriot, in New Jersey and throughout the Union, that he not only gave the sanction of his character to the validation of the fundamental law of 1776, but even elevated to a position of influence the impotent office that he held.

In New Jersey as in other states the first Constitution gave rise to a discussion about the distinction necessary to be made between mere legislation and fundamental law. Article 23 could plausibly be interpreted to mean that the legislature could alter the Constitution in any way save in respect to the three specified matters placed beyond its reach. Plausible or not, this interpretation collided with republican principles of government and also with deep-rooted convictions out of which the concept of fundamental law had arisen. The example of the Federal Constitution of 1787 and the forces leading to its adoption had a profound influence on this discussion. In 1790 Pennsylvania and Georgia revised their constitutions in a way to modify the democratic elements in their earlier ones and when the tendency of the first administrations of the national government showed a greater and greater inclination to magnify the powers of the executive, New Jersey also felt the pressure for revision. The advocates of revision argued that the principles and structure of government were far better understood than

* Quoted in C. R. Erdman, Jr., *The New Jersey Constitution of 1776* (Princeton, 1929), 39.

they had been when the Constitution of 1776 was drafted, but the impulse behind their advocacy reflected the tendency to curb the popular elements of government and to give greater strength to the executive branch. This widespread tendency also made its appearance in New Jersey in 1790, just at the close of William Livingston's long tenure of office, but it did not reach its height until the turbulent administration of President John Adams. Its chief protagonist—indeed the most prominent spokesman for constitutional reform between 1776 and 1844—was the Federalist lawyer William Griffith, who in 1797 began a series of newspaper articles over the signature *Eumenes*. These articles were published as a volume in 1799 in order to call attention to the errors and omissions of the Constitution and to establish the need for convoking a convention for its revision.

His object, Griffith declared, was to bring home to every man the actual evils arising from errors of theory:

There is no man, possessing tolerable conceptions of the first elements of a well-ordered republic, who will not admit, that the conformation of that charter contains no vestiges of dignity, wisdom or safety. No lines are drawn between the essential departments of government; no checks are provided against their encroachments upon each other; the executive is annihilated entirely in the legislative; the judiciary is rendered weak and dependent upon the same branch; and that again, in its turn, is corrupted and diverted from its proper functions, by the spoils which it has made from the other departments.*

These papers excited much attention, but the legislature refused to act on the ground that revision of the Constitution was beyond the scope of its powers. Yet that body was not so restrained when confronted with the question of interpreting the Constitution by statute. It conceived itself empowered to do this under the useful

* [William Griffith], *Eumenes* (Trenton, 1799), 9. Griffith's own copy, with corrections and marginalia in his own hand and with interleaved notes by others, is in the Princeton University Library.

fiction of explanatory enactments. The most notable of these was the Act of 1807. That statute denied the suffrage to Negroes, aliens, and women and substituted for the £50 property qualification a taxpayer's requirement. Thus a limitation produced by confusion actually had the effect of establishing by legislative construction the enfranchisement of all free, white, male citizens. In the preceding period of confusion all citizens of New Jersey having residence and property qualifications had been theoretically entitled to vote, and in fact many aliens, Negroes, and women capable of owning property had cast their ballots in New Jersey elections. This Act of 1807 was thus in substance if not in form a constitutional amendment. It anticipated by more than two decades the tidal wave of opinion that swept over the nation compelling one state after another to yield to the demand for universal manhood suffrage.

With this enactment there was resolved the one basic issue resulting from the theoretical imperfections of the first Constitution. The fabric of government erected in the very center of the revolutionary storm served the people of the State well for over six decades, not because of its virtues but because of their experience in grappling with the problems of self-government that had begun long before the Constitution of 1776 came into existence. But even though the men of New Jersey might make any constitution work, as Bagehot said of those of Massachusetts, that fabric could not withstand the turbulence of another era.

The Constitution of 1844

By 1844 the New Jersey Constitution of 1776 had become the oldest written constitution in existence, a fact that inspired neither veneration nor confidence in those who lived under it. In the second quarter of the nineteenth century that fundamental law was no longer a useful or realistic basis of government. The emergence of manufacturing towns, the beginning of railroads and canals, the multiplication of corporations, the growth of trade unions, the demand for the extension of the franchise, the deepening conflict between the rights of the citizen and the rights of property, the awakening social consciousness over the plight of the poor, the mentally ill, and the less fortunate members of society—all of these impulses and clashing interests of an enterprising people prompted the demand for constitutional revision.

Different as the issues were from those of the Revolutionary era, the two periods had one significant aspect in common. In both there was a profound discussion of the purposes of government and of the best means of achieving those purposes. On the eve of the Revolution, so John Adams had said, the fundamental principles of government were discussed at every hearth and fireside in America. The agitation of the public mind under the administrations of Andrew Jackson had a similar effect. "The controversy we have witnessed," wrote Theodore Sedgwick, Jr. in 1835, "sprang from the discussion . . . of those fundamental maxims of the science of government and of political economy, which it is absolutely essential that a free people should understand. . . . It has urged forward the whole American mind." * Just as John Adams and Thomas Paine had led the discussion of the fundamental maxims of government in the earlier period, so in the later there appeared men like Francis Lieber and Henry Vethake proclaiming that government was a science and urging in their respective ways that men would be prudent to attend its precepts. Unfortunately, as in earlier and later periods, neither the proponents of the new science of government nor the spokesmen for clashing aims and interests could reach agreement on the exact nature or application of those precepts.

The most salient of the pressures urging the American mind forward in this period was the demand for the

---

* Theodore Sedgwick, Jr., "What is a Monopoly?" in Joseph L. Blau (ed.), *Social Theories of Jacksonian Democracy* (New York, 1947), 220.

extension of the suffrage, a proposition implicit in the assumptions of the Declaration of Independence and indeed in the realities of colonial experience. New Jersey had long since come to terms with this issue, enjoying in this respect an almost unique distinction among the states of the union. The guarantee of universal white manhood suffrage was first given constitutional expression in New Jersey in 1844, but this was only a reflection of the legislative construction of 1807 that had given approximate reality to the idea. Extension of the franchise was not a burning issue in the move for constitutional revision in New Jersey. Such a bitter conflict over the abandonment of property qualifications for voting as took place in the Virginia constitutional convention of 1831 had no echoes in the convention of 1844. The state did not experience such a convulsion as Dorr's Rebellion which caused Rhode Island's colonial charter of 1663 to give way before insistent demands for the extension of the franchise.

But on other issues agitating the public mind New Jersey's fundamental law of 1776 stood more exposed to the prevailing winds of Jacksonian democracy. Its most conspicuous fault was that it contained no Bill of Rights. Freedom of the press, liberty of conscience, separation of church and state, trial by jury, habeas corpus, due process of law, the right of petition and of peaceable assembly— these in substance had been an integral part of New Jersey polity from the very beginning. But the Constitution of 1776 did not explicitly declare all of these ancient rights and liberties. To men who had been brought up on the philosophy of the Declaration of Independence, this was an intolerable omission. Both the philosophy and its various expressions in state and national constitutions served as examples for the Convention of 1844 to emulate. The resultant declaration of Rights and Privileges borrowed affirmations of individual liberty from the Virginia Declaration of Rights of 1776, doctrines of natural rights and of government by consent from the Declaration of Independence, and guarantees against oppression from the Bills of Rights of the Federal Constitution. But there were also significant elements added from the State's own distinctive experience. There was no declaration of the right of the people to keep and to bear arms. The strict subordination of the military to the civil authority was made emphatically clear. And imprisonment for debt was abolished. Thus the New Jersey affirmation of rights asserted in 1844 the doctrines of individual liberty universally acclaimed by Americans as axiomatic and at the same time reflected the humanitarian impulses that were the legacy of William Penn and others of the Society of Friends.

The example first set by Massachusetts in 1780 and given the force of compelling precedent by the Federal Convention of 1787 made it imperative that the revision should be undertaken by a convention especially called for that purpose. There was general agreement not only on this point but also on the assumption that, since fundamental law concerned the principles and structure of government for all of the people, the conflicting aims of political parties should be as far removed from the composition of the convention as possible. The Act providing for the calling of the Convention of 1844 therefore stipulated that quotas of delegates should be allocated in equal division to the Democratic and Whig parties. This high-minded aim was marred only by the lack of restraint on the part of the Democrats of Monmouth who filled the county quota both for themselves and for the Whigs. The unseemly maneuver allowed their party a technical majority of two in the convention, but that body was not deflected from its evident desire to preserve the spirit of non-partisanship. In New Jersey as in other states, in that era and afterward, the mere act of convoking an assembly to deal with the great task of framing a fundamental law seemed to have the effect of inspiring the people to choose their ablest and wisest men and of causing their deputies in this solemn act of sovereignty to rise above party consideration. There were deep cleavages in the Convention of 1844, as was to be expected, but the division was not basically along party lines. The members of the convention were men of considerable distinction and ability. Almost all of them had had experience in public affairs both in state and nation, and a number of them reflected the humanitarian ideals of the day in their activities in education, religion, and social welfare. Theirs was a conscientious and, on the whole, successful effort to lift their deliberations above the arena of partisan politics. In doing so, both they and the people who chose them paid a high and appropriate tribute to the concept of fundamental law.

In no respect did the Constitution of 1844 typify the aims of Jacksonian democracy more than in its stringent limitation on the authority of the legislature to create charters of incorporation for banks. Some in that period had gone so far as to declare that the principle of granting corporate rights of any sort was wholly adverse to the genius of American institutions, if not indeed in direct contravention of the doctrine of equal rights. This, they insisted, was a legislative practice inherited from England and one that Americans theretofore had unwisely allowed to go unexamined. It was high time, so some thought, to make an end of the practice. New Jersey had not been the first to legislate a corporation into existence, but in creating the Society for Useful Manufactures in 1791 she had established a shining target for the Jacksonian foes of monopoly and to this she had added many others. Special acts in the 1820's and 1830's incorporating banks, railroads, and canal companies, together with a mounting public debt and catastrophic bank failures, had helped focus attention on the need for constitutional restraints of one sort or another. Two significant provisions in the Constitution of 1844 reflected the public concern over these matters. The first of these was the crippling limit placed upon the capacity of the state to borrow money. The second was the requirement that acts incorporating banks could only be passed by three-fifths majority and should be limited in duration to twenty years. The last echoed the Jeffersonian maxim of 1789 that "the earth belongs in usufruct to the living," that one generation had no right to impose its will upon those that followed—a maxim that found its way into more than one of the state constitutions in one form or another.

The Constitution of 1844 also reflected the general acceptance of the doctrine of separation of powers and in its allocation of authority to the executive, the legislature, and the judiciary it redressed the imbalance of its predecessor. Yet it represented no fundamental or drastic break with the past. The weak veto given to the governor, the diffusion of the appointive power, and the retention of the equal representation granted to each county in the upper house indicated the conservative nature of the new structure of government. Like all constitutions growing out of the realities of conflicting aims and interests, that of 1844 was the result of compromise. No doubt its compromises were well suited to the predominantly agricultural and more or less homogeneous people of New Jersey at mid-century. But the society for which this fundamental law was fabricated was very far indeed from being static.

The Constitution of 1947

That society in fact was on the eve of violent change, one threatening the existence of the Union itself and bringing in its wake a vast expansion of industrial power, a phenomenal growth of large urban centers, an influx of new ethnic and religious groups having little experience with the basic concepts of Anglo-American institutions, and a proliferation of the number and power of corporations that was quite unprecedented. All of these changes posed social, economic, and political problems of constantly increasing dimension and gravity, among which the most urgent, if not the best understood, was the lack of anything approximating an adequate system of education. With these changes, too, came the opportunities that bred corruption in politics, including the new figure of the political boss serving special interests in an atmosphere of graft and legislative manipulation. Before such problems as these the Constitution of 1844 stood as an outmoded and even dangerous document within a quarter of a century after its drafting. Yet it survived for more than a century, not because its authors were prophetic, but precisely because they did not anticipate the remarkable alterations about to take place in the structure and nature of society. Its difficulty of amendment, its decentralized executive powers, its limitation on borrowing capacity, and especially its failure to define the relations of state and local government, actually served to make it the interest of some to perpetuate its life, while increasingly it tended to augment rather than to alleviate the growing problems. To these handicaps inherent in the provisions of the organic law was added the effect of the unusual political composition of the state which often placed the executive under the control of one party and the legislature under that of another. The limitation on executive tenure also served to increase the obstacles to the development of anything like a coherent and effective administration. In an era of often violent conflict between labor and capital, of multiplied special legislation, of growing religious intrusions into political decisions—an era in which no general legislation existed either in the constitution or in statutory law for the establishment and government of corporations—it was not surprising that the staunchest defenders of the Constitution of 1844 were those individuals and groups whose special interests stood to benefit most from its perpetuation.

A wide and deep resentment against abuses and neglect of the public interest led to the first demand for revision. In 1776 fear of abuse of the executive powers had found expression in the Constitution and a century later the public apprehended—with just cause—that the danger to its welfare proceeded from another source, its own representatives in the legislature. In 1873, following exposure of political and financial corruption in Jersey City, the governor of the state proposed the calling of a convention to alter the fundamental law so as to limit the enactment of special or private laws, to prohibit the irrevocable grants of special privileges to individuals or corporations, to require equitable property assessments, and to provide general laws for the government of municipalities.* The legislature authorized the appointment of a non-partisan commission to propose amendments to the Constitution of 1844. The reforms urged by the commission were salutary, but those forbidding the use of public money for sectarian purposes, providing the guarantee of a system of free public education in perpetuity, and prohibiting special legislation encountered religious opposition of a determined character. This—added to the growing resentment against legislative abuses—so aroused public sentiment that every one of the 28 amendments submitted to the people at a special election was adopted.*

The victory was both incomplete and costly. The amendments were aimed at the more glaring abuses of special legislation, at abuses in the area of municipal government, and at the growing threats to the principle of separation of church and state. But what was needed was a thorough revision, and the emphatic assault on the grosser invasions of the public interest only served to prolong the life of the Constitution another three-quarters of a century. The legislature blandly continued to enact special legislation and threw upon the judiciary the burden of disallowing great numbers of statutes that

* In his opening message to the legislature in 1873 Governor Joel Parker stated that the general public laws passed in the previous session occupied about a hundred pages in the printed statutes, whereas the special and private laws occupied over twelve hundred and fifty pages of the same volume.

* The amendments proposed by the Commission are to be found in *The Constitution of New Jersey as Proposed to be Amended by the Constitutional Commission* (Trenton, 1873). The texts of the amendments as adopted are given in the footnotes to the text of the Constitution of 1844.

clearly contravened the Constitution. Indeed in 1890 the General Assembly went so far as to submit to the people an amendment to repeal the prohibition against special legislation, but this was overwhelmingly defeated. In 1897 three amendments—one to prohibit gambling, one to limit the power of the governor to make appointments during the recess of the legislature, and one to enable women to vote for members of local boards of education —were voted upon at a special election. Only the first two were approved by the people, and these by very narrow margins.* From 1900 to 1940 amendments were proposed by the legislature on five separate occasions, but only two in this period were ratified by the people. In 1927 all amendments proposed were defeated save that enabling the legislature under general laws to permit municipalities to adopt zoning ordinances, and in 1939 an amendment allowing pari-mutuel betting at horse races was approved by a large majority.

In the first quarter of the twentieth century three governors of New Jersey, Woodrow Wilson among them, advocated the calling of a constitutional convention to provide a thorough revision of the substantive law of the State. In the 1920's two commissions called attention to the defects of the decentralized system of administration, though one thought the waste and inefficiency might be corrected by the consolidation of control in the executive without altering the Constitution, while the other proposed an original but unrealistic alteration of the legislature—a small unicameral body chosen by proportional representation from three or four districts into which the state would be divided.** Public commissions, private agencies, and students of government all began to focus public attention on the defects of the document

* The amendment against lotteries and gambling passed by the narrow majority of 801 in a total vote of 140,085. That limiting recess appointments won by a vote of 73,722 to 66,296.

** On the first, see *Report of the Joint Legislative Survey Committee of New Jersey* (1925); on the second, see National Institute of Public Administration, *Survey of the Organization and Administration of the State Government of New Jersey* (1929).

that was now approaching its centenary.* No disinterested person or thoughtful student of affairs wished to see its life extended.

While the need for laying the ancient instrument to rest was crystal clear, the process of interment was uncertain. The amending clause in the Constitution of 1844 left doubt whether the legislature could legally call a convention into being. This was a doubt magnified—if not invented—by many who employed it as a barrier to revision. The real obstacle was the principle of equal representation, for the revolutionary growth in population that had come about in the preceding century gave to the less populous counties a weight in public decisions far out of proportion to the number of their inhabitants. Some advocates of revision thought that the legislature could not act as a constituent assembly—as the Provincial Congress of 1776 had done—without first having public approval. It was also suggested that the governor might be obliged to call a convention without legislative sanction. In the end New Jersey tried all three available methods for drafting a constitutional law—by special commission, by the legislature sitting as a constituent assembly, and by convention.

The year 1940 marked the beginning of the end for the venerable Constitution that had served so long beyond its day. In the election campaign of that year the opposing gubernatorial candidates both urged constitutional reform and advocated the calling of a convention to achieve it. The victorious Democratic governor renewed the attack in his inaugural address, but the defeated Republican candidate had already introduced a bill in the Senate providing for the election of delegates to a constitutional convention. Thereafter, though hesitation and delay marked the course, the Republican

---

*Among these, see especially the Commission to Investigate County and Municipal Taxation and Expenditures, *Report No. 1*, and C. R. Erdman, Jr., *The New Jersey Constitution—a Barrier to Governmental Efficiency and Economy* (Princeton, 1934); *Report of the Judicial Council of New Jersey* (May 31, 1932).

party took the lead in the movement for constitutional revision. Early in 1941 the New Jersey Committee for a Constitutional Convention was organized and soon became the channel through which the most influential individuals and civic agencies made their views known. That same year the legislature created a seven-man Commission on the Revision of the New Jersey Constitution, and in the next two years this Commission carried on its studies with the aid of a staff that included a specialist never before seen in the state's long history with written constitutions—a public relations expert. A majority of the Commission seemed to feel—much as some statesmen had felt in 1787 about the Articles of Confederation—that only a few amendments were needed to make the venerable fabric adequate to the exigencies of a new day. Nevertheless the unanimous report submitted in 1942 contained the draft of a wholly new constitution.*

This document was the product of careful and disinterested study. It continued the separation of powers principle, but gave formal expression to the theory that state constitutions—unlike the Federal Constitution—merely limit but do not grant sovereign powers. Thus all powers of government not vested by the constitution in the executive and the judiciary or specifically proscribed or in conflict with rights reserved by the people—an undefined area extending beyond those enumerated in the Constitution—were to be embraced within the legislative power. The importance of this clarification is that it would have freed the legislature from any implication that, like the Congress of the United States, it could not act unless the power it wished to exercise was one of the enumerated grants of power. Had such an article existed in the Constitution of 1844, for example, no attorney general could have ruled—as one did in 1913—that the legislature had no authority to convoke a constitutional convention. The draft constitution of the Commission greatly enlarged the appointive power of the governor,

* *Report to the Commission on Revision of the New Jersey Constitution 1942* (Trenton, 1942).

centralized the administration of various departments, increased the governor's tenure to four years with eligibility for re-election for one term, and strengthened the veto power. But it was in the judiciary that the draft made its most drastic revision. This was because, as the Commission declared without exaggeration, "New Jersey has the most complicated scheme of courts existing in any English speaking state." The judiciary system in some of its aspects reflected its origins in medieval England. It had been imported into the province at its founding and had been perpetuated almost unchanged in the Constitutions of 1776 and 1844, whereas England and almost all other American states had long since simplified the court structure so as to consist generally of a supreme court with appellate jurisdiction only, a trial court of general jurisdiction with appellate divisions, and lower courts of limited jurisdiction created by the legislature. As a perceptive English observer of America wrote about the time the Commission made its report:

if you want to see the old common law in all its picturesque formality, with its fictions and its fads, its delays and uncertainties, the place to look for them is not London, not in the Modern Gothic of the Law Courts in the Strand, but in New Jersey. Dickens, or any other law-reformer of a century ago, would feel more at home in Trenton than in London, where, despite the survival of wigs and miniver and maces, the law has been modernized, simplified, made more rapid and efficient; in fact, everything that is desirable except cheap.*

Law reformers had not been lacking in New Jersey, but the difficulty of amending the Constitution of 1844 had interposed an almost insuperable barrier to their efforts to bring about a simplification of the judicial structure.

A joint legislative committee studied the Commission's report, held public hearings in 1942, and recommended that the subject be postponed until the close of the war. This led to the formation of the New Jersey Constitu-

* D. W. Brogan, *The English People, Impressions and Observations* (New York, 1943), 108.

tional Foundation which that same year began an intensive campaign, aided by all of the devices of mass communication, that "flooded the state with factual information and non-partisan discussions on the Constitution of 1844 and the then current proposals for changing it." * Newspapers, radio stations, educational institutions, and organizations lent support to this campaign. The effort of the Foundation took on the aspect of a mass assault, led by a volunteer corps of speakers trained in 52 training conferences held throughout the state. Champions of revision gained strength as leading citizens and the heads of both parties spoke out with increasing vigor. "The most important problem before the State of New Jersey," declared Governor Charles Edison in 1943, "is an old one . . . how to obtain modern, effective, responsible, and economical state government under the Constitution of 1844."

In 1943 a bill was passed—largely through the intervention of the late Walter E. Edge, an ardent proponent of revision who soon became governor. This Act enabled the people to vote in the coming election on the question of authorizing the 1944 legislature to act as a constituent assembly, though the Senate had amended the referendum Act so as to prevent any change in the Bill of Rights or in the system of equal representation of counties in the Senate. The measure was approved by a large majority at the election which placed Governor Edge and the Republican Party in control of both the executive and legislative branches. Early in 1944 the legislature, sitting as the 1944 Constitutional Convention of New Jersey, began its work toward the broad objectives outlined by the Governor: a unified court system, an increase and definition of executive authority, and a reorganization of administrative departments. The constitution drafted by this body incorporated the principal features recommended by the Commission of 1942 but rejected the proposal for a mandatory vote on revision every twenty years and some other recommendations of the

* Robert A. Petito, "A Constitutional History of New Jersey" (Unpublished thesis, Princeton University, 1948), 87.

New Jersey Committee for Constitutional Revision. The legislature—significantly by a strict party vote—approved the draft constitution and submitted it to the people. A desperate and embittered struggle over its adoption followed, in which unfortunately the opposition forces of Mayor Frank Hague of Jersey City and the intrusion of sectarian arguments did much to cloud the issue and to make any opposition seem to be an alliance with bigotry and corruption. In the ensuing election the cause of revision suffered a dismaying defeat when the proposed new fundamental law was rejected by an emphatic majority.

The entrenched political opposition in urban centers of the northern part of the state, resentful of any efforts to place limitations upon its control of municipal government, accounted in large part for the defeat. So, undoubtedly, did the attempt to arouse the forces of religious bigotry. But among the major causes, if not indeed the decisive one, must be reckoned the failure to follow one precedent of the Constitution of 1844 that was eminently worthy of emulation—that is, the conscientious attempt to remove the Convention that framed it from the arena of partisan politics. This precedent, so intimately connected with the very concept of fundamental law, was disregarded. Governor Edison and other leaders of his party had committed themselves to the movement for constitutional revision. But from 1941 on the Republican Party had appropriated the cause as its own. Despite its clear merits, the document submitted for public approval as the basic law of all the people and all parties was almost exclusively a Republican product. This partisan identification was an unnecessary and, indeed, an improper intrusion in a matter so fundamental as the framing of an organic law for the State. Since Governor Edge was not favorably disposed to the idea of a constitutional convention—and soon announced that he would proceed with administrative reorganization anyway—the movement for revision came to a standstill.

But some groups that had opposed the new constitution —such as organized labor—and those committed to the cause of constitutional reform kept the movement alive. In 1945 a joint legislative committee reported for consideration 13 amendments to the Constitution of 1844 and in 1946 the General Assembly adopted three proposed amendments intended for submission to that body in the ensuing year. But these attempts proved unnecessary. In his inaugural address early in 1947 Governer Alfred E. Driscoll recommended that a convention be called to draft a constitution in time to be submitted to the voters in the November general election. The legislature promptly passed the Constitutional Reform Act providing for a simultaneous vote in the primary on the question of holding a convention and on the delegates to be chosen. This time a determined effort was made to remove the stamp of party from the proceedings. Candidates were permitted to use the party label only with the approval of the county committees and Governor Driscoll urged that outstanding persons be selected regardless of party affiliation. In 13 of the 21 counties they were in fact selected by party organizations on a bipartisan basis.* Opposition to revision seemed to have collapsed—even Mayor Hague abandoned his former stand. The referendum calling the Constitutional Convention of 1947 into existence had a majority of five to one.**

The Convention met at Rutgers on June 12. In anticipation of its meeting Governor Driscoll had appointed a Committee on Preparatory Research for the New Jersey Constitutional Convention. Under the leadership of Sidney Goldmann, then Director of the State Library, this unpaid group of distinguished scholars, lawyers, and officials prepared a large number of special studies for the guidance of the delegates. The New Jersey Committee for Constitutional Revision also made available the services of its committee on research and drafting. Over two hundred persons accepted the invitation to be

* Exactly two-thirds of the 81 members elected to the Convention were Republicans.
** The total vote was one-fifth of that in 1944, when a presidential election was involved. The reversal of attitude in Hudson County resulted in a fifteen-to-one majority.

heard at the committee hearings. During the first few weeks the Convention met its task through the work of the committees, but by mid-August general debate began with the sessions continuing throughout the week. On September 8 the proposed constitution was adopted by a vote of 74 to 1. When submitted to the people at the general election on November 4, this document became the new fundamental law of the State by an overwhelming majority of votes.

The Constitution of 1947 was a revision rather than a new document. Its changes were important but not drastic. The Bill of Rights was altered to extend its protections to all persons regardless of religious principles, race, color, ancestry, or national origin. The structure of government was preserved as before but with modifications. The governor's tenure was extended to four years with eligibility to succeed himself for one term—an alteration that provoked more debate in the Convention than in the ensuing public discussion. The veto was strengthened and the time allowed the governor for considering legislation was extended in order to circumvent abuses. On the key question of administrative reorganization that had been at the heart of the drive for revision in the previous decade, the Constitution embraced a compromise, permitting some agencies such as the Department of Agriculture and the Department of Institutions and Agencies to retain independent status. The provisions of the Constitution of 1844 governing the legislature were little changed. The terms for which members were elected were altered, salaries were left to legislative determination, and a full calendar day made necessary between the second and third readings of a bill unless by a three-fourths vote it should be declared an emergency measure. There was no such definition and clarification of the legislative power as the Commission of 1942 had recommended.

The greatest departure related to the structure and administration of the judiciary, but here too the long effort to bring about a thorough simplification and unification of the court system failed in large measure to achieve its goal. The highest level of the judiciary, however, was drastically altered by the abolition of equity as a separate system and the creation of a new Supreme Court of seven justices with appellate jurisdiction to take the place of the old Supreme Court and the Court of Errors and Appeals. Upon this Supreme Court was thrown the duty of governing the administration, practice, and procedure in all state courts. A Superior Court divided into appellate, law, and chancery divisions was also created. County courts were given constitutional status with the jurisdiction formerly held by the Court of Common Pleas, the Orphans' Court, the Court of Oyer and Terminer, the Court of Quarter Sessions, and the Court of Special Sessions. In view of these changes the reorganization of the judiciary might in fact be regarded as the primary achievement of the Constitutional Convention of 1947.

It has become a commonplace that constitutions are the result of compromise, that in the complex task of accommodating conflicting aims and interests little that is innovative or drastic can be expected. But some who had long hoped for revision felt that many years, perhaps decades, would have to pass before so fair an opportunity to fabricate a wholly modern structure on the old foundations would again be presented. The other states had shown in their long, detailed, and complex constitutions that the distinction between legislation and fundamental law had become blurred. New Jersey had lagged far behind in reform, chained to the weight of archaic institutions and a basic law generally recognized to be obsolete. The opportunity for creating a fresh and challenging instrument seemed to some even more auspicious than that existing when the Federal Convention assembled in 1787, under authority to revise the Articles of Confederation, and then proceeded to draft a new constitution adequate to the exigencies of the Union. But that document had been wrought in an age of profound political experimentation when the people and their leaders were prepared for innovation and were daring enough to experiment. The New Jersey Constitution of 1947 was born in an age of political adjustment.

The responsibility cannot be placed upon the members of the Convention for the shortcomings of the new instrument. That responsibility lies upon every citizen. Few seemed to resent or even to notice the affront given by the representatives to the people in the Constitutional Reform Act of 1947 that authorized a solemn referendum on the most important task a people could face in the realm of self government—that of exercising their basic right to alter or reform their government. For the Act declared in effect that, though the people were sovereign and though the Convention might discard the Bill of Rights or do anything else the delegates deemed wise, there was one thing they could not do—they could not change the system of equal representation in the upper house of the legislature. Such a feudal limitation was to be expected in the seventeenth century when fundamental law was handed down from above, but it ill became an age that had before it the example set almost three centuries earlier in the Concessions and Agreements of 1677 in which even proprietors surrendered their legal prerogative for the sake of preserving the concept of the sovereignty of the people. To the legislature of 1947 that dared to interpose such a restriction and to the people of New Jersey who accepted it in almost silent acquiescence, then, belongs the unenviable distinction of having given such an affront to the idea of fundamental law.*

---

* On June 15, 1964 the Supreme Court of the United States handed down the most far-reaching of its decisions on legislative apportionment, concluding that "legislators represent people, not trees or acres" and that they were elected "by voters, not farms or cities or economic interests." The effect of this decision is almost certainly to render unconstitutional the one county-one vote composition of the Senate of New Jersey on which the people of the State were not permitted to vote in 1947. The reaction to this decision was prompt and predictable. A movement was begun at once to reverse this decision by amendment to the Constitution of the United States—an amendment requiring approval only by the legislatures.

This protected remnant of an earlier day thus remains not merely as an affront to democratic procedure but as a shackle on progress. Other elements of the Constitution also retained give unnecessary reinforcement to its power to retard. Old items of legislation that had crept into the Constitution of 1844 were not only preserved but some new ones were added to a document from which statutory enactments should by definition be excluded. The tax clause that had been a major objective of those leading the struggle for revision was vague in expression. The example of other states in providing for revision at periodic intervals was not followed. In brief, though some advances had been made in the executive and judicial departments, there were great losses. Perhaps the greatest was that the people of New Jersey had discarded the best weapon in their possession for achieving a truly creative statement of the fundamental principles of their society and a durable instrument of government adapted to the exigencies of the modern world. The Constitution of 1844 was buried, while its major elements lived on in the new organic law, not as an ally of progress but as an encumbrance.

It was an irony of history rather than a responsibility of the people of the state that the formidable weapon was discarded at a moment of impending need transcending all that had gone before. For once again, as in 1844, a new fabric of law had been created on the very eve of revolutionary change. This time, in fact, the climactic compromise with the century-old document came at the very moment that a new epoch in history began. With empires crumbling, populations multiplying, power of untold dimensions being released, continents shrinking, and explorations beyond the earth beginning, it was not to be expected that old structures of government could suffice. Yet down across the centuries came an unmistakable voice: not the fabric of government but the rights of men are to be regarded as precious and inviolable. "No Men nor number of Men upon Earth," so ran the Concessions and Agreements of 1677, could encroach upon these rights. Yet to preserve the great heritage more was needed than keeping the well-worn phrases on parchment. They needed to be cherished in the hearts of men, so Algernon Sidney and a host of others had declared. But they also needed to be understood. Once understood, the courage to experiment in new forms of government and to fit these to new exigencies would follow as it had when the people of New Jersey and of other states had thought of themselves as inaugurating a new order of the ages and then had gone on to fabricate forms of federalism never before known that would be appropriate to that new age. Now, at mid-century, a new order among the peoples of the earth was indubitably here. Men had met and triumphed over many challenges before. They were even now achieving feats of the intellect, and of the heart, also, never before realized.

There was no reason to doubt that they could perform equal wonders in the realm of government by consent if they dared. For on this all else depended, including first and above all the only aspect of organized society that Thomas Jefferson considered to be absolute and unchangeable—"the inherent and unalienable rights of man."

I

THE
CONCESSIONS AND AGREEMENT
OF THE
LORDS PROPRIETORS OF THE
PROVINCE OF NEW-JERSEY
FEBRUARY 10, 1664/1665

[Text from the engrossed and signed parchment copy in The New Jersey Historical Society, collated with the text in Aaron Leaming and Jacob Spicer, *The Grants, Concessions, and Original Constitutions of the Province of New-Jersey* (Philadelphia, [1756]), 12-26. A manuscript consisting only of the text of "Item 9" is in the Public Record Office, London, CO 5/952, f. 169, being a transcript sent over from America in 1728.]

The Concessions and Agreement of the Lords Propriators of the Province of New Cesaria or New Jersey to and with all and every the Adventurers and all such as shall settle or plant there.

1 INPRIMIS wee doe consent and agree That the Governor of the said Province hath power by the advice of his Councell to depute one in his place and Authority in case of death or removall, To continue untill our further order unles wee have Commissionated one before.

2 ITEM that hee hath (likewise) power to make choice of and to take to him six Councellors at least, or twelve at most, or any even number between six and twelve with whose advice and consent, or with at least three of the Six, or foure of a greater number (all being sumoned) hee is to governe according to the limitatons and instructions following during our pleasure.

3 ITEM that a Cheife Secratary or Register which wee have chosen or shall choose (wee failing that hee shall chuse) shall keep exact entries in faire bookes of all publique affaires, And to avoid deceipts and Law Suites shall record and enter all grannts of Land from the Lords to the Planters, and all Conveyances of Land house or houses from man to man As alsoe all Leases for Land House or houses made or to be made by the Landlord to any Tenant for more than one yeare, Which Conveyance or Lease shall be first acknowledged by the Grantor or Lessor, or proved by the Oath of two witnesses to the Lease or Conveyance before the Governor or some cheife Judge of a Court for the time being, who shall under his hand upon the backside of the said Deed or Lease Attest the acknowledgment or proofe as aforesaid which

shalbe a Warrant for the Register to record the same, which Conveyance or Lease soe recorded shalbe good and effectual in Law notwithstanding any other Conveyance Deed or Lease for the said Land house or houses or for any part thereof, although dated before the Conveyance Deed or Deeds or Lease soe Recorded as aforesaid; And the said Register shall doe all other thing or things that wee by our instructions shall direct, and the Governor Councell and assembly shall ordeine for the good and welfare of the said Province.

4 ITEM That the Surveyor Generall that wee have chosen or shall choose (wee failing that the Governor shall chose) shall have power by himselfe or Deputy to Survey lay out and bound all such Lands as shall be grannted from the Lords to the Planters, and all other Land within the said Province which may concerne perticular men as hee shalbe desired to doe, And a particular thereof Certifie to the Register to be recorded as aforesaid, **Provided** that if the said Register and Surveyor or either of them shall misbehave themselves as that the Governor and Councell or Deputie Governor and Councell or the major part of them shall find it reasonable to suspend their Actings in their respective imployments it shall be lawfull for them soe to doe, untill further order from us.

5 ITEM That the Governor Councellors Assembly men Secretary Surveyor and all other officers of Trust shall sweare or subscribe (in a booke to bee provided for that purpose) That they will beare true Allegiance to the King of England his heires and successors, and that they will be faithfull to the interest of the Lords Propriators of the said Province and their heires executors and assignes And endeavor the peace and welfare of the said Province And that they will truely and faithfully discharge their respective trusts in their respective Offices, and doe equall Justice to all men according to their best skill and Judgment without corrupton favour or affecton And the names of all that have sworne or subscribed to be entred in a Booke And whosoever shall subscribe and

not sweare, and shall violate his promise in that subscripton shall be liable to the same punishment that the persons are or may bee that have sworne and broken their Oathes.

6 ITEM That all persons that are or shall become subjects to the King of England and sweare or subscribe Allegiance to the King and faithfulnes to the Lords shalbe admitted to Plant and become Freemen of the said Province and enjoy the Freedomes and Imunities hereafter expressed untill some stopp or contradiction bee made by us the Lords or else the Governor Councell and Assemblie, which shalbe in force untill the Lords see cause to the contrary, Provided that such stopp shall not any way prejudice the right or continuance of any person that hath been received before such stopp or order came from the Lords or generall Assemblie.

7 ITEM That noe person qualified as aforesaid within the said Province at any time shalbe any waies molested punished disquieted or called in Question for any difference in opinion or practice in matters of Religious concernements, who doe not actually disturbe the civill peace of the said Province, but that all and every such person and persons may from time to time and at all times freely and fully have and enjoy his and their Judgments and Consciences in matters of Religion throughout all the said Province; They behaveing themselves peaceably and quietly and not using this liberty to Licentiousnes, nor to the civill injury or outward disturbance of others, any Law Statute or clause conteyned or to be conteined usage or custome of this Realme of England to the contrary thereof in any wise notwithstanding.

8 ITEM That noe pretence may be taken by us our heires or assignes for or by reason of our right of Patronage and power of Advowson grannted by his Majesties Letters Pattents unto his Royall Highnes James Duke of Yorke, and by his said Royall Highnes unto us, thereby to infringe the generall clause of Libertie of Conscience aforementioned Wee doe hereby grannt unto the Generall assembly of the said Province power by Act to

Constitute and appoint such and soe many Ministers or Preachers as they shall think fitt, and to establish their maintenance, Giving liberty besides to any person or persons to keep and maintaine what Preachers or Ministers they please.

9 ITEM That the inhabitants being Freemen or cheife Agents to others of the Province aforesaid doe as soone as this our Comission shall arrive by virtue of a writt in our names by the Governor to be for the present (untill our Seale comes) sealed and signed make choice of Twelve Deputies or Representatives from amongst themselves who being chosen are to joine with the said Governor and Councell for the makeing of such Lawes Ordinances and Constitutions as shalbe necessary for the present good and welfare of the said Province, But so soone as Parishes Divisions Tribes or other Distinctions are made That then the Inhabitants or Freeholders of the severall and respective Parishes Tribes Devisions and distinctions aforesaid doe (by our writts under our seale which wee engage shall be in due time issued) Anually meet on the first day of January and choose Freeholders for each respective division Tribe or Parish to be the Deputies or Representatives of the same Which body of representatives or the major part of them shall with the Governor and Councell aforesaid bee the generall Assembly of the said Province, the Governor or his Deputy being present unles they shall wilfullie refuse, in which case they may appoint themselves a President dureing the absence of the Governor or his Deputy Governor.

Which Assemblies are to have power

To appoint their own times of meeting, and to adjorne their Sessions from time to time, to such times and places as they shall think convenient, As alsoe to ascertaine the number of their Quorum Provided that such numbers be not lesse then the third part of the whole in whom (or more) shall be the full power of the generall Assembly vizt. To enact and make all such Lawes Acts and Constitutons as shalbe necessarie for the well Government of the said Province, and them to repeale, Provided that the same be consonant to reason, and, as neere as may be conveniently agreeable to the Lawes and Customes of his Majesties Kingdom of England, Provided also that they be not against the interest of us the Lords Propriators our heires or assignes nor any of these our Concessions, especiallie that they be not repugnant to the Article for Libertie of Conscience above mentioned, Which Lawes &c. soe made shall receive Publication from the Governor and Councell (but as the Lawes of us and our generall Assembly) and be in force for the space of one yeare and no more) unles contradicted by the Lords Propriators, within which time they are to bee presented to us our heires &c. for our Ratification, and being confirmed by us they shall be in continuall force till expired by their own limitaton or by Act of Repeale in like manner to be passed as aforesaid and confirmed.

3 By Act as aforesaid to constitute all Courts together with the limitts powers and Jurisdictions of the same, as alsoe the severall Offices and number of Officers belonging to each Court, with their respective Sallaries Fees and perquisits, their appellatons and dignities, with the penalties that shall be due to them for the breach of their severall and respective duties and Trusts.

4 By Act as aforesaid to lay equall taxes and assessments equally to raise money's or goods upon all Lands (excepting the Lands of us the Lord Propriators before setling) or persons within the severall Precincts Hundreds Parishes Manors or whatsoever other Divisions shall hereafter be made and established in the said Province as oft as necessity shall require and in such manner as to them shall seem most equall and easie for the said inhabitants in order to the better supporting of the publique charge of the said Government, and for the mutuall safetye defence and securitie of the said Province.

5 By Act as aforesaid to erect within the said Province such and soe many Manors with their necessarie Courts Juris-

dictions freedoms and Priviledges as to them shall seem meet and convenient, as alsoe to devide the said Province into Hundreds Tribes Parishes or such other Divisions or distinctions as they shall think fitt, and the said Divisions to distinguish by what names wee shall order or direct, And in default thereof by such names as they please, As alsoe within the said Province to create and appoint such and soe many Ports Harbors Creekes and other places for the convenient lading and unlading of goods and Merchandizes out of Shipps Boates and other Vessells as shalbe expedient, with such Jurisdictions priviledges and Franchises to such Ports &c. belonging as they shall judge most conducing to the generall good of the said Plantatons or Province.

By their Enacting to be confirmed as aforesaid to erect raise and build within the said Province or any part thereof such and soe many Forts Fortresses Castles Citties, Corporations Burroughs, Towns, Villages, and other places of Strength and defence, and them or any of them to incorporate with such Charters and Priviledges as to them shall seem good, and the Grant made unto us will permitt, and the same or any of them to Fortifie and furnish with such Provisions and proportions of Ordinance powder shott Armour and all other weapons Amunition and Habiliments of warr both offensive and deffensive as shall be thought necessary and convenient for the safety and welfare of the said Province; But they may not at any time demolish dismantle or disfurnish the same without the consent of the Governor and the major part of the Councell of the said Province.

By Act as aforesaid to constitute Trained bands and companies with the number of Soldiers for the safety strength and defence of the said Province; and of the Forts Castles Citties &c. to suppresse all Mutinies and Rebellions, To make warr Offensive and Defensive with all Indians Strangers and Foreigners, as they shall see cause; And to pursue an Enemye by Sea aswell as by Land if need be out of the limitts and Jurisdictions of the said Province,

	with the perticuler consent of the Governor or under his conduct or of our Comander in cheife, or whom he shall appoint
8	By Act as aforesaid to give unto all Strangers as to them shall seem meet A naturalization, and all such freedomes and priviledges within the said Province as to his Majesties subjects doe of right belong they Swearing or subscribeing as aforesaid Which said Strangers soe naturalized and priviledged shall be in all respects accompted in the said Province as the Kings naturall subjects.
9	By Act as aforesaid to prescribe the quantities of Land which shall be from time to time allotted to every head, free or Servant, Male or Female, and to make and ordeine rules for the casting of lotts for Land and the layeing out of the same, Provided they doe not in their prescriptions exceed the severall proportions which are hereby grannted by us to all persons arriving in the said Province or Adventuring thither.
10	The generally Assembly by Act as aforesaid shall make provision for the maintenance and support of the Governor, and for the defrayeing all necessarie charges of the Goverment As alsoe that the Constables of the said Province shall Collect the Lords Rent, and shall pay the same to the Receivor that the Lords shall appoint to receive the same, unles the said generall assembly shall prescribe some other way whereby the Lords may have their Rents duely collected without charge or trouble to them.
11	Lastlie to enact constitute and ordeine all such other Lawes Acts and Constitutions as shall or may be necessary for the good property and settlement of the said Province (excepting what by these presents is excepted And conforming to the limitations herein exprest.

The Governor with his Councell before exprest is

i	To see that all Courts established by the lawes of the Generall Assembly and all Ministers and Officers civill and military doe and execute their severall Duties and

Offices respectively according to the Lawes in force, and to punish them for Swerving from the Lawes or Acting contrary to their Trust, as the nature of their offence shall require.

i According to the Constitutions of the generall Assembly to nominate and Comissionate the severall Judges members and officers of Courts whither Magistraticall or Ministeriall and all other civell officers Coroners &c. and their Comissions powers and authorities to revoke at pleasure Provided that they appoint none but such as are Freeholders in the Province aforesaid unles the generall Assembly consent.

ii According to the Constitutions of the generall assembly to appoint Courts and Officers in Cases criminall, and to impower them to inflict penalties upon offenders against any of the Lawes in force in the said Province, as the said Lawes shall ordeine, whither by Fine imprisonment, banishment corporall punishment, or to the takeing away of member or of life itselfe if there be cause for it.

iii To place Officers and Soldiers for the safetie, strength, and defence of the Forts Castles Cities &c. according to the number appointed by the generall Assembly to nominate place and comissionate all Military Officers under the dignitie of the said Governor who is Commissionated by us over the severall Trained bands and Companies, Constituted by the generall Assembly as Colonells Captaines &c. and their Comissions to revoke at pleasure, the Governor with the advice of his Councell, unles some present Danger will not permitt him to advice, to muster and traine all the forces within the said Province, to prosecute War, pursue an Enemye, suppresse all Rebellions and Mutinies, as well by Sea as by Land, and to exercise the whole Militia as fully as wee by the Grannt from his Royall Highnes can impower him or them to doe, Provided that they appoint noe military forces but what are freeholders in the said Province, unles the Generally Assembly shall consent.

Where they see cause after Condemnation to Repreive

vi   untill the Case be Presented, with a coppie of the whole Tryall and proceedings and proofes to the Lords who will accordingly either pardon or comand execution of the sentence on the Offender who is in the meane time to be kept in safe custodie till the pleasure of the Lords be knowne.

vi   In case of death or other removall of any of the representatives within the yeare to issue Sumons by writt to the respective Division or Divisions for which he or they were chosen comanding the Freeholders of the same to choose others in their stead.

vii   To make Warrants and to Seale grants of Lands according to these our Concessions and the prescriptions by the advice of the generall Assembly in such forme as shall be at large sett down in our Instructions to the Governor in his Comission, and which are hereafter exprest.

viii   To Act and doe all other thing or things that may conduce to the safetie peace and well Government of the said Province, as they shall see fitt, soe as they bee not contrary to the Lawes of the said Province.

For the better security of the Propriators and all the Inhabitants.

1 They are not to impose nor suffer to be imposed any Taxe Custome Subsidie Talladge, Assessment or any other duty whatsoever upon any colour or pretence upon the said Province and inhabitants thereof other then what shall be imposed by the Authority and consent of the generall Assembly and then only in manner as aforesaid.

2 They are to take care that Land quietlie held planted and possessed seaven yeares after its being first duely Surveyed by the Surveyor Generall or his Order shall not be subject to any reveiw or Survey or alteration of bounds on what pretence soever by any of us or any officer or Minister under us.

3 They are to take care that noe man if his Cattell Stray, Range or Graze on any Ground within the said Province not actually appropriated or sett out to per-

ticular persons shall be lyable to pay any Trespasse for the same to us our heires &c. Provided that Custome of Commons be not thereby pretended to; nor any person hindred from taking up and appropriating any Lands soe grased upon, And that noe person doe purposely suffer his Cattle to graze on such Lands.

And that the planting of the said Province may be the more speedily promoted

1 Wee doe hereby Grannt unto all persons who have alreadie Adventured to the Province of New Cesaria or new Jersey or shall transport themselves or Servants before the first day of January which shall be in the yeare of our Lord 1665. These following proportions vizt. to every Freeman that shall goe with the first Governor from the Port where he imbarques (or shall meet him at the Randevouze hee appoints) for the Settlement of a Plantaton there, armed with a good Muskett boare twelve bulletts to the Pound, with Tenn pounds of powder, and Twenty pound of Bulletts with bandeleers and match convenient, and with six months provision for his own person arriving there 150 acres of Land English measure. And for every able man Servant that he shall carry with him armed and provided as aforesaid and arriving there, the like quantity of 150 acres of land English measure; And whoever shall send Servants at that time, shall have for every able man Servant hee or she soe sends armed and provided as aforesaid and arriving there the like quantity of 150 acres And for every weaker Servant or Slave male or female exceeding the age of Fourteen yeares which any one shall send or carry arriveing there 75 acres of Land And to every Christian Servant exceeding the age aforesaid after the expiraton of their time of service 75 acres of Land for their own use.

2 ITEM to every Master or Mistris that shall goe before the first day of January which shalbe in the yeare of our Lord 1665 120 acres of land and for every able man Servant that hee or she shall carry or send armed and

provided as aforesaid and arriving with the time aforesaid the like quantity of 120 acres of land, and for every weaker Servant or Slave male or female exceeding the age of 14 yeares arriving there 60 acres of land, and to every Christian Servant to their owne use and behoofe 60 acres of land.

3 **Item** to every Freeman and Freewoman shall arrive in the said Province armed and provided as aforesaid within the second yeare from the first day af January 1665. to the first of January 1666. with an intenton to plant 90 acres of land English measure, and for every able man Servant that hee or she shall carry or send armed and provided as aforesaid 90 acres of land of like measure.

4 **Item** for every weaker Servant or Slave aged as aforesaid that shall be soe carried or sent thither within the second yeare as aforesaid 45 acres of land of like measure And to every Christian Servant that shall arrive the second yeare 45 acres of land of like measure after the expiration of his or their time of Service for their own use and behoofe.

5 **Item** to every Freeman and Freewoman Armed and provided as aforesaid That shall goe and arrive with an intenton to plant within the third yeare from January 1666 to January 1667. 60 acres of land of like measure And for every able man Servant that he or they shall carry or send within the said time armed and provided as aforesaid the like quantitie of 60 acres of land, And for every weaker Servant or Slave aged as aforesaid that hee or they shall carry or send within the third yeare 30 acres of land and to every Christian Servant soe carried or sent in the Third yeare 30 acres of land of like measure after the expiraton of his or their time of Service. All which Land and all other that shall be possessed in the said Province are to be held on the same termes and Conditons as is before mentoned and as hereafter in the following Paragraphs is more at large expressed.

Provided alwaies that the before mentoned Land and all other whatsoever that shall be taken up and soe settled in the said Province shall afterward from time to time for the space of thirteen yeares from the date hereof be held upon the Conditons aforesaid continueing one able man Servant or two such weaker Servants as aforesaid on every 100 acres a Master or Mistris shall possess; besides what was granted for his or her own person; In failer of which upon notificaton to the present occupant or his assignes there shall be three yeares given to such for their compleating the said number of persons, or for their Sale or other Disposure of such part of their Lands as are not soe peopled within which time of three yeares if any person holding any Lands shall faile by himself his Agents executors or assignes, or some other way to provide such number of persons, unles the generall Assembly shall without respect to poverty judge it was impossible for the party soe failing to keep or procure his or her number of Servants to be provided as aforesaid; In such case wee the Lords to have power of disposing of soe much of such Land as shall not be planted with its due number of persons as aforesaid to some other that will plant the same; **Provided alwaies** that noe person arriving into the said Province with purpose to settle (they being Subjects or naturalized as aforesaid) bee denied a Grant of such proportons of Land as at the time of their arrivall there, are due to themselves or Servants by Commission from us as aforesaid, but have full licence to take up and settle the same in such Order and manner as is granted or prescribed; All Lands (notwithstanding the powers in the Assembly aforesaid) shall be taken up by Warrant from the Governor, and confirmed by the Governor and Councell under a Seale to be provided for that purpose in such Order and method as shalbe set down in this declaraton and more at large in the instructions to the Governor and Councell.

And that the Lands may be the more regularlie laid out and all persons the better ascertained of their Titles and possessions.

The Governor and Councell (and Assembly if any be) are to take care and direct that all Lands be devided by Generall Lotts, none lesse than 2100 acres, nor more then 21000 Acres in each lott, excepting Citties Townes &c. and the near lotts of Townshipps, And that the same be devided into Seaven parts one Seaventh part by Lott to us our heires and assignes, the remainder to persons as they come to plant the same in such proportons as is allowed.

ii   ITEM that the Governor, or whom he shall depute in case of Death, or absence, if some one be not before Commissionated by us as aforesaid doe give to every person to whom Land is due, a Warrant Signed and sealed by himselfe, and the Major part of his Councell, and directed to the Surveyor Generall or his Deputie comanding him to lay out limitt and bound   acres of land (as his due proporton is) for such a person in such Allottment, according to which Warrant the Register haveing first Recorded the same, and attested the record upon the Warrant, The Surveyor Generall or his Deputy shall proceed and certifie to the cheife Secretary or Register the name of the person for whom he hath laid out land by virtue of what Authority, the date of the Authoritie or Warrant, the number of acres, the bounds, and on what point of the Compasse the severall limitts thereof lye; which Certificate the Register is likewise to enter in a booke to be prepared for that purpose with an Alphabeticall table referring to the booke, that soe the Certificate may bee the easeir found, and then to file the Certificates and the same to keep safelye, The Certificate being entred a Warrant comprehending all the perticulars of the Land mentoned in the Certificate aforesaid is to bee signed and sealed by him and his Councell or the major part of them as aforesaid (they haveing seen the entry) and directed to the Register or cheife Secretary for his prepareing a Grannt of the Land to the partie for whom it is laid out, which grannt shall bee in the forme following vizt.

The Lords Propriators of the Province of New Cesaria or New Jersey doe hereby Grannt unto A B of the   in the Province aforesaid A plantation conteyn-

ing   acres English measure bounding (as in the Certificates) To hold to him (or her) his (or her) heires and assignes for ever, Yeilding and payeing yearely to the said Lord Propriators their heires or assignes every 25th day of March according to the English account, One halfe penny or One penny of lawfull money of England for every of the said acres To be holden of the Manor of   in free and comon Soccage, the first payment of which Rent to begin the 25th day of March which shall be in the yeare of our Lord according to the English account 1670. Given under the seale of the said Province the   day of   in the yeare of our Lord 16

iii To which Instrument the Governor or his deputy hath hereby full power to put the Seale of the said Province and to subscribe his name as alsoe the Councell or the major part of them are to subscribe their names, And then the Instrument or Grant is to be by the Register recorded in a booke of Records for that purpose, All which being done according to those instructions Wee hereby declare that the same shall be effectuall in Law for the enjoyment of the said Plantation, and all the benefitts and profitts of and in the same (except the halfe part of mines of Gold and Silver) paying the Rent as aforesaid Provided that if any Plantaton soe grannted shall by the space of these yeares be neglected to be planted with a sufficient number of Servants as is before mentoned That then it shall be lawfull for us otherwise to dispose thereof in whole or in part, this Grannt notwithstanding.

iii ITEM wee doe alsoe grannt convenient proportons of Land for highwaies and for Streets not exceeding 100 foote in bredth in Citties Town's and Villages &c. for Churches Forts Wharfes Keyes Harbours and for publique houses, And to each Parish for the use of their Minister 200 acres in such places as the Generall Assembly shall appoint.

ITEM the Governor is to take notice that all such Lands laid out for the uses and purposes aforesaid in the next preceding Article shall be free and exempt from all Rents

Taxes and other charges and duties whatsoever payable to us our heires or assignes.

vi **Item** that in layeing out Lands for Cities Townes Villages Burroughs or other Hamletts, the said lands be devided into seaven parts, one seaventh part whereof to be by Lott laid out for us and the rest devided to such as shalbe willing to build thereon, they paying after the rate of one halfe penny or one penny ℔ acre according to the value of the Lands yearely to us as for their other Land as aforesaid which said Lands in Citties Townes &c. is to be assured to each possessor by the same way and instrument as is before mentoned.

vii **Item** that the Inhabitants of the said Province have free passage through or by any Seas, bounds creeks rivers rivuletts &c. in the said Province through or by which they must necessarilie passe to come from the maine Ocean to any part of the Province aforesaid.

viii **Lasteie** it shall be lawfull for the Representatives of the ffreeholders to make any Addresse to the Lords touching the Governor and Councell or any of them for or concerning any Greivances whatsoever, or for any other thing they shall desire, without the consent of the Governor and Councell or any of them.

Februarie 10th, 1664

John Berkeley
Geo: Carterett

II

A DECLARATION OF THE TRUE INTENT AND MEANING OF THE CONCESSIONS AND AGREEMENT DECEMBER 6, 1672

[Text from Aaron Leaming and Jacob Spicer, *The Grants, Concessions, and Original Constitutions of the Province of New-Jersey* (Philadelphia, [1756]), 55-57, collated with an attested clerk's copy that probably dates from the late seventeenth century and is found in a volume entitled "East Jersey Deeds, &c." Liber 3, 59-60, in the New Jersey Bureau of Archives and History.]

A DECLARATION *of the true Intent and Meaning of us the* LORDS PROPIETORS, *and Explanation of theire Concessions made to the Adventurers and Planters of New-Caesarea or New-Jersey*

1. THAT as to the 6th Article, it shall be in the Power of the Governor and his Council to admit of all Persons to become Planters and free Men of the said Province, without the General Assembly; but no Person or Persons whatsoever shall be counted a Freeholder of the said Province, nor have any Vote in electing, nor be capable of being elected for any Office of Trust, either Civil or Military, until he doth actually hold his or their Lands by Patent from us, the Lords Proprietors.

II. As to the 8th Article, it shall be in the Power of the Governor and Council, to constitute and appoint such Ministers and Preachers as shall be nominated and chosen by the several Corporations, without the General Assembly, and to establish their Maintenance, giving Liberty besides to any Person or Persons to keep and maintain what Preachers or Ministers they please.

As to the General Assembly.

I. THAT it shall be in the Power of the Governor and the Council to appoint the Times and Places of meeting of the General Assembly, and to adjourn and summon them together again when and where he and they shall see Cause.

II. To the *Third;* That it is to be understood, that it is in the Power of the Governor and his Council to constitute and appoint Courts in particular Corporations already settled, without the General Assembly; but for the Courts of Sessions and Assizes to be constituted and established by the Governor Council and Representatives together: And that all Appeals, shall be made from the Assizes, to the Governor and his Council, and thence to the Lords Proprietors; from whom they may appeal to the King, and that no more Corporations be confirm'd but by or with the special order of us the Lords Proprietors.

III. To the ninth Article: That the Governor and his Council may dispose of the Allotments of Land to each particular Person, without the General Assembly according to our Directions, as he and they shall think fit.

Concerning the Governor.

I. As to the second and third Article; all Officers Civil and Military (except before excepted) be nominated and appointed by the Governor and Council, without the General Assembly, unless he the said Governor and Council shall see occasion for their Advice and Assistance.

II. As to the fourth Article, in case of foreign Invasion or intestine Mutiny or Rebellion; it shall be lawful for the Governor and his Council to call in to their Aid, any Persons whatsoever whether Freeholder or not.

III. That in the Sixth Article, concerning the regular laying out of Lands, Rules for Building each Street in Townships, and Quantities of Ground for each House Lot, the same is left to the Freeholders or first undertakers thereof, as they can agree with the Governor and Council, and not to the General Assembly, but to be laid out by the Surveyor General.

IV. That all Warrants for Lands not exceeding the Proportions in the Concessions, being only sign'd by the Governor and Secretary shall be effectual in Case his Council or any Part of them be not present.

We the Lords Proprietors do understand that in all

General Assembly's, the Governor and his Council are to set by themselves, and the Deputies or Representatives by themselves, and whatever they do propose to be presented to the Governor and his Council, and upon their Confirmation to pass for an Act or Law when Confirm'd by us. WITNESS our Hands and Seals the 6th day of *December,* 1672.

JOHN BERKELEY.
G. CARTERET

III

THE CONCESSIONS AND AGREEMENTS OF THE PROPRIETORS, FREEHOLDERS, AND INHABITANTS OF THE PROVINCE OF WEST NEW JERSEY MARCH 3, 1676/1677

[Text from the engrossed and signed original manuscript, a bound volume of ninety numbered pages and three additional pages of signatures, in the archives of the Council of Proprietors of the Western Division of New Jersey at Burlington; collated with the text in Aaron Leaming and Jacob Spicer, *The Grants, Concessions, and Original Constitutions of the Province of New-Jersey* (Philadelphia, [1756]), 382-411. The latter contains 151 signatures, the former 152. It is clear that Leaming and Spicer printed their text from this original manuscript, hence it follows that the additional signature was added after 1756. The quality of the ink and the handwriting indicate that this was done at a much later date. In 1951 Henry H. Bisbee proved that in fact it was done during the second quarter of the twentieth century, for he possessed a facsimile of the final page of the manuscript that had been made about 1925, showing that the signature in question was not on the document at that time (Henry H. Bisbee, ed., *The Concessions and Agreements of the Proprietors, Freeholders and Inhabitants of the Province of West New Jersey* [Burlington, 1951], vii). This signature, having no relevance to the original manuscript, can only be characterized as a defacement. It is therefore omitted in the present text in which facsimiles of the signatures of the 151 persons who signed the original document are presented.]

The Concessions and Agreements of the Proprietors Freeholders and Inhabitants of the Province of West New Jersey in America:

Chapter 1

WEE DOE CONSENT AND AGREE as the best present expedient that such persons as shall be from time to time deputed nominated and appointed Comissioners by the present Proprietors or the major parte of them by writeing under their hands and seales shall be Comissioners for the time being and have power to order and manage the Estate and affairs of the said Province of West New Jersey according to these our Concessions hereafter following and to depute others in their place and Authority in case of death or removeall and to continue untill some other persons be deputed nominated and appointed by the said proprietors or the Major parte of them to succeed them in that Office and service. And the Comissioners for the time being are to take care for setting forth and dividing all the Lands of the Said Province as be allready taken up or by themselves shall be taken up and contracted for with the Natives and the said land soe taken up and contracted for to divide into one hundred parts as occasion shall require that is to say for every quantity of Land that they shall from time to time lay out to be planted and setled upon they shall first for expedition divide the same into tenn equall parts or shares and for distinction Sake to marke in the Register and upon some of the trees belonging to every tenth parte with the letters **A B** and so end at the letter **K**. And after the same is so divided and marked the said

Comissioners are to grant unto Thomas Hutchinson of Beverley Thomas Pearson of Bonwicke Joseph Helmsley of great Kelke George Hutchinson of Sheffield and Mahlon Stacy of Hansworth all of the County of Yorke or their Lawfull deputies or particuler Comissioners for themselves and their friends who are a Considerable number of people and may speedily promote the Planting of the said Province that they may have free liberty to make choice of any one of the said tenth parts or shares which shall be first divided and set out being also done with their consent that they may plant upon the same as they see meet and afterward any other person or persons who shall goe over to inhabitt and have purchased to the number of tenn proprieties they shall and may have Liberty to make choice of any of the remaineing Parts or Shares to settle in and all other Proprietors who shall goe over to settle as aforesaid and cannot make up amongst them the number of tenn Proprietors yet nevertheless they shall and may have Liberty to make choice of settleing in any of the said tenth shares that shall not be taken up before and the Comissioners have hereby power to see the said one tenth parte that they shall soe make choice of laid out and divided into tenn Proprieties and to allott them so many Proprieties out of the same as they have order for and the said Comissioners are to follow these Rules untill they receive contrary order from the major parte of the Proprietors under their hands and seales.

The said Comissioners for the time being have hereby power for appointing and setting out fitt places for Townes and to limitt the bounderies thereof and to take care they be as Regular built as the present occasion time and conveniency of the places will admit of and that all Townes to be erected and built shall be with the consent of the Comissioners for the time being or the major parte of them. And further the said Comissioners are to order the affaires of the said Province according to these concessions and any other instructions that shall be given them by the major parte of the Proprietors untill such time as more or other Comissioners shall be chosen by the Inhabitants of West Jersey as here in these Concessions is mentioned and appointed.

And it is further expressly provided and agreed to that whereas there is a contract or agreement granted by William Penn Gawen Lawry And Nicholas Lucas unto Thomas Hutchinson Thomas Pearson Joseph Helmsly George Hutchinson and Mahlon Stacy Dated the second day of the month called March 1676 instant wherein they grant unto the said persons certaine priviledges for a Towne to be built whereby they have Liberty to choose their owne Magistrates and officers for executing the Laws according to the Concessions within the said Towne which said Contract or agreement is to be held firme and good to all intents and purposes and we doe by these our Concessions confirme the same.

CHAPTER 2

And that all and every person and persons May enjoy his and their just And equall propriety and purchase of lands in the said Province it is hereby agreed concluded and ordained that the Survey or Surveyors that the said Proprietors have deputed and appointed or shall depute or appoint they faileing that the Comissioners shall depute & appoint or that the generall free Assembly hereafter shall depute and appoint shall have power by him or themselves or his or their Lawfull Deputie or Deputies to Survey lay out or bound All the Proprietors Lands and all such lands as shall be granted from any of the Proprietors to the Freeholders Planters or inhabitants and a particuler or Terryor thereof to Certifie to the Register to be recorded.

Chapter 3

That hereafter upon further settlement of the said province the Proprietors Freeholders and Inhabitants resident upon the said Province shall and may at or upon the five and twentieth day of the month Called March which shall be in the yeare according to the English account One thousand six hundred and Eighty and soe thenceforward upon the five and twentieth day of March yearly by the ninth houre in the morning of the said day assemble themselves together in some publick place to be ordered and appointed by the Comissioners for the time being and upon default of such appointment in such place as they shall see meet and then and there elect of and amongst themselves tenn honest and able men fitt for Government to officiate and execute the place of Comissioners for the yeare ensueing and untill such time as tenn more for the yeare then next following shall be elected and appointed which said elections shall be as followeth that is to say the Inhabitants Each tenn of the one hundred Proprieties shall elect and choose one and the one hundred proprieties shall be divided into tenn divisions or Tribes of Men.

And the said elections shall be made and distinguished by ballating trunks to avoid noise and confusion and not by voices holding up of the hands or otherwise howsoever which said Comissioners so yearly to be elected shall likewise Governe and order the affairs of the said Province pro tempore for the good and wellfare of the said people and according to these our concessions Untill such time as a generall free assembly shall be elected and deputed in such manner and wise as is hereafter expressed and conteined.

Chapter 4

And that the planting of the said province be the more speedily promoted it is consented granted concluded agreed and declared first   That the proprietors of the said Province have and doe hereby grant unto all persons who by and with the consent of one or more of any of the proprietors of the said Province Attested by a certificate under his or their hands and seales Adventure to the said Province of West New Jersey and shall Transport themselves or servants before the first day of the month commonly called Aprill which shall be in the yeare of our Lord one thousand six hundred seaventy and seaven these Following propsitions vizt. for his owne person Arriveing Seaventy Acres of Land English Measure and for every Able man servant that he shall carry with him and arriveing there the like Quantity of seaventy Acres of land English Measure and whoever shall send Servants before that time shall have for every able man servant he or they so send as aforesaid and arriveing there the like Quantity of Seaventy Acres And for every weaker servant male or female Exceeding the Age of fourteen yeares which any one shall send or carry Arriveing there Fifty Acres of Land and after the expiration of their time of service Fifty Acres of Land for their owne use and Behoofe to hold to them and their heires forever all such persons and persons Freemen or servants and their respective heires and assignes afterwards paying yearely to the Proprietor his heires and assignes to whom the said Lands belong one penny an acre for what shall be laid out in Townes and one halfe penny an acre for what shall be laid out elsewhere the first yearly payment to begin within two yeares after the said lands are laid out.

2   To every Master or Mistress that by and with such consent aforesaid shall goe hence the second yeare before the first day of the month called Aprill which shall be in the yeare one thousand six hundred Seaventy and eight Fifty Acres of Land and for every able man servant that he or she shall carry or send and arriveing there the like quantity of Fifty acres of Land and for every weaker servant Male or female exceeding the age of fourteen yeares arriveing there Thirty acres of land and after the

expiration of their service Thirty acres of land for their owne use and behoofe to hold to them and their heires forever all the said persons and their respective Heires and Assignes yearely paying as aforesaid to the Proprietor his heires and assignes to whom the land belongs one penny farthing the acre for all such lands as shall be laid out in Townes and three farthings the acre for all that shall be laid out elsewhere.

To every Freeman that shall arrive in the said Province within the third yeare from the first day of the month commonly called Aprill in the yeare one thousand six hundred seaventy and eight to the first of the said month called Aprill one thousand six hundred seaventy and nine (with an intention to plant) Forty acres of Land English measure and for every able man servant that he or she shall carry or send as aforesaid forty acres of land of like measure and for every weaker servant aged as aforesaid that shall be soe carried or sent thither within the third yeare as aforesaid twenty acres of land of like measure and after the expiration of his or their time of service twenty acres of land for their owne use and behoofe to hold to them and their heires forever all the said persons and their heires and assignes paying yearly as aforesaid to the Proprietor his heires or assignes with whom they contract for the same One penny halfe penny the acre for what shall be laid out in Townes and one penny the acre for what shall be laid out elsewhere. All which lands that shall be possessed in the said province are to be held under and according to the concessions and conditions as is before mentioned and as hereafter in the following Paragraph is more at large expressed **provided** always that the before mentioned land that shall be taken up and so setled in the province as aforesaid shall from the date hereof be held upon the conditions aforesaid conteining at least two able Men servants or three such weaker servants as aforesaid for every hundred acres and so proportionably for a lesser or greater quantity as one hundred acres besides what a Master or

Mistress shall posess which was granted for his or her owne person in failer of which upon notation to the present occupant or his assignes there shall be three yeares given to such for the compleating the said number of servants and for their sale or other disposure of such part of their lands as are not so peopled within which time of three yeares if any person holding any land shall faile by himselfe his agents executors or assignes or some other way to provide Such number of persons unless the Generall Assembly shall without respect to poverty Judg it was impossible for the partie so faileing to keep his or her number of servants to be provided as aforesaid in such case the Comissioners are to summon together twelv men of the neighbourhood upon such inquest verdict and Judgment past of such default they are and have power of disposeing of soe much of such land for any terme of yeares not exceeding twenty yeares as shall not be planted with it's due number of persons as aforesaid to some other that will plant the Same reserveing and preserveing to the Proprietor or his lawfull assignes the rents to become due and owing for or in respect of the same according to the tenure and effect of these concessions. And further that every proprietor that goeth over in person and inhabitt in the said Province shall keep and maintaine upon every lott of land that they shall take up one person at least and if the lot shall exceed two hundred acres he shall keep and maintaine for every two hundred acres the like quantity of one person at the least.

And for all other proprietors that doth but goe over in person and inhabit in the said province shall keep and maintaine upon every lot of land that shall fall to them one person at the least and if the said lott exceed one hundred acres then upon every hundred acres that fall to them as aforesaid they shall keep and maintaine one person at the least and if any neglect or deficiency shall be found in any of the proprietors of their keeping and maintaineing the number of persons before mentioned that then and in that case the Comissioners are to dispose upon the said lands for any terme of yeares not exceeding twenty to any person or persons that will keep and maintaine upon the said lands the number of persons as before is mentioned reserving alwaies unto the said proprietors the rents that shall fall due for the same as before is reserved and appointed to be so Alwaies provided that the keeping and maintaineing of the said number of persons upon the severall lots and number of acres before mentioned is to continue for ten yeares from the date of the concessions and no longer except wher there have been any deficiency so as the comissioners have lett the lands for a longer time to any person or persons they are to enjoy the same dureing the term granted them by the Comissioners any thing in this last proviso to the contrary notwithstanding.

Chapter 5

And for the regular laying out of all lands whatsoever in the said province this method is to be followed by the Register and Surveyor

That the Register to be appointed as aforesaid haveing recorded any grant from any of the Proprietors to any person for any quantity or quantities of acres shall make out a Certificate to the surveyor or his deputie enjoying him to lay out limit and bound

Acres of land for **A B** out of the several lotts of **C D** one of the Proprietors in the proportions following that is to say   part there of in the lott of the said **C D** in   which the Surveyor or his deputie shall lay out limitt and bound accordingly and shall certifie back to the Register on what point of the Compass the severall limitts thereof lie and on whose lands the severall parcells Butt and bound which last certificate shall be entered by the said Register or his deputie in a booke for that purpose with an Alphabeticall table of the Proprietors names and the name of the planter or purchaser referring to the said Certificate shall by the said Register be endorsed on the back of the grant with the folio of the booke in which it is entered and his name subscribed to the said Indorsement.

And that the Commissioners for the time being are hereby impowered to asertaine the rates and fees of the publick Register Surveyor and other officers as they shall see meet and reasonable how much or what every one shall pay for Registering any conveyance Deed lease specialty Certificate or other writeing as also what shall be paid by every proprietor for surveying divideing and laying out of any lands in the said province which said Register Surveyor or other officer is not to exact or demand any more or greater rates as shall be established as aforesaid.

CHAPTER 6

Wee doe also grant convenient Portions of Land for Highwaies and for streets not under one hundred foote in breadth in Citties Townes and Villages.

And for wharfes Keys Harbours and for public houses in such places as the Comissioners for the time being (untill there be a generall assembly) shall appoint and that all such lands laid out for the said uses and purposes shall be free and exempt from all rents taxes and other charges and duties whatsoever as also that the Inhabitants of the said Province have free passage through or by any Seas Bounds Creeks Rivers Rivoletts in the said Province through or by which they must necessarily pass to come from the maine Ocean to any part of the Province aforesaid as also by Land in waies laid out or through any Lands not planted or enclosed.

That all the Inhabitants within the said Province of

West Jersey have the Liberty of Fishing in Delaware River or on the sea coast and the Liberty of Hunting and Killing any Deer or other wild beasts the Liberty to Shoot or Take any wild Fowles within the said Province provided alwaies that they doe not Hunt Kill Shoot or Take any such Deer wild Beasts or Fowles upon the Lands that is or shall be surveyed taken up inclosed sowen and planted except the owners of the sd lands or their assignes.

Chapter 7

The Comissioners are to take care that Lands quietly held planted and posessed seaven years after it's being first duely Surveyed by the Survey or surveyors his or their Lawfull deputies which shall be appointed by the said Proprietors and Registred in manner as aforesaid shall not be subject to reveiw resurvey or alteration of bounds upon any pretence or by any pretence or by any Person or persons whatsoever.

Chapter 8

The Commissioners are to take care that no man if his cattell stray range or graze on any ground within the said province not actually approprieted or set out to particular persons shall be lyable to pay any trespass for the same provided that custome of Commons be not thereby pretended to nor any person hindred from legally takeing up and approprieteing any land so grazed upon.

Chapter 9

The Commissioners are to see that all Courts established by the Laws and Constitutions of the Generall Assembly and pursuant unto those Concessions doe execute their severall duties and offices respectively according to the laws in force and to displace or punish them for violate-ing the said Laws or acting contrary to their duty and trusts as the nature of their offences shall require and where they see cause after condemnation or sentence past upon any person or persons by any Judg Justice or court whatsoever the said Comissioners have power to reprieve and suspend the execution of the sentence untill the Cause be presented with a Coppie of the whole Tryall proceedings and proofs to the next generall assembly who may accordingly either pardon or command execution of the sentence on the offendor or offendors (who are to be kept in the meane time in safe custody untill the sence of the Generall assembly be knowne therein.

CHAPTER 10

To act and doe all other thing or things that may conduce to the safety peace and well Government of the said Province and these present concessions and that all inferior officers be accountable to the Comissioners and they to be accountable to the generall Assembly The Comissioners are to take care that the Constables of the said Province shall collect such of Proprietors rents who dwell not in the said province but in England Ireland or Scotland and shall pay it to the receiver that they shall appoint to receive the same unless the Generall assembly shall prescribe some other way whereby they may have their rents duely collected without charg and trouble to the said Proprietors.

CHAPTER 11

They are not to impose or suffer to be imposed any Tax Customs or Subsidie Tollage Assessment or any Other duty whatsoever upon any colour or pretence how specious soever upon the said Province and Inhabitants thereof without their owne consent first had or other then what shall be imposed by the authority and consent of the Generall Assembly and that only in manner and for the good ends and uses as aforesaid.

Chapter 12

That the said Comissioners Registers Surveyors and all and every other publicke officers of trust whatsoever already deputed and chosen are * hereafter from time to time to be deputed and chosen shall subscribe (in a booke or bookes to be provided for that purpose that they will truely and faithfully discharge their respective trusts according to the law of the said Province and Tenour of these Concessions in their respective offices and duties and doe equall Justice and right to all men according to their best skill and Judgment without Corruption favour or affection And the names of all that shall subscribe to be entered in the said booke And whosoever shall subscribe and shall violate breake or any wise falsifie his promise after such subscription shall be lyable to be punished or fined and also be made Incapeable of any publick office within the said Province.

The Charter or fundamentall Laws of West New Jersey agreed upon

Chapter 13

That these following concessions are the common Law or fundamentall Rights of the province of West New Jersey
That the common Law or fundamentall Rights and priviledges of West New Jersey are Individually agreed upon by the Proprietors and freeholders thereof to be the foundation of the Government which is not to be altered by the Legislative Authority or free Assembly hereafter mentioned and constituted But that the said Legislative Authority is constituted according to these fundamentalls to make such Laws as agree with and maintaine the said fundamentalls and to make no Laws that in the least contradict differ or vary from the said fundamentalls under what pretence or allegation soever.

* Thus in MS; "or" was intended. [Ed.]

Chapter 14

But if it so happen that any person or persons of the said free Assembly shall therin designedly willfully and Malitiously move or excite any to move any matter or thing whatsoever that contradicts or any wayes subverts any fundamentall of the said Laws in the constitution of the Government of this province it being proved by seaven honest and reputeable persons he or they shall be proceeded against as Traitors to the said Government.

Chapter 15

That these Concessions Law or great Charter of fundamentalls be recorded in a faire table in the assembly house and that they be read at the beginning and disolveing of every Generall free assembly And it is further agreed and Ordained that the said Concessions Common Law or great Charter of fundamentalls be writt in faire tables in every Common Hall of Justice within this Province and that they be read in sollemn manner foure times every yeare in the presence of the People by the chiefe Magistrates of those places.

Chapter 16

That no Men nor number of Men upon Eearth hath power or Authority to rule over mens consciences in religious matters therefore it is consented agreed and ordained that no person or persons whatsoever within the said Province at any time or times hereafter shall be any waies upon any pretence whatsoever called in question or in the least punished or hurt either in Person Estate or Priveledge for the sake of his opinion Judgment faith or worship towards God in matters of Religion but that all and every such person and persons may from time to time and at all times freely and fully have and enjoy his and their Judgments and the exercise of their consciences in matters of religious worship throughout all the said Province.

Chapter 17

That no proprietor Freeholder or Inhabitant of the said Province of West New Jersey shall be deprived or condemned of Life limb Liberty estate Property or any wayes hurt in his or their Priveledges Freedoms or Frachises upon any account whatsoever without a due tryall and Judgment passed by twelve good and Lawfull men of his neighbourhood first had and that in all causes to be tried and in all tryalls the person or persons araigned may except against any of the said Neighbourhood without any reason Rendred (not exceeding thirty five) and in case of any vallid reason alledged against every person nominated for that service.

Chapter 18

And that no proprietor Freeholder free denison or Inhabitant in the said Province shall be attached arrested or imprisoned for or by reason of any debt dutie or other thing whatsoever (cases fellonious criminall and treasonable excepted) before he or she have personall summon or summons left at his or her last dwelling place if in the said Province by some legall Authorized Officer constituted and appointed for that purpose to appear in some Court of Judicature for the said Province with a full and plaine account of the cause or thing in demand as alsoe the name or names of the person or persons at whose suite and the Court where he is to appeare And that he hath at least fourteen dayes time to appeare and answer the said suite if he or she live or inhabitt within forty Miles English of the said Court and if at further distance to have for every twenty miles two dayes time more for his and their appeareance and so proportionably for a larger distance of place.

That upon the recording of the summons and non appeareance of such person and persons a writt or attachment shall or may be issued out to arrest or attach the person or persons of such defaulters to cause his or their appeareance in such Court returnable at a day certaine to answer the penalty or penalties in such suite or suites and if he or they shall be Condemned by legal tryall and Judgement the penalty or penalties shall be paid and satisfied out of his or their reall or personall Estate so Condemned or cause the person or persons soe condemned to lie in execution till satisfaction of the debt and damages be made **Provided** alwaies if such person or persons soe condemned shall pay and deliver such Estate Goods and Chattells which he or any other person hath for his or their use and shall sollemnly declare and averr that he or they have not any further Estate Goods or chattells wheresoever to satisfie the person or persons (at whose suite he or they are Condemned) their respective Judgments and shall alsoe bring and produce three other persons as Compurgators who are Well knowne and of honest reputation and approved of by the Commissioners of that division where they dwell or inhabitt which shall in such open Court likewise sollemnly declare and averr that they believe in their Consciences such person and persons soe Condemned hav not wherewith further to pay the said condemnation or Condemnations he or they shall be thence forthwith discharged from their said imprisonment any Law or custome to the contrary thereof heretofore in the said Province notwithstanding and upon such summons and default of appeareance recorded as aforesaid and such person and persons not appeareing within forty dayes after it shall and may be lawfull for such Court of Judicature to proceed to tryall of twelve Lawfull men to Judgment against such defaulters and issue forth execution against his or their estate real and personall to satisfie such penalty or penalties to such debt and damages soe recorded as farr as it shall or may extend.

CHAPTER 19

That there shall be in every Court three Justices or Comissioners who shall sitt with the twelve men of the Neighbourhood with them to heare all causes and to assist the said twelve men of the neighbourhood in case of Law and that they the said Justices shall pronounce such Judgment as they shall receive from And be directed by the said twelve men in whom only the Judgment resides and not otherwise. And in case of their neglect and refusall that then one of the twelve by consent of the rest pronounce their owne Judgment as the Justices should have done. And if any Judgement shall be past in any case civill or Criminall by any other person or persons or any other way then according to this agreement and appointment it shall be held null and void and such person or persons soe presumeing to give Judgment shall be severely fined and upon complaint made to the generall Assembly by them be declared incapeable of any office or trust within this Province.

CHAPTER 20

That in all matters and causes civill and Criminall proofe is to be made by the sollemn and plaine averrment of at least two honest and reputeable persons And in case that any person or persons shall beare false witness and bring in his or their evidence contrary to the truth of the matter as shall be made plainly to Appeare that then every such person or persons shall in civill causes suffer the penalty which would be due to the person or persons he or they beare witness against. And in case any witness or witnesses on the behalfe of any person or persons indicted in a criminall cause shall be found to have borne false witness for feare gaine Mallice or favour and thereby hinder the due execution of the Law and deprive the suffering person or persons of their due satisfaction That then and in all other cases of false evidence such person or persons shall be first severely fined and next that he or they shall forever be disabled from being admitted in Evidence or into any publick office employment or service within this Province.

Chapter 21

That all and every person and persons whatsoever who shall prosecute or prefere any indictment or information against others for any personall injuries or matter Criminall or shall prosecute for any other Criminall cause (Treason Murther and Fellony only excepted) shall and may be Master of his owne process and have full power to forgive and remitt the person or persons offendeing against him or herselfe only as well before as after Judgment and Condemnation and pardon and remitt the sentence fine and punishment of the person or persons offending be it personnall or other whatsoever.

Chapter 22

That the tryalls of all Causes Civill and Criminall shall be heard and decided by the vardict or Judgment of twelve honest men of the neighbourhood only to be summoned and presented by the Sherriffe of that division or propriety where the fact or trespass is Committed and that no person or persons shall be compelled to fee any Attorney or Councellor to plead his cause but that all persons have free liberty to plead his owne cause if he please And that no person nor persons imprisoned upon any account whatever within this Province shall be obliged to pay any Fees to the officer or officers of the said prison either when committed or discharged.

Chapter 23

That in all public Courts of Justice for tryalls of causes Civill or criminall any person or persons inhabitants of the said Province may freely come into and attend the said Courts and heare and be present at all or any Such tryalls as shal be there had or passed that Justice may not be done in a corner nor in any Covert manner (being intended and resolved by the help of the Lord and by these our Concessions and fundamentalls that all and every person and persons Inhabiting the said Province shall as farr as in us lies be free from oppression and slavery.

CHAPTER 24

For the preventing of frauds deceits collusions in bargaines Sailes trade and traffick and the usuall contests quarrells debates and utter ruine which have attended the people in many nations by costly tedious and vexatious Law suites And for a due Settlement of estates

It is agreed concluded and ordained that there be kept a Register at *London* within the nation of *England* and also another Register witin the Province of *New West Jersey* and that all deeds evidences and conveyances of land in the said province of *New West Jersey* that shall be executed in *England* may also be there registred and once every yeare the register of the said deeds and conveyances so registered shall be duely transmitted under the hands of the Register and three proprietors unto the comisioners in *New West Jersey* to be enrolled in the publick Register of the said province as alsoe that the cheife Register which the said Proprietors have deputed or chosen or shall depute or choose faileing that the Comissioners shall depute or choose or which the Generall assembly of the said Province hereafter mentioned shall depute or choose shall keep exact entries and Registries in faire bookes or rolls for that purpose to be provided of all publick affaires and therein shall record and enter all grants of land from the proprietors to the planters and all Conveyances of land house or houses from man to man as alsoe all assignments Mortgages Bonds and specialties whatsoever and all leases for land house or houses made or to be made from Landlord to Tennant and from person to person which conveyances Leases Assignments Mortgages Bonds and Specialties which shall be executed in *West New Jersey* shall be first acknowledged by the granter Assignor and obligor before the said Comissioners or two of them at least or some two of their lawfull deputies for the time being who shall under their hands upon the back side of the said deed Lease Assignment Mortgage or specialty Attest the acknowledgment thereof as aforesaid which shall be a warrant for the Register to record the same and such Conveyance or specialty if sealed executed acknowledged before three proprietors in the nation of *England* or *Ireland* and recorded or registred there within three months after the date thereof or if sealed executed and acknowledged in the said Province or elsewhere out of England and recorded or registered within six months after the date thereof shall be good and effectuall in Law and for passing or transferring of Estates in Lands Tennements or hereditaments shall be as effectuall as if delivery and seizin were executed of the same and all other conveyances Deeds Leases or specialties not recorded as aforesaid shall be of no force nor effect and the said Register shall doe all other thing or things the said Proprietors by their instructions shall direct or the Comissioners of Assembly shall ordaine for the good and welfare of the said Province.

Chapter 25

That there may be a good understanding and friendly correspondence between the proprietors freeholders and inhabitants of the Said province and the Indian Natives thereof

It is concluded and agreed that if any of the Indian natives within the said province shall or may doe any wrong or injury to any of the Proprietors Freeholders or inhabitants in person estate or otherwayes howsoever upon notice thereof or Complaint made to the comissioners or any two of them they are to give notice to the Sachim or other chiefe person or persons that hath authority over the said Indian native or natives that Justice may be done and satisfaction made to the Person or persons offended according to Law and Equitie and the nature and quallitie of the offence and injury done or comitted.

And also in case any of the Proprietors Freeholders or Inhabitants shall any wise wrong or injure any of the Indian natives there in person estate or otherwise the Comissioners are to take care upon complaint to them made or any one of them either by the indian natives or others that Justice be done to the Indian Natives and plenary satisfaction made them according to the nature and quallitie of the offence and Injury. And that in all tryalls wherein any of the said Indian Natives are concerned the tryall to be by six of the neighbourhood and six of the said Indian Natives to be indifferently and impartially Chosen by order of the Comissioners and that the Comissioners use their endeavour to persuade the Natives to the like way of tryall when any of the Natives doe any waies wrong or injure the said proprietors Freeholders or inhabitants that they choose six of the Natives and six of the Freeholders or Inhabitants to Judge of the wrong and injury done and to proportion satisfaction accordingly.

Chapter 26

It is agreed when any land is to be taken up for settlements of towns or otherwayes before it be Surveyed the Comissioners or the major part of them are to appoint some persons to goe to the chiefe of the natives concerned in that land soe intended to be taken up to acquaint the Natives of their Intention and to give the Natives what present they shall agree upon for their good will or consent and take a grant of the same in writeing under their hands and seales or some other publick way used in those parts of the world which grant is to be Registered in the public register allowing also the Natives (if they please) a coppie thereof and that noe Person or persons take up any land but by order from the Comissioners for the time being.

Chapter 27

That no shipp Master or commander of any Shipp or vessell shall receive into his shipp or vessell to carry unto any other Nation Country or plantation any person or persons whatsoever without a Certificate first had and obtained under the hands and seales of the Comissioners or any two of them that the said person or persons are cleare and may be taken on board signifieing that the said person or persons name have been put up in three publick places of the Province Appointed by the Comissioners for that purpose for the space of three weekes giveing notice of his or their intention to transport themselves.

Chapter 28

That men may peaceably and quietly enjoy their estates

It is agreed if any person or persons shall steale Robb or take any goods or chattells from or belonging to any person or persons whatsoever he is to make restitution two fold out of his or their estate and for want of such estate to be made worke for his theft for such time and times as the nature of the offence doth require or untill restitution be made double for the same or as twelve men of the neighbourhood shall determine being appointed by the Comissioners not extending either to Life or Limb. If any person or persons shall willfully beat hurt wound assault or otherwayes abuse the person or persons of any man woman or child they are to be punished according to the nature of the offence which is to be determined by twelve men of the neighbourhood appointed by the Commissioners.

Chapter 29

For Securing estates of persons that die and takeing care of orphans

1   If any person or persons die the Comissioners are to take care that the will of the deceased be duely performed and security given by those that prove the will and that all wills or Testaments be registered in a publick Register appointed for that purpose and the person or persons that prove the same to bring in one true Inventory under their hands of all the estate of the deceased and to have a warrant under the hand of three Comissioners and the publick seale of the Province Intimateing that they have brought in an Inventory of the Estate and given securitie then and not before are they to dispose upon the Estate

2   If any person die intestate leaveing a wife and children the Comissioners are to take security from the person that shall Administer to secure two parts of the Estate for the Children and the third to the Wife if there be any and if ther be no Child, then halfe to the next of Kin and the other to the Wife

3   If the parents of Children be dead and no Will made then the Comissioners are to appoint two or more persons to take the charge of the Children and Estate and to bring in an Inventory of the Estate to be registered and that the said persons are to make good to the children what part of the Estate shall come unto their hands and to give a true account of their receipts and disbursements to be approved of by the Comissioners

4   If parents die leaveing Child or Children and no estate or not sufficient to maintain and bring up the said Child or children in that case the comissioners are to appoint persons to take care for the child or Children to bring them up in such manner as the Comissioners shall appoint and the charges thereof to be borne by the publick stock of the Province and if none be established then by a tax to be leavied by twelve men of the neighbourhood with the consent of the Comissioners or the maine part of them

Chapter 30

In cases when any person or persons kill or destroy themselves or be killed by any other thing

It is agreed if man or woman shall willfully put hand and kill him or her selfe the Estate of such person or persons is not to be forfeited but the kindred heires or such other as of Right the estate belongs to may enjoy the same or if any Beast or Shipp Boat or other thing should occasion the death of any person or persons nevertheless the said Beast Shipp Boat or other thing is not to be forfeited but those to whom they belong may enjoy the same provided alwayes that the said Beast did not willfully kill the said person or hath been knowne to attempt or addicted to mischief or hath been found to hurt or kill any person then the said beast is to be killed.

Chapter 31

All such person or persons as shall be upon tryall found guilty of Murder or Treason the sentence and way of execution thereof is left to the Generall Assembly to determine as they in the wisdome of the Lord shall Judg meet and Expedient

The Generall Assembly and their Power

Chapter 32

That so soone as divisions or Tribes or other such like distinctions are made that then the inhabitants Freeholders and Proprietors resident upon the said Province or severall and respective Tribes or Divisions or Distinctions aforesaid doe yearely and every yeare meet on the first day of October or the Eighth month and choose one Proprietor or Freeholder for each respective Propriety in the said province (the said Province being to be divided into one hundred Proprieties) to be deputies Trustees or Representatives for the benefitt service and behoofe of the people of the said province which body of deputies trustees or Representatives Consisting of one hundred persons chosen as aforesaid shall be the generall free and supream Assembly of the said province for the yeare ensueing and no longer And in Case any member of the said assembly dureing the said yeare shall decease or otherwise be rendred incapeable of that service that then the Inhabitants of the said Proprietie shall elect a new member to serve in his Roome for the remainder of the said yeare.

Chapter 33

And to the end the respective members of the yearely assembly to be chosen may be regularly and impartially elected

That no person or persons who shall give bestow or promise directly or indirectly to the said parties electing any meat drinke money or moneys worth for procurement of their choice and consent shall be capeable of being elected a member of the said Assembly And if any person or persons shall be at any time corruptly elected and sufficient proofe thereof made to the said Free Assembly such person or persons soe electing or elected shall be reckoned incapeable to choose or sitt in the said Assembly or execute any other publick office of trust within the said province For the space of seaven yeares thence Next ensueing and also that all such elections as aforesaid be not determined by the common and confused way of cries and voices but by putting balls into ballating boxes to be provided for that purpose for the prevention of all partiallity and whereby every man may Freely choose according to his owne Judgment and honest intention.

Chapter 34

To appoint their owne times of meting and to adjourne their sessions from time to time (within the said yeare to such times and places as they shall thinke fitt and convenient as also to ascertaine the number of their Qorum provided that such numbers be not less than one halfe of the whole in whome (or more) shall be the full power of the Generall assembly and that the voates of two thirds of the said Qorum or more of them if assembled together as aforesaid shall be determinative in all cases whatsoever comeing in question before them Consonant and Conformable to the Concessions and fundamentalls.

Chapter 35

That the said Proprietors and Freeholders at their choice of persons to serve them in the Generall and Free Assemblys of the Province give their Respective Deputies or Trustees their instructions at large to represent their grievances or for the improvement of the Province and that the persons chosen doe by indentures under hand and seale Covenant and oblidge themselves to act nothing in that capacity but what shall tend to the fitt service and behoofe of those that send and employ them and that in case of failer of trust or breach of Covenant that they be questioned upon complaint made in that or the next Assembly by any of their respective Electors

And that each member of the assembly Chosen as aforesaid be allowed one shilling ℔ day dureing the time of the sitting of the assembly that thereby he may be knowne to be the servant of the people which allowance of one shilling ⅌ day is to be paid him by the inhabitants of the propriety or division that shall elect him

Chapter 36

That in every generall Free Assembly every respective member hath Liberty of speech that no man be interupted when speakeing that all questions be stated with deliberation and Liberty for amendments that it be put by the chaire man by them to be chosen and determined by plurallity of voates also that every Member has power of entering his protest and reasons of protestations And that if any member of such assembly shall require to have the persons names registered according to their YYs and Noe's that it be accordingly done and that after debates are past and the question agreed upon the doores of the house be sett open and the people have Liberty to come in to heare and be witnesses of of the voates and the inclinations of the persons voating.

Chapter 37

And that the said Assembly doe elect Constitute and appoint tenn honest and able men to be Comissioners of Estate for manageing and carrying on the affaires of the said Province according to the Law therein established dureing the Adjournments and dissolutions of the said Generall Free Assembly for the conservation and tranquillitie of the same.

Chapter 38

That it shall be lawfull for any person or persons dureing the session of any generall Free Assembly in that Province to address remonstrate or declare any suffering danger or grievance or to propose tender or request any priveledge proffit or advantage to the said Province they not

exceeding the Number of one hundred persons.

Chapter 39

To enact and make all such Laws Acts and Constitutions as shall be necessary for the well Government of the said Province (and them to repeale) provided that the same be as neare as may be conveniently agreeable to the primitive antient and Fundamentall Lawes of the nation of England **provided** alsoe that they be not against any of these our Concessions and Fundamentalls before or hereafter mentioned.

Chapter 40

By Act as aforesaid to Constitute all Courts together with the limits powers and Jurisdictions of the same (consonant to these consessions) as also the severall Judges Officer and Number of Officers belonging to each court to continue such time as they shall see meet not exceeding one yeare or two at the most with their respective Sallaries Fees and perquisites and their appellations with the penalties that shall be inflicted upon them for the breach of their severall and respective duties and Trusts And that noe person or persons whatsoever inhabitants of the said Province shall susteyn or beare two offices in the said province at one and the same time.

Chapter 41

That all the Justices and Constables be chosen by the people and all Comissioners of the publick seales Treasuries and chiefe Justices Embassadors and Collectors be chosen by the Generall Free Assembly.

Chapter 42

That the Comissioners of the Treasury of the said province bring in their account at the end of their yeare unto the generall Free Assembly there to be seen and adjusted and that every respective member carry a coppie thereof unto that hundred or propriety he serves for to be Registred in the Capitall publick court of that Propriety.

Chapter 43

By Act as aforesaid to lay equall Taxes and Assesments and equally to raise moneys or goods upon all lands or persons within the severall proprieties precincts Hundreds Tribes or whatsoever other divisions Shall hereafter be made and established in the said Province as oft as necessity shall require and in such manner as to them shall seem most equall and easie for the inhabitants in order to the better supporting of the publick charge of the said Government as alsoe for the publick benefitt and advantage of the said People and province.

Chapter 44

By Act as aforesaid to subdivide the said Province into Hundreds proprieties or such other divisions and distinctions As they shall thinke fitt and the said Divisions to distinguish by such names as shall be thought good as also within the said Province to direct and appoint places for such and so many Townes Citties Ports Harbours Creeks and other places for the convenient Ladeing and unladeing of Goods and merchandise out of the Shipps Boates and other Vessells as shall be expedient with such Jurisdictions priveledges and Franchises to such Citties Ports Harbours Creekes or other places as they shall Judge most conduceing to the Generall Good of the said Province and people thereof and to erect raise and build within the said Province or any parte thereof such and soe many Market Townes and villages and also appoint such and soe many Martes and faires and in such place and places as they shall see meet from time to time as the Grant made and assigned unto the said Proprietors will permitt and admit

In Testimony *and witness of our consent to and affir-*

mation of these present Laws Concessions and Agreements **Wee** the Proprietors Freeholders and Inhabitants of the said Province of West New Jersey whose names are under written have to the same voluntarily and freely set our hands dated this third day of the month commonly called March in the year of our Lord one thousand six hundred and seaventy six

Mahlon Stacy
Thomas Budd
Samll Jenings

Lambert
Thomas Hooton
Henry Stacy

John Lambert
William Bealings
George Denon
[illegible] Crompton

Hert J Jansen
John o Swiyre

Edward Bradway
Richard Guy
James Nevill
Mantwell
Jeffra [illegible]
[illegible] Barron
Casp Herman
Henry Hoff
Robert Kombs
John Cornelis
garret van jumne

Thomas Smith
Seams yranes
Edward + Web:
John Hodger
Rew M wilkison
Cristopher C Sanders:
Reneare: RH vanhust:
William Johns
Charles C Bagley
Samuel Wade
Tho: Woodrofe
John Smith

the mark's
of William ⋈ Gillsonson
Mickaell + Lackerouse
Markos M. Algus
Ewert ✶ Aldricks

Hendrick ᚺ Enerson
Gilles Douwesen
Claus Jansen
Paul Jacquet

Richard Morgan

Cristopher White
John Maddocks
John Howrist
James ?iccary
William Rumsey
Richard ? Robison
Mark Roone
the mark T. ⋈ of Watson (thomas)
Samuell Nicholson
Daniel Smith

Tho: Pewell
William ?
Joseph Mans
Isack Smart
Androw Thompson
Thomas ?
Seowry Jennings

Henry Stubbens
his ⋈ marke
Wm + Willis
George Haselwood
Roger Povvith
William ?
Abraham Vanhigst
Hypolitos Lefever
William Wilkinson
Androw Thomok
his ⋈ marke

102

Richard Daniell   Lacy [mark]   Pendlious
William N Penton   his   marke

william danndl   Sam'll Hedge
Robert Zane

Walter   Peterson   Will Malster
Anthony Page
Andrew A Bartleson   John Grubb
Wooley   Woolison   John wordrigo
Anthony Dixson   R. Muje
John Erme
Thomas Benson
                            Thomas Barker
Vining arne   Robert Powell
Rich'd Buffington   Thomas Harding
Samll Jowett   Walter Clare

Barnard Devenish   T Wright
Thomas Stokes
Thomas French   Godfrey Hancock
Isaac Marriott
                   John Petty
John Hutton
Geo: Hutchinson   Abraham Houlings
                   John Newbold

Thomas Gardner
Thomas Ewes   John While
  John Horton   the marke I of Jn° Robarts
  John Paine   John ◯ Wood marke
  Charge ffenton
    Samwell Ouldale   John Gosling
   Willm Blake Kirnarby   Tho Lovell
  Anthony Woodhouse
  Daniel Leeds
  John Manroagt
  Francis Boswitho
  William Lugwell

    John Snowden
  Richard Fenimore
  Zurriuacab
  Tho Scholes

IV

THE
FUNDAMENTAL AGREEMENTS
OF THE
GOVERNOR, PROPRIETORS,
FREEHOLDERS, AND INHABITANTS
OF THE
PROVINCE OF WEST NEW JERSEY
NOVEMBER 25, 1681

[Text from a manuscript copy apparently dating from the late seventeenth century in the New Jersey Bureau of Archives and History, bound with a copy of the West New-Jersey Concessions and Agreements of 1677; text collated with that in Aaron Leaming and Jacob Spicer, *The Grants, Concessions, and Original Constitutions of the Province of New-Jersey* (Philadelphia, [1756]), 423-425. There is no copy of the Fundamental Agreements of 1681 among the records of the Proprietors of West New Jersey at Burlington.]

Att A Generall Free Assembly held in the Towne of Burlington the 25th day of the ninth Month called November in the Yeare 1681.

FORASMUCH as itt hath pleased God to bring us into this Province of West New Jersey, and Settle us here in safety, that we may be a people to the praise and honour to his name who hath so dealt with us, and for the good and welfare of our posterity to come Wee the Governor Propriators Freeholders and Inhabbittants of West Jersey by mutuall consent and agreement for the prevention of innovacion and opression either upon us or our posterity, and for the preservation of the peace and tranquility of the same. And that all may be encouraged to goe on Chearfully in their Severall places, Wee doe make and constitute these our agreements to be as fundamentals to us and our posterity, to be held and kept inviolable. And that no person or persons whatsoever shall or may make voyd or disanull the same upon any pretence whatsoever.

1st That there shall be a generall Free Assemblye for the Province aforesaid yearly and every year at a day certaine chosen by the free people of the said Province wherein all the representatives of the said Province shall be summoned to apeare to consider of the affaires of the said Province, and to make and ordaine such acts and lawes as shall be requisite and necessary for the good Government and prosperity of the Free people of the said Province, and if necessity shall require the Governor for the time being with the consent of his Councell, may and shall Issue out Writts to convene the Assembly sooner, to consider and answer the necessities of the people of the said Province.

2dly That the Governor of the Province aforesaid his heirs or Successors for the time being shall not susspend or deferr the signeing sealeing and confirmeing all such acts and laws as the Generall assembly (from time to time to be Elected by the Free people of the Province aforesaid) shall make or Act for the secureing the libberties, and properties of the said free people of the Province aforesaid.

3dly That itt shall not be lawfull for the Governor of the said Province his heires or Sucsessors for the time being and Councell or any of them at any time or times hereafter to make or raise Ware uppon any accompt or pretence whatsoever, or raise any Millitary Forces within the Province aforesaid without the Consent and act of the General Free Assembly for the time being.

4^{thly} That itt shall not be lawfull for the Governor of the said Province his heires or Sucsessors for the time being and Counsell or any of them at any time or times hereafter to make or enact any law or lawes for the said Province without the Consent act and Concurrance of the Generall Assembly. And if the Governor for the time being his heires or sucsessors and Councell or any of them, shall attempt to enact or make any such law or lawes of him or them selfes without the consent act and Concurrance of the Generall Assembly, That from thenceforth he, they, or so many of them as shall be guilty thereof, shall upon legall conviction be demed and taken for enimies to the Free people of the said Province, and it shall and may be lawfull for the Generall Free Assembly for the time being, to punish such ofender or ofenders, according to the nature of the Offence, and such act soe attempted to be made to be of no force.

5^{thly} That the Generall Free Assembly from time to time, to be Chosen as aforesaid, as the Representatives of the people, shall not be prorouged or dissolved (before the expiracion of one whole yeare, to commence from the day of there Electcion) without their owne Free Concent.

6thly That it shall not be lawfull, for the Governor of the said Province, his heires or sucsessors for the time being, and Councell or any of them, to levey or raise any Summ or Summs of money, or any other tax, without the act consent and concurrance of the Generall Free Assembly.

7thly That all Officers of State or trust relateing to the said Province, shall be nominated and elected by the Generall Free Assembly for the time being, or by their appoyntment, which Officer and Officers shall be accomptable to the Generall Free Assembly, or such as the said Assembly shall appoynt.

8thly That the Governor of the Province aforesaid his heires or Sucsessors, for time being, or any of them shall not send Embassadors or make Treaties or enter into alience upon the publique accompt of the said Province, without the consent of the Generall Free Assembly.

9thly That no Generall Free Assembly hereafter to be Chosen by the Free people of the Province aforesaid shall give to the Governor of the said Province for the time being his heires or Sucsessors, any Tax or Custome for a longer time then one whole yeare.

10thly That libberty of Conscience in matters of faith and Worshipp towards God shall be granted to all people within the Province aforesaid who shall live peaceably and quietly therein, and that none of the Free people of the said Province shall be rendered incapable of Office in respect of their faith and Worshipp. In Testimony whereof I have hereunto put my hand and Seale the day and yeare above written.

Subscribed and Sealed by
SAMUELL JENINGS Deputie Governor.
Upon the Governors acceptance and performance of the proposealls before expressed, We the Generall Free Assembly, Propriators and Freeholders of the Province of West New Jersey aforesaid doe accept and recive Samuell Jenings as Deputie Governor.

THOMAS OLIVE Speaker to the General Free Assembly. By Order of the Whole Assembly

V

THE FUNDAMENTAL CONSTITUTIONS FOR THE PROVINCE OF EAST NEW-JERSEY 1683

[Text from Aaron Leaming and Jacob Spicer, *The Grants, Concessions, and Original Constitutions of the Province of New-Jersey* (Philadelphia, [1756]), 153-166, signed by fourteen of the Proprietors. Of the text here employed, Leaming and Spicer said: "It appears on Reading the foregoing Instrument, that in sundry Places the Sense is not compleat, but it is likely to be occasioned by Omissions and neglects in Recording, and therefore if the Original can be come at, it will be proper to re-examine the foregoing copy therewith." No such original is know to be extant.

It should be noted that the Fundamental Constitutions of 1683 never actually became operative as an organic law. See Introduction, p. 17-18.]

The Fundamental Constitutions for the Province of *East New-Jersey* in *America*, Anno Domini 1683.

SINCE the Right of Government, as well as Soil, is in the Four and Twenty Proprietors, and that the same is confirmed to them a new by a late Patent from JAMES Duke of *York*, Pursuant of Patent granted to him from the King; the Proprietors for the well ordering and governing of the said Province, according to the Powers conveyed to them, do grant and declare that the Government thereof shall be as followeth, viz.

1. That altho' the Four and Twenty Proprietors have formerly made choice of *Robert Barclay*, Esq; for Governor, during his natural Life, and to serve by a Deputy to be approved of by sixteen of the Proprietors, until he himself shall be upon the Place, which is by these Presents ratified and confirmed, to all Intents and Purposes: Yet after the Decease of the said *Robert Barckly*, or by Reason of his Malverstation, the Proprietors shall find Cause to divest him of the Government, the Four and Twenty Proprietors shall choose a Governor; in order to which it shall be in the Power of each of them to name One, and Sixteen of the Four and Twenty shall determine it: Which Governor shall be obliged to serve and reside upon the Place, and shall only continue for three Years; and if any shall directly or indirectly propound or advise the Continuance for any longer Time, or of new to choose him again, or his Son, within the three Years, it shall be esteemed a betraying of the publick Liberty of the Province; and the Actors shall be esteemed as publick Enemies; and the said Governor

that shall be so continued, shall be reputed guilty of the same, not only by Reason of his acceptance of that Continuation, but also by Reason of any kind of Solicitation which he may directly or indirectly have endeavoured. If the Governor so do die before the three Years be expired, the Proprietors shall choose one to supply his Place, for the Time the other should held it, and no longer. *Provided,* that this Limitation of three Years abovementioned, do not extend to the Deputy Governor of *Robert Barclay,* for seven Years after the passing of those Constitutions, who may be for a longer Time than three Years, if the Proprietors see meet.

II. That for the Government of the Province, there shall be a great Council, to consist of the Four and Twenty Proprietors, or their Proxies in their Absence, and One Hundred Forty four to be chosen by the Freemen of the Province. But forasmuch as there are not at present so many Towns built as there may be hereafter, nor the Province divided into such Counties as it may be hereafter divided into, and that consequently no certain Division can be made how many shall be chosen for each Town and County; at present Four and Twenty shall be chosen for the eight Towns that are at present in being, and Eight and Forty for the County, making together Seventy two, and with the Four and Twenty Proprietors, Ninety six Persons, till such Times as the great Council shall see meet to call the above mentioned Number of One Hundred Forty four, and then shall be determined by the great Council, how many shall come out of each Town and County; but every year they shall choose one third, and the first chosen shall remain for three Years, and they that go out shall not be capable to come in again for two Years after, and therefore they shall not be put in the Ballot in Elections for that Year: And in order to this Election, they shall in course meet in their several Boroughs and Counties the Six and Twentieth Day of *March,* beginning in the Year One Thousand Six Hundred Eighty four, and choose their several Representatives; whose first Day of meeting shall be the Twentieth Day of *April* afterwards; and they shall sit upon their own Adjournments, if they see meet, till the Twentieth of *July* following, and then to be disolved till the next Year, unless the Governor and common Council think fit to continue them longer, or call them in the Intervail; but if any of those Days fall on the first Day of the Week, it shall be deferred until the next Day.

III. The Persons qualified to be Freemen, that are capable to choose and be chosen in the great Council, shall be every Planter and Inhabitant dwelling and residing within the Province, who hath acquired Rights to and is in Possession of Fifty Acres of Ground, and hath cultivated ten Acres of it; or in Boroughs, who have a House and three Acres; or have a House and Land only hired, if he can prove he have Fifty Pounds in Stock of his own: And all Elections must be free and voluntary, but were any Bribe or indirect Means can be proved to have been used, both the giver and acquirer shall forfeit their Priviledge of electing and being elected forever: And for the full preventing of all indirect Means, the Election shall be after this Manner, the Names of all the Persons qualified in each County, shall be put in equal pieces of Parchment, and prepared by the Sheriff and his Clerk the Day before, and the Day of Election shall be put in a Box, and Fifty shall be taken out by a boy under Ten Years of age; these Fifty shall be put into the Box again, and the first Five and Twenty then taken out shall be those who shall be capable to be chosen for that Time; the other Five and Twenty shall by Plurality of Votes, name (of the aforesaid Twenty five) twelve, if there be three to be chosen, and eight if there be two to stand for it; these nominators, first solemnly declaring before the Sheriff, that they shall not Name any known to them to be guilty for the Time, or to have been guilty for a Year before, of Adultery, Whoredom, Drunkeness, or any such Immorality, or who is Insolvent or a Fool; and then out of the Twelve or

Eight so nominated, three or two shall be taken by the Ballot as abovesaid.

IV. It shall be the Priviledge of every Member of the great Council, to propose any Bill in Order to a Law, which being admitted to be debated, shall be determined by the Vote, wherein two Parts of three shall only conclude; but of this, twelve of the Proprietors, or their Proxies, must be assenting; which shall also be requisite after the Number of Freemen are double: Nor shall any Law be made or enacted to have force in the Province, which any ways touches upon the Goods or Liberties of any in it, but what thus passeth in the great Council; and whoever shall levy, collect or pay any Money or Goods without a Law thus passed, shall be held a publick Enemy to the Province, and a betrayer of the publick Liberty thereof: Also the Quorum of this great Council shall be half of the Proprietors, or their Proxies, and half of the Freemen at least; and in Determination, the proportionable assent of both Proprietors and Freemen must agree, viz. two Parts of whatever Number of Freemen, and one half of whatever Number of Proprietors are present.

V. For the constant Government of the Province there shall be with the Governor a common Council, consisting of the Four and Twenty Proprietors, or their Proxies, and Twelve of the Freemen, which shall be chosen by the Ballot out of the Freemen of the great Council, and shall successively go off each Year as they do; which Common Council will thus consist of Six and Thirty, whereof they shall be three Committees; twelve for the publick Policy, and to look to Manners, Education and Arts; Twelve for Trade and Management of the publick Treasury; and Twelve for Plantations and regulating of all Things, as well as deciding all Controversies relating to them: In each Committee Eight shall be of the Proprietors, or their Proxies, and four of the Freemen; Each of these Committees shall meet at least once a Week, and all the Thirty six once in two Months, and oftner, in such Places and at such Times as they shall find most convenient. And if it happen the Number of Freemen in the great Council to be doubled, there shall also be Twelve more of them be added to the Common Council; in this Common Council and those several Committees the one half shall be a Quorum, as in the former Article.

VI. All Laws shall be published and run in the Name of the Governor, Proprietors and Representatives of the Freemen of the Province, and shall be signed by two of the Proprietors, two of the Freemen, the Secretary and the Governor, or Deputy Governor for the Time being, who shall preside in all Meetings, and have two Votes, but shall no ways pretend to any negative Vote: But if he or they refuse to do his or their Duty, or be accused of Malversation, he shall be liable to the Censure of the Proprietors, and if turned out, there shall be another chosen to fullfil his Time as is abovesaid.

VII. Forasmuch as by the Concessions and Agreements of the former Proprietors, *(to wit)* the Lord *Berkeley* and Sir *George Carteret,* to and with all and every the Adventurers and all such as shall settle and plant in the Province in *Anno* 1664, it is consented and agreed by the six and seven Articles, that the great Assembly should have Power, by Act confirmed as there expressed, to erect, raise and build within the said Province, or any Part thereof, such and so many Forts, Castles, Cities and other Places of Defence, and the same, or any of them, to fortify and furnish with such Provisions and Proportions of Ordinance, Powder, Shot, Armour and all other Weapons, Ammunition and Abilments of War, both Offensive and Defensive, as shall be thought necessary and convenient for the Safety and Wellfare of the said Province; as also to constitute Train Bands and Companies, with the Number of the Soldiers, for the Safety, Strength and Defence of the aforesaid Province; to suppress all

Mutinies and Rebellions; to make War Offensive and Defensive, against all and every one that shall infest the said Province, not only to keep the Enemy out of their Limits, but also, in Case of necessity, the Enemy by Sea and Land to pursue out of the Limits and Jurisdiction of the said Province. And that amongst the present Proprietors there are several that declare, that they have no freedom to defend themselves with Arms, and others who judge it their Duty to defend themselves, Wives and Children, with Arms; it is therefore agreed and consented to, and they the said Proprietors do by these Presents agree and consent, that they will not in this Case force each other against their respective Judgments and Consciences; in order whereunto it is Resolved, that on the one Side, no Man that declares he cannot for Conscience sake bear Arms, whether Proprietor or Planter, shall be at any Time put upon so doing in his own Person, nor yet upon sending any to serve in his stead, And on the other side, those who do judge it their Duty to bear Arms for the publick Defence, shall have their Liberty to do in a legal Way. In pursuance whereof, there shall be a fourth Committee erected, consisting of six Proprietors, or their Proxies, and three of the Freemen, that are to set in the other three Committees, which shall be such as do understand it their Duty to use Arms for the publick Defence; which Committee shall provide for the publick Defence without and Peace within, against all Enemies whatsoever; and shall therefore be stiled, the Committee for the Preservation of the publick Peace: And that all Things may proceed in good Order, the said Committee shall propound to the great Council what they judge Convenient and Necessary for the keeping the Peace within the said Province, and for publick Defence without, by the said great Council to be approved and corrected, as they, according to exigence of Affairs, shall judge fit; the Execution of which Resolutions of the great Council shall be committed to the Care of the said Committee. But because through the Scruples of such of the Proprietors, or their Proxies, as have no freedom to use Arms, the Resolutions of the great Council may be in this Point obstructed, it is resolved and agreed, and it is by these Presents resolved and agreed, that in Things of this Nature, the Votes of these Proprietors shall only be of Weight at such Time or Times as one of these two Points are under Deliberation, which shall not be concluded where Twelve of the Proprietors and two Thirds of the whole Council, as in other Cases, are not consenting, (that is to say) First, whether, to speak after the Manner of Men, (and abstractly from a Man's Perswasion in Matters of Religion) it be convenient and suitable to the present Condition or Capacity of the Inhabitants, to build any Forts, Castles or any other Places of Defence? If yea; where and in what Places (to speak as Men) they ought to be erected. Secondly, whether there be any present or future foreseen Danger, that may, (to speak as Men without respect to ones particular Perswasion in Matters of Religion) require the putting the Province into a Posture of Defence, or to make use of those Means which we at present have, or which, from time to time as occasion may require, according to the Capacity of the Inhabitants, we may have; which Ability and Conveniency of those Means of Defence, and (to speak as Men without respect to any Man's Judgment in Matters of Religion) the necessity of the actual Use thereof, being once resolved upon; all further Deliberations about it, as the raising of Men, giving of Commissions both by Sea and Land, making Governors of Forts, and providing Money necessary for maintaining the same, shall belong only to those Members of the Great Council who judge themselves in Duty bound to make Use of Arms for the Defence of them and theirs. PROVIDED, that they shall not conclude any Thing but by the Consent of at least five Parts out of six of their Number; and that none of the Proprietors and other Inhabitants may be forced to contribute any Money for the Use of Arms, to which for Conscience sake they have not freedom, that which is necessary for the publick Defence, shall be borne by such as judge themselves in Duty bound to use Arms. PROVIDED, that the other, that for Conscience sake do oppose the bearing of Arms, shall on the other Hand bear so much in other Charges, as may make up that Proportion in the general Charge of the Province. And as the refusing to subscribe such Acts concerning the Use and Exercise of Arms abovesaid, in the Governor and Secretary, if scrupulous in Conscience so to do, shall not be esteemed in them an Omission of neglect of Duty, so the wanting thereof shall not make such Acts invalid, they being in lieu thereof, subscribed by the major Part of the six Proprietors of the Committee for the Preservation of the publick Peace.

VIII. The choosing the great and publick Officers, as Secretary, Register, Treasurer, Surveyor General, Marshal, and after Death or turning out of those now first to be nominated, shall be in the Governor and Common Council; as also of all Sherifs, Judges, and Justices of the Peace. But upon any Malversation or Accusation, they shall be liable to the Examination and Censure of the great Council, and if condemn'd by them, the Governor and Common Council must Name others in their Places.

IX. PROVIDED, That all Boroughs shall choose their own Magistrates, and the Hundreds in the County, their Constables or under Officers, in such Manner as shall be agreed to by the great Council.

X. Forasmuch as by the Patent, the Power of pardoning in capital Offences, is vested in the Four and Twenty Proprietors; it is hereby declared, that the said Power of pardoning shall never be made Use of but by the Consent of Eighteen of the Proprietors, or their Proxies: Nevertheless, it shall be in the Power of the Governor, in Conjunction with four Proprietors, who for the Time are Judges of the Court of Appeals, to repreive any Person after the Day of Execution appointed, for some time, not exceeding a Month.

XI. The four and Twenty Proprietors, in their Absence, may Vote in the Great and Common Council by their Proxies; One Proprietor may be Proxy for another, yet so as not but for one, so that none can have above two Votes: The Proxies of the Proprietors must be such as has Shares in Properties not under a Twentieth Part.

XII. That whoever has any Place of publick Trust in another Province, tho' a Proprietor, shall not sit in the great or common Council, but by their Proxies, unless thereunto particularly called by the one or other Council.

XIII. Whatever Proprietor doth not retain at least one fourth Part of his Propriety, *viz.* one Ninety sixth Part of the Country, shall loose the Right of Government, and it shall pass to him who has the greatest Share of that Propriety, exceeding the above mentioned Proportion: But if two or three has each one Ninety sixth Part, they shall have it successively Year about, like as when a Propriety is in two Hands, he who is upon the Place, if the other be absent, sick or under Age, shall still have it; but if both there, then by Turns as abovesaid; and if in a provided Propriety all be absent, the Proxies must be constituted by both; if but two or the greater Number if there be more. And if any who sells a Part of his Propriety, and retains one Ninety sixth Part and the Title of the Government Portion be absent, whoever has Shares for him, not under one Ninety sixth Part, being present, shall set for him, whether having a Proxy or not; and if there be more than one, it shall go by Turns as above. But because after sometime by Division among Children, it may happen that some one Twenty fourth Part may be so divided, that not any one may have one fourth Part of a Propriety, or one Ninety sixth Part of the whole, in that Case the Proprietors shall elect one having not under one Ninety sixth Part, to bear the Character of the Government for that Propriety: But if the County shall fall to be so divided, that there shall not be found four and Twenty Persons who have one Ninety sixth Part each; then whoever has Five Thousand Acres, shall be capable to be chosen to be one of the four and Twenty, and that by the rest of the Proprietors, by the Ballot, each having priviledge to list one; but this not to take Place till Forty Years after the settling of these Constitutions: And if Twenty Years after the Expiration of the Forty Years above mentioned, it shall fall out that four and Twenty Persons cannot be found who have each Five Thousand Acres, it shall be then in the Power of the great Council to make a less Number of Acres sufficient to carry the Character of the Government, provided they bring it not under three Thousand Acres (the Proprietors being always Electors as aforesaid) No Proprietor under One and Twenty Years shall be admitted to Vote, but during Nonage there shall be a Proxy appointed by the Tutor, and failing that, by the other Proprietors.

XIV. In all Civil and Ordinary Actions, the Proprietors shall be judged after the same manner, and lyable to the same censure with any other; but in all cases that are Capital, or may inferr for Forfeiture of their Trust or Proprietorship, they shall be adjudged by a Jury of Twelve of the Proprietors, or their Proxies, or such as has Share in a Propriety not under one Twentieth Part; the Bill being first found relievant against them by a Grand Jury of Twelve Proprietors and Twelve free Men to be chosen by the Ballot, as in Article nineteen.

XV. For preserving a right ballance, no Proprietor shall at any Time require or purchase more than his one Four and Twentieth Part of the Country; but if by any accident, more fall into the Hands of any of the Proprietors, he may be allowed to dispose of it to his Children, tho' under Age, yet not so as to acquire to himself more than one Vote besides his own; but if such an acquirer have no Children he shall be obliged to sell it within one Year after he has acquired it, nor shall he evade this by putting in anothers Name in Trust for him; but shall upon his Assignment solemnly declare himself to be realy and effectually divested of it for the proper use of him it is assign'd to: And if within three Years he find not a Merchant, he shall be obliged to dispose of it at the Current Rate to the rest of the Proprietors, to be holden in common by them, who shall appoint one to bear that Character in the Government, untill such a Share of it fall in one Hand, by a former Article may render him capable, by the consent of two Parts of the other Proprietors, to have the Power devolved in him; and if by this or any other Accident one or more Votes be wanting in the Interem, the Proprietors shall name others quallified as above to supply their Places.

XVI. All Persons living in the Province who confess and acknowledge the one Almighty and Eternal God, and holds themselves obliged in Conscience to live peaceably and quietly in a civil Society, shall in no way be molested or prejudged for their Religious Perswasions and Exercise in matters of Faith and Worship; nor shall they be compelled to frequent and maintain any Religious Worship, Place or Ministry whatsoever: Yet it is also hereby provided, that no Man shall be admitted a Member of the Great or Common Council, or any other Place of publick Trust, who shall not profess Faith in *Christ-Jesus,* and solemnly declare that he doth no ways hold himself obliged in Conscience to endeavour alteration in the Government, or seeks the turning out of any in it or their ruin or prejudice, either in Person or Estate, because they are in his Opinion Hereticks, or differ in their Judgment from him: Nor by this Article is it intended, that any under the Notion of this Liberty shall allow themselves to avow Atheism, Irreligiousness, or to practice Cursing, Swearing, Drunkeness, Prophaness,

Whoring, Adultery, Murdering or any kind of violence, or indulging themselves in Stage Plays, Masks, Revells or such like abuses; for restraining such and preserving of the People in Deligence and in good Order, the great Council is to make more particular Laws, which are punctually to be put in Execution.

XVII. To the end that all Officers chosen to serve within the Province, may with the more Care and deligence Answer the Trust reposed in them; it is agreed, that no such Person shall enjoy more than one publick Office at one Time: But least at first before the Country be well Planted, there might be in this some Inconveniency, it is declared, that this shall not necessarily take Place till after the Year 1685.

XVIII. All Chart, Rights, Grants and Conveyances of Land (Except Leases for three Years and under) and all Bonds, Wills, and Letters of Administration and Specialties above *Fifty Pounds*, and not under six Months, shall be Registred in a publick Register in each County, else be void in Law: Also there is to be a Register in each County for Births, Marriages, Burials and Servants, where their Names, Times, Wages and Days of Payment shall be registered; but the Method and Order of settling those Registers is recommended to the great Council; as also the Fees which are to be moderate and certain, that the taking of more in any Office, directly or indirectly by himself or any other, shall forfeit his Office.

XIX. That no Person or Persons within the said Province shall be taken and imprisoned, or be devised of his Freehold, free Custom or Liberty, or be outlawed or exiled, or any other Way destroyed; nor shall they be condemn'd or Judgment pass'd upon them, but by lawful Judgment of their Peers: Neither shall Justice nor Right be bought or sold, defered or delayed, to any Person whatsoever: In order to which by the Laws of the Land, all Tryals shall be by twelve Men, and as near as it may be, Peers and Equals, and of the Neighbourhood, and Men without just Exception. In Cases of Life there shall be at first Twenty four returned by the Sheriff for a Grand Inquest, of whom twelve at least shall be to find the Complaint to be true; and then the Twelve Men or Peers to be likewise returned, shall have the final Judgment; but reasonable Challenges shall be always admitted against the Twelve Men, or any of them: But the Manner of returning Juries shall be thus, the Names of all the Freemen above five and Twenty Years of Age, within the District or Boroughs out of which the Jury is to be returned, shall be written on equal Pieces of Parchment and put into a Box, and then the Number of the Jury shall be drawn out by a Child under Ten Years of Age. And in all Courts Persons of all Perswasions may freely appear in their own Way, and according to their own Manner, and there personally plead their own Causes themselves, or if unable, by their Friends, no Person being allowed to take Money for pleading or advice in such Cases: And the first Process shall be the Exhibition of the Complaint in Court fourteen Days before the Tryal, and the Party complain'd against may be fitted for the same, he or she shall be summoned ten Days before, and a Copy of the Complaint delivered at their dwelling House: But before the Complaint of any Person be received, he shall solemnly declare in Court, that he believes in his Conscience his Cause is just. Moreover, every Man shall be first cited before the Court for the Place where he dwells, nor shall the Cause be brought before any other Court but by way of Appeal from Sentence of the first Court, for receiving of which Appeals, there shall be a Court consisting of eight Persons, and the Governor (protempore) President thereof, (*to wit*) four Proprietors and four Freemen, to be chosen out of the great Council in the following Manner, *viz.* the Names of Sixteen of the Proprietors shall be written on small pieces of Parchment and put into a Box, out of which by a Lad under Ten Years of Age, shall be drawn eight of them, the eight remaining in the Box shall choose four; and in like Manner shall be done for the choosing of four of the Freemen.

XX. That all Marriages not forbidden in the Law of God, shall be esteemed lawful, where the Parents or Guardians being first acquainted, the Marriage is publickly intimated in such Places and Manner as is agreeable to Mens different Perswasions in Religion, being afterwards still solemnized before creditable Witnesses, by taking one another as Husband and Wife, and a certificate of the whole, under the Parties and Witnesses Hands, being brought to the proper Register for that End, under a Penalty if neglected.

XXI. That all Witnesses coming or called to testify their Knowledge in or to any Matter or Thing in any Court or before any lawful Authority within the Province, shall there give and deliver in their Evidence by solemnly promising to speak the Truth, the whole Truth and nothing but the Truth, to the Matter in Question. And in Case any Person so doing shall be afterwards convict of willful Falsehood, both such Persons as also those who have proved to have suborn, shall undergo the Damage and Punishment both in Criminal and in Civil; the Person against whom they did or should have incurred, which if it reach not his Life, he shall be publickly exposed as a false Witness, never afterwards to be credited before any Court; the like Punishment in Cases of Forgery, and both Criminals to be stigmatized.

XXII. Fourteen Years quiet Possession shall give an unquestionable Right, except in Cases of Infants, Lunaticks or married Women, or Persons beyond Sea or in Prison. And whoever forfeits his Estate to the Government by committing Treason against the Crown of *England*, or in this Province, or by any other capital Crime, the nearest of Kin may redeem it within two Months after the Criminals Death, by paying to the publick Treasury not above one Hundred Pounds, and not under five Pounds Sterling, which Proportion the common Council shall determine, according to the Value of the Criminals Estate, and to the Nature of the Offence; Reparation to any who have suffered by him, and Payment of all just Debts being always allowed.

XXIII. For avoiding innumerable Multitude of Statutes, no Act to be made by the great Council shall be in Force above Fifty Years after it is enacted; but as it is then *de novo* confirmed, allways excepting these four and twenty Fundamental Articles, which, as the primitive Charter, is forever to remain in force, not to be repealed at any Time by the great Council, tho' two Parts of the Council should agree to it, unless two and Twenty of the four and Twenty Proprietors do expressly also agree, and Sixty six of Seventy two Freemen; and when they are one Hundred Forty four, one Hundred Thirty two of them; and also this assent of the Proprietors must be either by their being present in their own Persons, or giving actually their Votes under their Hands and Seals (if elsewhere) and not by Proxies; which solemn and express assent must also be had in the opening of Mines of Gold and Silver; and if such be opened, one third Part of the Profit is to go to the publick Treasury; one third to be divided among the four and Twenty Proprietors, and one third to Proprietor or Planter in whose Ground it is; the Charges by each proportionably borne.

XXIV. It is finally agreed, that both the Governor and the Members of the great and common Council, the great Officers, Judges, Sheriffs and Justices of the Peace, and all other Persons of publick Trust, shall before they enter actually upon the Exercise of any of the Employs in the Province, solemnly promise and subscribe to be true and faithful to the KING of *England,* his Heirs and Successors, and to the Proprietors, and he shall well and faithfully discharge his Office in all Things according to his Commission, as by these Fundamental

Constitutions is confirmed, the true Right of Liberty and Property, as well as the just Ballance both of the Proprietors among themselves, and betwixt them and the People: It's therefore understood, that here is included whatever is necessary to be retained in the first Concessions, so that henceforward there is nothing further to be proceeded upon from them, that which relates to the securing of every Man's Land taken up upon them, being allways excepted. *And Provided also,* that all judicial and legal Proceedings heretofore done according to them, be held, approved and confirmed.

VI

THE INSTRUCTIONS FROM THE QUEEN IN COUNCIL TO THE GOVERNOR OF THE PROVINCE OF NEW JERSEY NOVEMBER 16, 1702

[Text from the records of the Board of Trade, Public Record Office, London, CO 5/994, f. 43-90. This is the text as finally approved but before being signed and sealed; collated with Aaron Leaming and Jacob Spicer, *The Grants, Concessions, and Original Constitutions of the Province of New-Jersey* (Philadelphia, [1756]), 619-646), and the date in the caption supplied from that source.]

INSTRUCTIONS *for our Right Trusty and Well beloved* EDWARD LORD CORNBURY *Our Captain General and Governor in Chief in and over Our Province of Nova Caesarea or New-Jersey in America. Given at Our Court at* St. James's *the* 16th *day of* November, 1702,* *in the first year of Our Reign.*

1. With these Our Instructions You will receive Our Commission under Our Great Seale of England, constituting you Our Captain General and Governour in Chief of Our Province of New Jersey.

2. You are with all convenient speed to repair to Our said Province, and being there arrived, you are to take upon you the Execution of the Place and Trust We have reposed in You, and forthwith to call together the following Persons, whom we do by these presents appoint and Constitute Members of Our Councill in and for that Province vizt. Edward Hunlock, Lewis Morris, Andrew Bowne, Samuel Jennings, Thomas Revell, Francis Davenport, William Pinhorne, Samuel Leonard, George Deacon, Samuel Walker, Daniel Leeds, William Sandford, and Robert Quary Esqrs.

3. And you are with all due Solemnity, to cause Our said Commission under Our Great Seale of England constituting you Our Captain Generall and Governour in Chief as aforesaid, to be read and published at the said Meeting of Our Councill, and to Cause Proclamation to be made in the Several most publick places of Our said Province of your being constituted by us our Captain Generall and Governour in Chief as aforesaid.

* Date supplied from text in Leaming and Spicer (Ed.).

4. Which being done, you shall yourself take, and also administer to each of the Members of Our said Council so appointed by Us, the Oaths appointed by Act of Parliament to be taken instead of the Oaths of Allegiance and Supremacy, and the Oath mentioned in an Act Entituled *An Act to declare the alteration in the Oath appointed to be taken by the Act Entituled an Act for the further Security of his Majesty's Person and the Succession of the Crown in the Protestant Line and for Extinguishing the hopes of the pretended Prince of Wales and all other Pretenders and their open and Secret Abettors and for declaring the Association to be determined;* As also the Test mentioned in an Act of Parliament made in the 25th year of the Reign of King Charles the 2d. Entituled *An Act for preventing Dangers which may happen from Popish Recusants,* Together with an Oath for the due Execution of your and their Places and Trusts, as well with regard to the Equal and impartial Administration of Justice in all Causes that shall come before you as otherwise; And likewise the Oath required to be taken by Governours of Plantations, to do their utmost that the Laws relating to the Plantations be observed.

5. You are forthwith to communicate unto Our said Council such and so many of these Our Instructions wherein their Advice and Consent are mentioned to be requisite; As likewise all such others from time to time, as you shall find convenient for Our Service to be imparted to them.

6. And whereas the Inhabitants of Our said Province have of late years been unhappily divided, and by their Enmity to each other Our service and their own Wellfare has been very much obstructed You are therefore in the Execution of Our Commission to avoid the engaging yourself in the Parties which have been form'd amongst them, and to use such Impartiallity and Moderation to all as may best conduce to Our Service and the good of the Colony.

7. You are to permit the Members of our said Councill

to have and enjoy freedome of Debate and Vote in all Affaires of Publick concerne that may be debated in Councill.

8. And altho' by Our Commission aforesaid, We have thought fit to direct that any three of Our Counsellors make a Quorum, it is nevertheless Our Will and Pleasure, that you do not Act with a Quorum of less than five Members except in Case of Necessity.

9. And that We may be always informed of the Names and Characters of Persons fit to Supply the Vacancies which shall happen in Our said Councill, You are to transmit unto Us by One of Our Principal Secretarys of State, and to Our Commissioners for Trade and Plantations with all convenient Speed, the Names and Characters of Six Persons Inhabitants of the Eastern Division, and Six other Persons Inhabitants of the Western Division of Our said Province, whom You shall Esteem the best qualifyed for that Trust, and so from time to time when any of them shall Dye, depart out of Our said Province, or become otherwise unfit, You are to Nominate unto Us so many other Persons in their Stead, that the List of Twelve Persons fit to Supply the said Vacancies, Vizt. Six of the East, and six out of the West Division as aforesaid may be always Compleat.

10. You are from time to time to send to Us as aforesaid, And to Our Commissioners for Trade and Plantations, the Names and Qualities of any Members by you put into Our said Councill by the first Conveniency after your so doing.

11. And in the Choice and Nomination of the Members of Our said Council, as also of the Principal Officers, Judges, Assistants, Justices and Sheriffs, You are always to take care that they be Men of good life and well Affected to Our Government, of good Estates and Abilities, and not necessitous People or much in Debt.

12. You are neither to Augment nor diminish the Number of Our said Council as it is hereby Established, nor to Suspend any of the present Members thereof without good and sufficient Cause; And in Case of Suspension of

any of them, You are to cause your reasons for so doing together with the Charges and Proofs against the said Persons, and their Answers thereunto, (unless you have some Extraordinary reason to the Contrary) to be duly entred upon the Council Books; And you are forthwith to transmitt the same, together with your reasons for not Entring them upon the Council Books, (in case You do not so enter them) unto Us, and to Our Commissioners for Trade and Plantations as aforesaid.

13. You are to Signifye Our Pleasure unto the Members of Our said Council that if any of them shall at any time hereafter, Absent themselves, And continue absent above the space of two Months together from Our said Province without leave from You, or from Our Governor or Commander in Chief of Our said Province for the time being first Obtained, or shall remain Absent for the Space of Two Years, or the greater part thereof successively, without Our Leave given them under Our Royal Sign Manual, their place or places in Our said Councill, shall immediately there upon become void, And that We will forthwith appoint others in their Stead.

14. And in Order to the better Consolidating and Incorporating the two Divisions of East and West New Jersey into and under one Government Our Will and Pleasure is, that with all convenient Speed, You call together One General Assembly for the Enacting of Laws for the joint and Mutual Good of the whole: And that the said General Assembly do sit in the first place at Perth-Amboy in East New Jersey, and afterwards the same, or other the next Generall Assembly at Burlington in West New Jersey; And that all future General Assemblys do sit at one or the Other of those Places alternately Or (in case of extraordinary necessity) according as You with the Advice of Our foresaid Councill shall think fit to appoint them.

15. And Our further Will and Pleasure is, that the General Assembly so to be called, do *consist of four and Twenty Representatives* who are to be Chosen in the manner following, Vizt. Two by the Inhabitants House-

holders of the City or Town of Perth Amboy in East New Jersey; Two by the Inhabitants House-holders of the City and Town of Burlington in West New Jersey; Ten by the Freeholders of East New Jersey; And Ten by the Freeholders of West New Jersey; And that no person shall be capable of being Elected a Representative by the Free-holders of either Division, or afterwards of sitting in Generall Assemblies, who shall not have one Thousand Acres of Land of an Estate of Freehold in his own Right, within the Division for which he shall be chosen; And that no Freeholder shall be capable of Voting in the Election of such Representative, who shall not have One hundred Acres of Land of an Estate of Freehold in his own Right, within the Division for which he shall so Vote; And that this Number of Representatives Shall not be enlarged or Diminished, or the manner of Electing them altered, otherwise than by an Act or Acts of the General Assembly there, and confirmed by the Approbation of Us, Our Heires and Successors.

16. You are with all Convenient Speed to Cause a Collection to be made of all the Laws, Orders, Rules, or such as have hitherto served or been reputed as Laws amongst the Inhabitants of Our said Province of Nova-Cæsaria or New Jersey; And together with Our foresaid Council and Assembly; you are to revise, Correct, and Amend the same, as may be necessary, and accordingly to enact such and so many of them, as by You with the Advice of Our said Council and Assembly, shall be judged proper, and conducive to Our Service and the Welfare of Our said Province, that they may be transmitted unto Us in Authentick Form, for Our Approbation or Disallowance.

17. You are to observe In the passing of the said Laws, and of all other Laws that the Stile of Enacting the same, be by the Governor Councill and Assembly and no other.

18. You are also as much as possible to observe in the passing of all Laws, that whatever may be requisite upon each different matter be accordingly provided for by a different Law without intermixing in one and the same

Act, such things as have no proper relation to each other; And you are especially to take Care that No Clause or Clauses be inserted in, or annexed to any Act which shall be foreign to what the Title of Such respective Act Imports.

19. You are to transmitt, Authentick Copies of the aforementioned Laws that Shall be Enacted, and of all Laws, Statutes and Ordinances which Shall at any time hereafter be made, or Enacted within Our said Province, each of them Separately under the Publick Seal unto Us and to Our said Commissioners for Trade and Plantations within Three months or by the first opportunity after their being Enacted, together with Duplicates thereof by the next Conveyance, upon pain of Our High Displeasure, and of the Forfeiture of the Years Salary, wherein You shall at any time, or upon any pretence whatsoever, omit to send over the said Laws, Statutes and Ordinances as aforesaid, within the time above limitted, as also of such other Penalty as we shall please to inflict: But if it shall happen that during time of War, no Shipping shall come from Our said Province or other Our adjacent or Neighboring Plantations, within Three months after the making such Laws, Statutes and Ordinances, whereby the same may be transmitted as aforesaid, then the said Laws, Statutes and Ordinances are to be so transmitted as aforesaid by the next Conveyance after the making thereof, whenever it may happen, for Our Approbation or disallowance of the same.

20. You are to take Care that in all Acts or Orders to be passed within that Our Province in any Case for levying Mony or imposing Fines and Penalties, express mention be made that the same is granted or reserved to Us Our Heirs or Successors for the Publick uses of that Our Province and the Support of the Government thereof as by the said Act or Order shall be directed.

21. And we do particularly require and Command, that no Mony or Value of Mony whatsoever, be given or Granted by any Act or Order of Assembly to any Governor, Lieutenant Governor, or Commander in Chief

of Our said Province, which shall not according to the Stile of Acts of Parliament in England, be mentioned to be given and Granted unto Us, with the humble desire of such Assembly that the same be applyed to the Use and behoof of such Governor Lieutenant Governor, or Commander in Chief, if We shall so think fit; Or if We shall not approve of such Gift or application that the said Mony or Value of Mony be then disposed of and appropriated to such other Uses as in the said Act or Order Shall be mentioned; And that from the Time the same shall be raised, it remain in the Hands of the Receiver of Our Said Province untill Our Royal Pleasure Shall be known therein.

22. You shall also propose unto the said General Assembly, and use your utmost endeavours with them, that an Act be passed for raising and Settling a publick Revenue, for Defraying the Necessary Charge of the Government of Our said Province, in which Provision be particularly made for a Competent Salary to Yourself, as Captain General and Governor in Chief of Our said Province, and to other Our Succeeding Captain Generals for Supporting the Dignity of the said Office; As likewise due Provision for the Salarys of the respective Members of Our Council and Assembly, and of all other Officers necessary for the Administration of that Government.

23. Whereas it is not reasonable that any of Our Colonies or Plantations should by Virtue of any Exemptions or other Priviledges whatsoever, be allowed to seek and pursue their own particular Advantages, by Methods tending to undermine and prejudice Our other Colonies and Plantations, which have equal Title to Our Royal Care; And whereas the Trade and Welfare of Our Province of New Yorke would be greatly prejudiced if not intirely ruined, by allowing unto the Inhabitants of Nova Cæsaria or New Jersey, any Exemption from those Charges, which the Inhabitants of New Yorke are lyable to; You are therefore in the Settling of a Publick Revenue as before Directed, to propose to the Assembly, that such Customs, Duties and other Impositions be laid upon all

Commodities imported, or Exported in, or out of Our said Province of Nova Cæsaria or New Jersey, as may equal the Charge that is, or shall be laid upon the like Commodities in Our Province of New Yorke.

24. And Whereas We are willing in the best manner to provide for the Support of the Government of Our said Province by setting apart sufficient allowances to such as shall be Our Governour or Commander in Chief residing for the time being within the same. *Our Will and Pleasure* therefore is That when it shall happen that you shall be absent from the Territories of New Jersey and New Yorke of which We have appointed you Governor, one full Moyety of the Salary and of all Perquisites and Emoluments whatsoever, which would otherwise become due unto You, shall during the time of your Absence from the said Territories, be paid and Satisfied unto such Governor or Commander in Cheif, who shall be resident upon the Place for the time being, which We do hereby Order and allot unto him towards his maintenance, and for the better support of the Dignity of that Our Government.

25. Whereas great prejudice may happen to Our Service and the Security of Our said Province under Your Government, by Your absence from those parts without a sufficient Cause and especial Leave from Us, for prevention whereof You are not upon any Pretence whatsoever to come to Europe from Your Government with out first having Obtained Leave for so doing under Our Signet and Sign Manual, Or by our Order in our Privy Council.

26. You are not to permit any Clause whatsoever to be incerted in any Law for the Levying Mony, or the Value of Mony whereby the same shall not be made lyable to be accounted for unto Us here in England, and to Our High-Treasurer or to Our Commissioners of Our Treasury for the time being.

27. You are to take Care that fair Books of Accounts of all Receipts and Payments of all such Mony be duely

kept, and the Truth thereof attested upon Oath, and that the said Books be transmitted every half year, or oftener to Our High Treasurer or to Our Commissioners of Our Treasury for the time being, And to Our Commissioners for Trade and Plantations, And Duplicates thereof by the next Conveyance; In which Books shall be Specified every particular Summ raised or Disposed of, together with the Names of the Persons to whom any Payment shall be made, to the end We may be satisfyed of the Right and due Application of the Revenue of Our said Province.

28. You are not to suffer any Publick Mony whatsoever, to be Issued or disposed of otherwise than by Warrant under Your hand, by and with the Advice and Consent of Our said Council: But the Assembly may be nevertheless permitted from time to time to View and Examine the Accounts of Mony or Value of Mony disposed of by Virtue of Laws made by them, which You are to signifye unto them as there shall be occasion.

29. And it is Our Express Will and Pleasure that no Law for raising any imposition on Wines or other Strong Liquors be made to continue for less than one whole Year; As also that all Laws whatsoever for the Good Government and Support of Our said Province be made indefinite, and without limitation of time Except the same be for a Temporary End, which Shall Expire and have its full Effect within a Certain time.

30. And therefore You shall not re-enact any Law which shall have been once enacted there by you except upon very urgent Occasions, But in no Case more than Once without Our Express Consent.

31. You shall not permit any Act or Order to pass in Our said Province, whereby the price or Value of the Current Coyne within Your Government (whether it be Foreign or belonging to Our Dominions) may be altered, without Our particular leave or direction for the same.

32. And You are particularly not to pass any Law or do any Act by Grant, Settlement, or otherwise whereby

our Revenue after it shall be settled, may be lessened or impaired without our especial Leave or Commands therein.

33. You shall not remit any Fines or Forfeitures whatsoever above the Summ of Ten pounds, nor dispose of any Escheats, Fines or Forfeitures whatsoever, until upon Signifying unto Our High Treasurer or to Our Commissioners of Our Treasury for the time being, And to Our Commissioners for Trade and Plantations, the Nature of the Offence and the Occasion of such Fines, Forfeitures or Escheats with the particular Summs or Value thereof (which you are to do with all Speed) You shall have received Our Directions therein, But you may in the meantime suspend the payment of the said Fines and Forfeitures.

34. You are to require the Secretary of Our said Province or his Deputy for the time being to furnish You with Transcripts of all such Acts, and publick Orders as shall be made from time to time, together with a Copy of the Journals of the Council, to the End the same may be transmitted unto Us, and to Our Commissioners for Trade and Plantations as above directed, which he is duly to perform upon pain of incurring the forfeiture of his place.

35. You are also to require from the Clarke of the Assembly or other proper Officer Transcripts of all the Journalls and other proceedings of the said Assembly to the end the same may in like manner be transmitted as aforesaid.

36. *Our Will and Pleasure* is that for the better quieting the minds of Our Good Subjects Inhabitants of Our said Province, and for settling the Properties and Possessions of all Persons concerned therein, either as General Proprietors of the Soyle under the first Original Grant of the said Province made by the late King Charles the Second to the late Duke of Yorke, Or as particular Purchasers of any Parcells of Land from the said General Proprietors, You shall propose to the General Assembly of Our Said Province the passing of such Act, or Acts,

whereby the Right and Property of the said General Proprietors, to the Soyle of Our said Province may be confirmed to them according to their respective Rights and Titles; together with all such Quit-Rents as have been reserved or are or shall become due to the said General Proprietors from the Inhabitants of our said Province, and all such Priviledges as are exprest in the Conveyances made by the said Duke of Yorke; Excepting only the Right of Government, which remains in Us; And You are further to take care that by the said Act or Acts so to be passed the particular Titles and Estates of all the Inhabitants of that Province and other Purchasers claiming under the said General Proprietors be confirmed and Settled as of Right does appertain, under such obligations as shall tend to the best and speediest Improvement or Cultivation of the same. Provided always that you do not consent to any Act or Acts to lay any Tax upon Lands that lye unprofitable.

37. You shall not permit any other Person or Persons, besides the said General Proprietors, or their Agents to purchase any Land whatsoever from the Indians within the Limits of their Grant.

38. You are to permit the Surveyors and other Persons appointed by the aforementioned General Proprietors of the Soile of that Province, for Surveying and recording the Surveys of Land granted by, and held of them, to Execute accordingly their respective Trusts, And You are likewise to permit and, if need be, aid and Assist such other Agent or Agents, as shall be appointed by the said Proprietors for that End, To Collect and Receive the Quit-Rents which are or shall be due unto them, from the particular Possessors of any parcells or Tracts of Land from time to time. *Provided always* that such Surveyors, Agents, or other Officers appointed by the said General Proprietors, doe not only take proper Oaths for the due Execution and performance of their respective Offices or Employments, and give good and Sufficient Security for their so doing, but that they likewise take the Oaths appointed by Act of Parliament to be taken

instead of the Oaths of Allegiance and Supremacy; And the Oath mentioned in the aforesaid Act Entituled *An Act to declare the alteration in the Oath appointed to be taken by the Act Entituled an Act for the further Security of his Majesty's Person and the Succession of the Crown in the Protestant Line and for extinguishing the hopes of the pretended Prince of Wales, and all other Pretenders and their open and Secret Abettors and for declaring the Association to be determined,* as also the Forementioned Test, And you are more particularly to take Care that all Lands purchased from the said Proprietors be cultivated, and Improved by the Possessors thereof.

39. You shall transmit unto Us, and to Our Commissioners for Trade and Plantations by the first opportunity a Map with the Exact Discription of Our whole Territory under Your Government, and of the severall Plantations that are upon it.

40. You are likewise to send a List of Officers imployed under your Government together with all publick Charges.

41. You shall not displace any of the Judges Justices, Sheriffs, or other Officers or Ministers within Our said Province, without good and Sufficient Cause, to be Signifyed unto Us, and to Our said Commissioners for Trade and Plantations: And to prevent Arbitrary removal of Judges and Justices of the Peace, You shall not express any limitation of time in the Commissions which you are to Grant, with the Advice and consent of the Council of Our said Province to Persons fit for those Imployments; Nor shall you Execute yourself, or by Deputy, any of the said Offices, Nor suffer any Person to Execute more Offices than one, by Deputy.

42. Whereas we are given to understand that there are severall Offices within Our said Province granted under the great Seal of England, and that Our Service may be very much prejudiced by reason of the Absence of the Patentees, and by their appointing Deputies not fit to Officiate in their Stead, You are therefore to inspect the

said Offices, and to inquire into the Capacity and behaviour of the persons now exercising them, and to report thereupon to Us and to Our Commissioners for Trade and Plantations, what you think fit to be done or altered in relation thereunto; And you are upon the Misbehaviour of any of the said Patentees or their Deputies to suspend them from the Execution of their Places, till you shall have represented the whole matter and received Our Directions therein. But you shall not by Colour of any Power or Authority hereby or otherwise granted or mentioned to be granted unto You, take upon you to give, grant or Dispose of any Office or Place, within Our said Province, which now is or shall be granted under the Great Seal of England, any further than that You may upon the Vacancy of any such Office or place, or Suspension of any such Officer by You as aforesaid, put in any fit Person to Officiate in the Intervall, till You shall have represented the matter unto Us and to Our Commissioners for Trade and Plantations as aforesaid (which You are to do by the first Opportunity) and till the said Office or Place be disposed of by Us, Our Heirs or Successors under the Great Seal of England, Or that Our further Directions be given therein.

43. In Case any Goods, Mony or other Estate of Pirates, or piratically taken, shall be brought in or found within Our said Province of Nova Cæsaria or New Jersey, or taken on board any Ships or Vessells, You are to cause the same to be Seized and Secured untill You shall have given Us an Account thereof, and received Our Pleasure concerning the Disposal of the same: But in Case such Goods or any part of them are perishable, the same shall be publickly sold and disposed of; And the Produce thereof in like manner Secured untill our further Order.

44. And whereas Commissions have been granted unto Several Persons in Our respective Plantations in America for the trying of Pirates in those parts pursuant to the *Act for the more effectual Suppression of Piracy,* And by a Commission already sent to Our Province of New Yorke, You (as Captain General and Governour in Cheif of

Our said Province of New Yorke) are impowered together with others therein mentioned to proceed accordingly in reference to Our Provinces of New Yorke, New Jersey, and Connecticut; *Our Will and Pleasure is,* That in all matters relating to Pirates, you govern yourself according to the intent of the Act and Commission aforementioned. But whereas Accessories in Cases of Piracy beyond the Seas are by the said Act left to be tryed in England according to the Statute of the 28th of King Henry the VIII, We do hereby direct further and require you to send all such Accessories in Cases of Piracy in Our aforesaid Province of Nova Cæsaria or New Jersey, with the proper Evidences that you may have against them into England in order to theire being tryed here.

45. You shall not erect any Court or Office of Judicature not before erected or established without Our especial Order.

46. You are to transmit unto Us and to Our Commissioners for Trade and Plantations with all convenient Speed a particular Account of all Establishments of Jurisdictions, Courts, Offices, and Officers, Powers, Authorities, Fees and Priviledges which shall be Granted or Settled within the said Province, by Virtue and in pursuance of Our Commission and Instructions to You, Our Captain Generall and Governour in Cheif of the same, to the end you may receive Our further Directions therein.

47. And You are with the Advice and Consent of Our said Council, to take Especial Care to regulate all Salaries and Fees belonging to Places, or paid upon Emergencies, that they be within the Bounds of Moderation, and that no Exaction be made on any occasion whatsoever; As also that Tables of all Fees be publickly hung up in all places where such Fees are to be paid; and You are to transmit Copies of all such Tables of Fees to us, and to Our Commissioners for Trade and Plantations as aforesaid.

48. Whereas it is necessary that our Rights and Dues be preserved and recovered, and that Speedy and Effectual Justice be administred in all Cases relating to Our

Revenue, you are to take Care that a Court of Exchequer be called and do meet at all such times as shall be needfull, and You are to inform Us and Our Commissioners for Trade and Plantations whether Our Service may require that a constant Court of Exchequer be Settled and established there.

49. You are to take care that no Mans life, Member, Freehold or Goods be taken away or harmed in Our said Province, otherwise than by Established and known Laws, not repugnant to, but as much as may be agreable to the Laws of England.

50. You shall Administer or Cause to be Administred the Oaths Appointed by Act of Parliament to be taken in Stead of the Oaths of Allegiance and Supremacy, and the Oath mentioned in the foresaid Act Entituled *An Act to declare the Alteration in the Oath appointed to be taken by the Act Entituled an Act for the further Security of his Majesty's Person and the Succession of the Crown in the Protestant Line and for extinguishing the Hopes of the pretended Prince of Wales and all other Pretenders, and their open and Secret Abettors, and for declaring the Association to be determined,* as also the aforementioned Test to the Members and Officers of the Council and Assembly, and to all Judges, Justices, and all other Persons that hold any Office or Place of Trust or Profit in the said Province, whether by Virtue of any Patent under Our Great Seale of England or otherwise, Without which You are not to admit any Person whatsoever into any Publick Office nor suffer those who have been admitted formerly to continue therein.

51. You are to permit a Liberty of Conscience to all Persons (except Papists) so they be contented with a Quiet and Peaceable Enjoyment of the same, not giving Offence or Scandal to the Government.

52. And whereas We have been informed that Divers of Our Good Subjects inhabiting those parts, do make a Religious Scruple of Swearing, and by reason of their refusing to take an Oath in Courts of Justice and other places, are or may be liable to many Inconveniences,

Our Will and Pleasure is that in Order to their Ease in what they conceive to be matter of Conscience, so far as may be consistent with good Order and Government, You take care that an Act be passed in the General Assembly of Our said Province to the like Effect as that past here in the 7th and 8th Year of His Majesty's Reign Intituled *An Act that the Solemn Affirmation and Declaration of the People called Quakers shall be accepted instead of an Oath in the usual form* and that the same be transmitted to Us and to Our Commissioners for Trade and Plantations as before directed.

53. And Whereas We have been further informed that in the first Settlement of the Government of our said Province it may so happen that the number of Inhabitants fitly qualifyed to serve in Our Councill, in the General Assembly, and in other Places of Trust or Profit there will be but Small; It is therefore Our Will and Please that, such of the said People called Quakers as Shall be found Capable of any of those Places or Employments, and accordingly be elected or appointed to Serve therein may upon their taking and signing the Declaration of Allegiance to Us in the form used by the same People here in England, together with a Solemn Declaration for the true discharge of their respective Trusts be admitted by you into any of the said Places or Employments.

You shall send an Account unto Us and to Our Commissioners for Trade and Plantations of the present Number of Planters and Inhabitants Men, Women and Children, as well Masters as Servants, Free and unfree, and of the Slaves in Our said Province, As also a Yearly Account of the Increase or Decrease of them, and how many of them are fit to bear Arms in the Militia of Our said Province.

You shall also Cause an Exact Account to be kept of all Persons, Borne, Christen'd and Buried, and You shall Yearly Send fair Abstracts thereof to Us and to Our Commissioners for Trade and Plantations as aforesaid.

You shall take care that all Planters and Christian

Servants be well and fitly provided with Armes, and that they be Listed under good Officers, and when and as often as shall be thought fit, Mustered and Trained, whereby they may be in a better readiness for the Defence of Our said Province under Your Government, And You are to endeavor to get an Act past (if not already done) for apportioning the Number of White Servants, to be kept by every Planter.

You are to take especial Care that neither the frequency nor unreasonableness of their Marches, Musters, and Trainings, be an unnecessary Impediment to the affairs of the Inhabitants.

You shall not upon any Occasion whatsoever establish or put in Execution any Articles of War, or other Law Martial upon any of Our Subjects, Inhabitants of Our said Province without the Advice and Consent of Our Councill there.

And Whereas there is no Power given you by your Commission to Execute Martial Law in time of Peace upon Soldiers in pay, and that nevertheless it may be necessary that some care be taken for the keeping of good Discipline amongst those that We may at any time think fit to send into Our said Province (which may properly be provided for by Legislative Power of the same) You are therefore to recommend to the General Assembly of Our said Province that they prepare such Act or Law for the punishing of Mutiny, Desertion, and false Musters, and for the better preserving of good Discipline amongst the said Soldiers as may best answer those ends.

And Whereas upon Complaints that have been made of the irregular Proceedings of the Captains of some of Our Ships of War in the pressing of Seamen in several of our Plantations, We have thought fit to Order, and have given Directions to Our High Admiral accordingly That when any Captain or Commander of any of Our Ships of War in any of Our said Plantations shall have occasion for Seamen to Serve on board Our Ships under their Command, they do make their application to the Governours and Commanders in Cheif of Our Plantations respectively, To whom, as Vice Admirals, We are pleased to Commit the sole Power of Impressing Seamen in any of Our Plantations in America; Or in Sight of any of them, You are therefore hereby required upon such Application made to you by any of the Commanders of Our said Ships of War within Our Province of Nova Cæsaria or New Jersey, to take care that Our Said Ships of War be furnished with the Number of Seamen that may be necessary for Our Service on board them from time to time.

And Whereas together with other Powers of Vice Admiralty, You will receive Authority from Our Dearest Husband Prince George of Denmark, Our High Admiral of England and of Our Plantations, upon the refusal or Neglect of any Captain or Commander of any of Our Ships of War to execute the Written Orders he shall receive from You for Our Service and the Service of Our Province under your Government, Or upon his negligent or undue Execution thereof to Suspend him Such Captain or Commander from the Exercise of his said Office of Captain or Commander, and to commit him into safe Custody, either on board his own Ship or elsewhere at Your discretion, in Order to his being brought to answer for such refusal or neglect by Commission, either under Our Great Seal of England, or from Our High Admiral or Our Commissioners for Executing the Office of High Admiral of England for the time being; And Whereas You will likewise receive Direction from Our said Dearest Husband, As Our High Admiral of England and of Our Plantations, that the Captain or Commander so by you suspended shall, during such his Suspension and Commitment, be succeeded in his said Office by such Commission or Warrant Officer of Our said Ship appointed by Our said High Admiral or by Our Commissioners for executing the Office of Our High Admiral of England for the time being, as by the known practice and discipline of Our Navy does and ought to Succeed him next as in Case of Death Sickness or other Ordinary disability happening to the Commander of any of Our Ships of

War and not otherwise. You standing also Accountable for the Truth and Importance of the Crime and Misdemeanour for which you shall so proceed, to the Suspending of such Our Captain or Commander, You are not to exercise the said Power of Suspending any such Captains or Commanders of Our Ships of War, otherwise than by Virtue of Such Commission or Authority from Our said High Admiral, any former Custome or Usage notwithstanding.

Whereas it is absolutely necessary that We be exactly Informed of the State of Defence of all Our Plantations in America, as well in relation to the Stores of War that are in each Plantation, as to the Fort and Fortifications there, and what more may be necessary to be built for the Defence and Security of the same, You are so soon as possible to prepare an Account thereof with relation to Our said Province of Nova Cæsaria, or New Jersey in the most particular manner; And you are therein to Express the present State of the Arms, Ammunition and other Stores of War, either in any Publick Magazines, or in the hands of Private Persons, together with the State of all Places either already Fortified or that You Judge necessary to be Fortifyed for the Security of Our said Province: And you are to transmit it the said Account, to Us, and to our Commissioners for Trade and Plantations by the first Opportunity and other like Accounts Yearly in the same manner.

And that We may be the better informed of the Trade of Our said Province, You are to take Especial Care that due Entries be made in all Ports in our said Province of all Goods and Commodities, their Species or Quantities, imported or Exported, from thence with the Names, Burden, and Guns, of all Ships Importing and Exporting the same; Also the Names of their Commanders, and likewise expressing from and to what Places the said Ships do come and goe, a Copy whereof the Naval Officer is to furnish you with. And you are to transmit the same unto Us, Our High Treasurer or Our Commissioners of Our Treasury for the time being, and to

Our Commissioners for Trade and Plantations Quarterly and Duplicates thereof by the next Conveyance.

And whereas great Losses have been sustained by Our Subjects trading to Our Plantations in America, by Ships sailing from those parts without Convoy, or without the Company of other Ships which might protect them from Our Enemies, by which means many of them have been taken by the French in their return to England; To the End therefore the Ships of Our Subjects may be the better Secured, in their return home, You are to take care that during this time of War, no Ships trading to Our Province of Nova Cæsaria or New Jersey be permitted to come from thence to England but in Fleets, or under the Convoy or protection of some of Our Ships of War, or at such a time as you shall receive notice from hence of their meeting such Convoys, as may be appointed for the bringing of them safe to some of Our Ports in this Kingdome and in Case of any danger, You are to expect Directions from hence, what Precautions shall be further Necessary for their Security.

You are likewise to examine what Rates and Duties are charged and Payable upon any Goods imported or Exported within our Province of Nova Cæsaria or New Jersey, whether of the Growth or Manufacture of the said Province or otherwise, and to use your best Endeavours for the Improvement of the Trade in those parts.

And Whereas Orders have been given for the Commissionating of fit Persons to be Officers of Our Admiralty and Customs in Our Several Plantations in America; And it is of great Importance to the Trade of this Kingdome, and to the Welfare of all Our Plantations, that Illegal Trade be everywhere discouraged, you are therefore to take especial Care that the Acts of Trade and Navigation be duly put in Execution. And in order thereunto you are to give constant Protection and all due Encouragement to the said Officers of Our Admiralty and Customs in the Execution of their respective Offices and Trusts within Our Territories under Your Government.

You are from time to time to give an Account as before directed what Strength your bordering Neighbours have, be they Indians or others, by Sea and Land, and of the Condition of their Plantations, and what Correspondence you do keep with them.

You shall take Especial Care, that God Almighty be Devoutly and duly Served throughout Your Government; The Book of Common Prayer as by Law Established read each Sunday and Holyday and the Blessed Sacrament Administred according to the Rites of the Church of England.

You shall be Carefull that the Churches already built there be well and Orderly kept, and that more be Built as the Colony Shall by Gods Blessing be Improved; And that besides a competent maintenance to be Assigned to the Minister of each Orthodox Church, a Convenient House be built at the Common Charge for each Minister, and a competent proportion of Land assigned to him, for a Glebe and Exercise of His Industry.

And You are to take Care that the Parishes be so limited and Settled, as you shall find most convenient for the Accomplishing this good Worke.

You are not to prefer any Minister to any Ecclesiasticall Benefice in that Our Province without a Certificate from the Right Reverend Father in God the Lord Bishop of London, of his being conformable to the Doctrine and Discipline of the Church of England, and of a good life and Conversation; And if any Person already prefer'd to a Benefice shall appear to you to give Scandal, either by His Doctrine, or Manners, You are to use the best means for the Removal of him, and to Supply the Vacancy in such manner as We have directed.

You are to give Order that every Orthodox Minister within your Government, be one of the Vestry in his respective Parish, and that no Vestry be held without him, except in Case of Sickness, or that after Notice of a Vestry Summoned, he omit to come.

You are to enquire whether there be any Minister within your Government who Preaches and Administers the Sacrament in any Orthodox Church or Chappel without being in due Orders, and to give Account thereof to the said Lord Bishop of London.

And to the End the Ecclesiastical Jurisdiction of the said Lord Bishop of London may take place in Our said Province, so far as conveniently may be, We do think fit that you give all Countenance and encouragement to the Exercise of the same, excepting only the Collating to Benefices, Granting Lycences for Marriages, and Probate of Wills, which We have reserved to You Our Governour, and the Commander in Cheif of Our said Province for the time being.

And You are to take Especial care that a Table of Marriages Established by the Cannons of the Church of England be hung up in every Orthodox Church, and duely observed, And you are to endeavor to get a Law passed in the Assembly of Our said Province (if not already don) for the Strict observation of the said Table.

You are to take Care that Drunkeness and Debauchery, Swearing and Blasphemy, be Discountenanced and punished; And for the further Discountenance of Vice and incouragement of Virtue and good living (that by such Example the Infidels may be invited and desire to partake of the Christian Religion) you are not to admit any Person to Publick Trusts and Employments in Our said Province under Your Government, whose ill Fame and Conversation may occasion Scandal.

You are to suppress the Engrossing * of Commodities, as tending to the prejudice of that freedom, which Commerce and Trade ought to have and to Settle such Orders and Regulations therein, with the Advice of the Council, as may be most conducive to the Benefit and Improvement of that Colony.

You are to give all due Encouragement and invitation to Merchants and others who shall bring Trade unto Our said Province, or any way contribute to the Advantage thereof, and in particular the Royal African Company of England.

* That is, monopolizing (Ed.).

And whereas we are willing to recommend unto the said Company that the said Province may have a Constant and Sufficient Supply of Merchantable Negroes at moderate Rates in mony or Commodities, so you are to take especial care that Payment be duly made, and within a competent time according to their agreements.

And You are to take care that there be no Trading from Our said Province to any place in Africa within the Charter of the Royal African Company, otherwise than prescribed by an Act of Parliament, Intituled *An Act to Settle the Trade to Africa*.

And You are yearly to give unto Us and to Our Commissioners for Trade and Plantations an Account of what number of Negroes our said Province is yearly supplied with, and at what Rates.

You are likewise from time to time to give unto Us, and to Our Commissioners for Trade and Plantations as aforesaid An Account of the want and Defects of Our said Province, what are the Cheif Products thereof, what New Improvements are made therein by the Industry of the Inhabitants or Planters, and what further Improvements You conceive may be made or advantages gained by Trade, and in what manner We may best advance the same.

You are not to grant Commissions of Marque or Reprizals against any Prince or State, or their Subjects, in Amity with Us, to any Person whatsoever without Our Especial Command.

Our Will and Pleasure is that Appeals be permitted to be made in Cases of Error from the Courts in Our said Province of Nova Cæsaria or New Jersey, unto You and the Council there, and in your Absence from Our said Province to Our Commander in Chief for the time being, and Our said Council, in Civil Causes, wherein such of Our said Council as shall be at that time Judges of the Court from whence Such Appeal shall be made to You Our Governour and Council or to the Commander in Chief for the time being and Council as aforesaid, shall not be admitted to Vote upon the said Appeal; But they may nevertheless be present at the hearing thereof, to give the reasons of the Judgment given by them in the Cause wherein such Appeal shall be made PROVIDED nevertheless that in all such Appeals the Summ or Value appeal'd for exceed One hundred pounds Sterling, and that Security be first duly given by the appellant to answer such Charges as shall be awarded, in case the first Sentence be affirmed.

And if either Party shall not rest satisfyed with the Judgment of You or the Commander in Cheif for the time being and Council, as aforesaid, Our Will and Pleasure is that they may then Appeal unto Us in Our Privy Council, Provided the Summ or Value so appealed for unto Us, do exceed Two hundred Pounds Sterling, and that such Appeal be made within fourteen days after Sentence, And that good Security be given by the Appellant that he will Effectually prosecute the same, and Answer the Condemnation as also pay such Costs and Damages, as shall be awarded by Us, in case the Sentence of you or the Commander in Cheif for the time being and Council be Affirmed, And *Provided* also that Execution be not Suspended by reason of any such Appeal to Us.

You are also to permit Appeals to Us in Council in all Cases of Fines imposed for Misdemeanours *Provided* the Fines so imposed amount to or exceed the Value of 200£, The Appellant first giving good Security that he will effectually prosecute the same and answer the Condemnation if the Sentence by which such Fine was imposed in Our said Province of Nova Cæsaria or New Jersey, shall be confirmed.

You are for the better Administration of Justice to Endeavour to get a Law passed (if not already done) wherein shall be set the Value of Mens Estates either in Good or Lands, under which they shall not be capable of Serving as Jurors.

You shall endeavour to get a Law past for the restraining of any Inhuman Severity, which by ill Masters or Overseers may be used towards their Christian Servants and their Slaves; And that provision be made therein, that the Wilful killing of Indians and Negroes may be punished with Death, and that a fit Penalty be Imposed for the maiming of them.

And You are also with the Assistance of the Council and Assembly to find out the best means to facilitate and incourage the Conversion of Negroes and Indians to the Christian Religion.

You are to endeavour with the Assistance of the Council to provide for the raising of Stocks and building of publick Work houses in convenient Places for the Employing of Poor and indigent People.

You are to propose an Act to be past in the Assembly whereby the Creditors of Persons becoming Bank-rupts in England and having Estates in Our aforesaid Province of New Jersey may be releived and satisfied for the Debts owing to them.

You are to incourage the Indians upon all occasions so as they may apply themselves to the English Trade and Nation rather than to any other of Europe.

And Whereas the preservation of the Northern Frontiers of Our Province of New Yorke against the Attempts of any Enemy by Land, is of great importance to the Security of Our other northern Plantations on the Continent of America, and more especially of Our said Province of New Jersey, which lyes so near adjoyning to Our Province of New Yorke, and the Charge of Erecting and repairing the Fortifications and of maintaining the Soldiers necessary for the Defence of the same is too great to be born by the Single Province of New Yorke, without due Contributions from others concerned therein, for which reason We have upon several occasions required such Contributions to be made, and accordingly Settled a Quota to regulate the Proportions thereof; You are therefore to take further Care to dispose the General Assembly of Our said Province of New Jersey to the raising of such other Supplies, as are or may be necessary for the Defence of Our Province of New Yorke, according to the Signification of Our Will and Pleasure therein, which has already been made to the Inhabitants of New Jersey, or which shall at any time hereafter be made to You Our Governour, or to the Commander in Chief of Our said Province for the time being.

And in Case of any distress of any of Our Plantations, You shall upon Application of the respective Governours to you, assist them with what Aid the Condition and safety of Your Government will permit; And more particularly in Case Our Province of New Yorke be at any time attacked by an Enemy, the Assistance You are to contribute towards the Defence thereof, whether in Men or Mony is to be according to the forementioned Quota or Repartition, which has already been Signifyed to the Inhabitants of Our foresaid Province under your Government, or according to such other Regulation as We shall hereafter make in that behalf; and signifye to you or the Commander in Cheif of Our said Province for the time being.

And for the greater Security of Our Province of New Jersey, You are to appoint fit Officers and Commanders in the several parts of the Country bordering upon the Indians, who upon any Invasion may raise Men and Arms to oppose them, untill they shall receive Your Directions therein.

And whereas We have been pleased by Our Commission to direct that in Case of your Death or Absence from Our said Province, and in case there be at that time no Person upon the Place Commissionated or appointed by Us to be Our Lieutenant Governour or Commander in Chief, the then present Council of Our said Province shall take upon them the Administration of the Government and Execute Our said Commission and the Several Powers and Authorities therein contained in the manner therein Directed; It is nevertheless Our Express Will and Pleasure, that in such Case the said Council shall forbear to pass any Acts but what are immediately necessary for the Peace and Welfare of Our said Province without Our particular Order for that purpose.

You are to take Care that all Writs be issued in Our Name throughout Our said Province.

For as much as great inconveniencies may arise by the Liberty of Printing in Our said Province, you are to provide by all necessary Orders, that no Person keep any press for printing, nor that any Book, Pamphlet or other matters whatsoever be printed without your especial Leave and License first obtained.

And if anything shall happen that may be of Advantage and Security to Our said Province which is not herein or by Our Commission to You provided for, We do hereby allow unto you with the Advice and Consent of Our Council of Our said Province to take Order for the present therein, giving unto Us by one of Our Principal Secretaries of State, and to Our Commissioners for Trade and Plantations, Speedy notice thereof that so You may receive Our Ratification if We shall approve of the same.

Provided always that you do not by any Colour of any Power or Authority hereby given You, Commence or declare War, without Our knowledg and particular Commands therein, except it be against Indians upon Emergencies, wherein the Consent of Our Councill shall be had, and speedy Notice given thereof unto Us as aforesaid.

And You are upon all Occasions to send unto Us by one of Our Principal Secretaries of State and to Our Commissioners for Trade and Plantations a particular Account of all your Proceedings and of the Condition of Affairs within Your Government.

And whereas the Lords Spiritual and Temporal in Parliament upon consideration of the great Abuses practised in the Plantation Trade, did by an humble Address Represent to his late Majesty the great Importance it is of, both to this Our Kingdome and to Our Plantations in America, that the many good Laws which have been made for the Government of the said Plantations, and particularly the Act passed in the Seventh and Eighth years of his said Majestys Reign Entituled *An Act for preventing Frauds and regulating Abuses in the Plantation Trade* be strictly observed. You are therefore to take notice, that whereas notwithstanding the many good

Laws made from time to time for preventing Frauds in the Plantation Trade, It is nevertheless manifest that very great abuses have been and continue still to be practised to the prejudice of the same, which Abuses must needs arise, either from the Insolvency of the Persons who are accepted for the Security, or from the remissness or Connivance of such as have been, or are Governours in the Several Plantations, who ought to take care that those Persons who give Bond should be duly prosecuted, in Case of Non performance; We take the Good of Our Plantations and the Improvement of the Trade thereof by a Strict and punctual Observance of the Several Laws in force concerning the same, to be of so great Importance to the Benefit of this Our Kingdom and to the advancing of the Duties of Our Customes here, that if We shall be hereafter informed that at any time there shall be any failure in the due Observance of those Laws within Our foresaid Province of Nova Cæsaria or New Jersey, by any Wilfull fault or Neglect on your part, We shall look upon it as a Breach of the Trust reposed in You by Us, which We shall punish with the loss of Your Place in that Government, and Such further Marks of Our Displeasure, as We shall Judg reasonable to be inflicted upon You, for Your Offence against Us, in a matter of this Consequence. That We now so particularly charge You with.

VII

THE CONSTITUTION OF THE STATE OF NEW JERSEY
JULY 2, 1776

[The first Constitution of the State of New Jersey was neither engrossed nor signed by the delegates to the Provincial Congress that framed it. The present text is taken from an attested copy signed by Samuel Tucker as President and by William Paterson as Secretary (recorded in Lib: AB, Commissions, f. 187, in the New Jersey Bureau of Archives and History); collated with the official printing issued by Isaac Collins at Burlington in 1777—*Acts of the General Assembly of the State of New-Jersey at a Session Begun at Princeton on the 27th Day of August, 1776, and continued by Adjournments. To Which is Prefixed the Constitution of the State.*]

Constitution of New Jersey

Whereas all the constitutional Authority, ever possessed by the Kings of Great Britain over these Colonies, or their other Dominions, was, by Compact, derived from the People, and held of them for the common Interest of the whole Society, Allegiance and Protection are, in the Nature of Things, reciprocal Ties, each equally depending upon the other, and liable to be dissolved by the other's being refused or withdrawn. And whereas George the Third, King of Great Britain, has refused Protection to the good People of these Colonies; and, by assenting to Sundry Acts of the British Parliament, attempted to subject them to the absolute Dominion of that Body; and has also made War upon them in the most cruel and unnatural Manner, for no other Cause than asserting their just Rights, all civil Authority under him is necessarily at an End, and a Dissolution of Government in each Colony has consequently taken Place.

And whereas in the present deplorable Situation of these Colonies, exposed to the Fury of a cruel and Relentless Enemy, some Form of Government is absolutely necessary, not only for the Preservation of good Order, but also the more effectually to unite the People, and enable them to exert their whole Force in their own necessary Defence; and as the Honourable the Continental Congress, the Supreme Council of the American Colonies, has advised such of the Colonies, as have not yet gone into the Measure, to adopt for themselves respectively such Government, as shall best conduce to their own Happiness and Safety, and the Well-Being of America in general; We the Representatives of the Colony of New Jersey, having been elected by all the Counties in the freest Manner, and in Congress assembled, have, after mature Deliberation, agreed upon a Set of Charter-Rights, and the Form of a Constitution in Manner following, viz.

1. That the Government of this Province shall be vested in a Governor, Legislative Council, and General Assembly.

2d. That the said Legislative Council and Assembly shall be chosen, for the first Time, on the second Tuesday of August next, the Members whereof shall be the same in Number and Qualifications as is herein after mentioned; and shall be and remain vested with all the Powers and Authority to be held by any future Legislative Council and Assembly of this Colony, until the second Tuesday in October, which will be in the Year of our Lord, one thousand seven hundred, and seventy seven.

3d. That on the said second Tuesday in October yearly and every Year forever, (with the Privilege of adjourning from Day to Day as Occasion may require) the Counties shall severally choose one Person to be a Member of the Legislative Council of this Colony, who shall be and have been for one whole Year next before the Election an Inhabitant and Freeholder in the County in which he is chosen, and worth at least one thousand Pounds Proclamation Money of real and personal Estate within the same County: that, at the same Time, each County shall also choose three Members of Assembly; provided, that no Person shall be entitled to a Seat in the said Assembly, unless he be and have been for one whole Year next before the Election, an Inhabitant of the County he is to represent, and worth five hundred Pounds Proclamation Money in real and personal Estate in the same County: that, on the second Tuesday next after the Day of Election, the Council and Assembly shall separately meet; and that the Consent of both Houses shall be necessary to every Law, provided, that seven shall be a Quorum of the Council for doing Business; and that no Law shall pass, unless there be a Majority of all the Representatives of each Body personally present and agreeing thereto. Provided always, That if a Majority of the Representatives of this Province in Council and General Assembly convened, shall, at any Time or Times hereafter, judge it equitable and proper to add to or diminish the Number or Proportion of the Members of the Assembly for any County or Counties in this Colony, then and in such Case the same may, on the Principles of more equal Representation, be lawfully done, any Thing in this Charter to the Contrary notwithstanding; so that the whole Number of Representatives in Assembly shall not at any Time be less than thirty nine.

4. That all Inhabitants of this Colony of full Age, who are worth Fifty Pounds proclamation Money clear Estate in the same, and have resided within the County in which they claim a Vote for twelve Months immediately preceding the Election, shall be entitled to vote for Representatives in Council and Assembly; and also for all other publick Officers that shall be elected by the People of the County at Large.

5thly. That the Assembly, when met, shall have Power to choose a Speaker, and other their Officers; to be Judges of the Qualifications and Elections of their own Members; sit upon their own Adjournments, prepare Bills to be passed into Laws, and to empower their Speaker to convene them, whenever any extraordinary Occurrence shall render it necessary.

6thly. That the Council shall also have Power to prepare Bills to pass into Laws, and have other like Powers as the Assembly, and in all Respects be a free and independant Branch of the Legislature of this Colony; save only that they shall not prepare or alter any Money-Bill, which shall be the Privilege of the Assembly; that the Council shall from Time to Time be convened by the Governor or Vice-President, but must be convened at all Times when the Assembly sits; for which Purpose the Speaker of the House of Assembly shall always immediately after an Adjournment give Notice to the Governor or Vice-President of the Time and Place to which the House is adjourned.

7. That the Council and Assembly jointly at their first Meeting, after each annual Election, shall, by a Majority of Votes, elect some fit Person within the Colony to be a Governor for one Year, who shall be constant President of the Council, and have a casting Vote in their Proceedings; and that the Council themselves shall choose a Vice-President, who shall act as such in the Absence of the Governor.

8. That the Governor, or, in his absence, the Vice-President of the Council shall have the Supreme executive Power, be Chancellor of the Colony, and act as Captain-General, and Commander in Chief of all the Militia, and other military Force in this Colony; and that any three or more of the Council shall at all Times be a Privy Council to advise the Governor in all Cases, where he may find it necessary to consult them; and that the Governor be Ordinary or Surrogate-General.

9. That the Governor and Council (seven whereof shall be a Quorum) be the Court of Appeals in the last Resort in all Causes of Law as heretofore; and that they possess the Power of granting Pardons to Criminals after Condemnation in all Cases of Treason, Felony, or other Offences.

10. That Captains, and all other inferior Officers of the Militia shall be chosen by the Companies in the respective Counties; but Field and General Officers by the Council and Assembly.

11. That the Council and Assembly shall have Power to make the Great Seal of this Colony, which shall be kept by the Governor, or, in his Absence, by the Vice-President of the Council, to be used by them as Occasion may require; and it shall be called the Great Seal of the Colony of New Jersey.

12. That the Judges of the Supreme Court shall continue in Office for seven Years, the Judges of the Inferior Court of Common Pleas in the several Counties, Justices of the Peace, Clerks of the Supreme Court, Clerks of the Inferior Courts of Common Pleas, and Quarter-Sessions, the Attorney-General, and Provincial Secretary shall continue in Office for five Years, and the Provincial

Treasurer shall continue in Office for one Year; and that they shall be severally appointed by the Council and Assembly in Manner aforesaid, and commissioned by the Governor or, in his Absence, by the Vice-President of the Council: provided always, That the said Officers severally shall be capable of being re-appointed at the End of the Terms severally before limited; and that any of the said Officers shall be liable to be dismissed, when adjudged guilty of Misbehaviour by the Council on an Impeachment of the Assembly.

13. That the Inhabitants of each County qualified to vote as aforesaid shall, at the Time and Place of electing their Representatives, annually elect one Sheriff, and one or more Coroners; and that they may re-elect the same Person to such Offices, until he shall have served three Years, but no longer; after which three Years shall elapse, before the same Person is capable of being elected again. When the Election is certified to the Governor or Vice-President, under the Hands of six Freeholders of the County, for which they were elected, they shall be immediately commissioned to serve in their respective Offices.

14. That the Townships, at their annual Town-Meetings for electing other Officers, shall choose Constables for the Districts respectively; and also three or more judicious Freeholders of good Character to hear and finally determine all Appeals relative to unjust Assessments in Cases of publick Taxation; which Commissioners of Appeal shall, for that Purpose, sit at some suitable Time or Times to be by them appointed, and made known to the People by Advertisements.

15. That the Laws of this Colony shall begin in the following Stile, viz. *"Be it enacted by the Council and General Assembly of this Colony, and it is hereby enacted by the Authority of the same."* That all Commissions, granted by the Governor or Vice President, shall run thus, *"The Colony of New Jersey to A. B. &c. Greeting:"* and that all Writs shall likewise run in the Name of the Colony; and that all Indictments shall conclude in the following Manner, viz. *against the Peace of this Colony, the Government, and Dignity of the same.*

16. That all Criminals shall be admitted to the same Privileges of Witnesses and Counsel, as their Prosecutors are or shall be entitled to.

17. That the Estates of such Persons, as shall destroy their own Lives, shall not, for that Offence, be forfeited; but shall descend in the same Manner as they would have done had such Persons died in a natural way; nor shall any Article, which may occasion accidentally the Death of anyone, be henceforth deemed a Deodand, or in any wise forfeited on Account of such Misfortune.

18. That no Person shall ever within this Colony be deprived of the inestimable Privilege of worshipping Almighty God in a Manner agreeable to the Dictates of his own Conscience; nor under any Pretence whatsoever compelled to attend any Place of Worship, contrary to his own Faith and Judgment; nor shall any Person within this Colony ever be obliged to pay Tithes, Taxes, or any other Rates, for the Purpose of building, or repairing any Church or Churches, Place or Places of Worship, or for the Maintenance of any Minister or Ministry, contrary to what he believes to be right, or has deliberately or voluntarily engaged himself to perform.

19. That there shall be no Establishment of any one religious Sect in this Province in Preference to another; and that no *Protestant Inhabitant* of this Colony shall be denied the Enjoyment of any civil Right merely on Account of his religious Principles; but that all Persons, professing a Belief in the Faith of any Protestant Sect, who shall demean themselves peaceably under the Government as hereby established, shall be capable of being elected into any Office of Profit, or Trust, or being a Member of either Branch of the Legislature, and shall fully and freely enjoy every Privilege and Immunity enjoyed by others their Fellow-subjects.

20. That the legislative Department of this Colony may, as much as possible, be preserved from all Suspicion of Corruption, none of the Judges of the Supreme or other Courts, Sheriffs, or any other Person or Persons possessed of any Post of Profit under the Government, other than Justices of the Peace, shall be entitled to a

Seat in Assembly; but that, on his being elected and taking his Seat, his Office or Post shall be considered as vacant.

21. That all the Laws of this Province, contained in the Edition lately published by Mr. Allinson, shall be and remain in full Force, until altered by the Legislature of this Colony, (such only excepted as are incompatible with this Charter) and shall be, according as heretofore, regarded in all Respects by all civil Officers, and others, the good People of this Province.

22. That the Common Law of England, as well as so much of the Statute-Law, as have been heretofore practised in this Colony, shall still remain in Force, until they shall be altered by a future Law of the Legislature, such Parts only excepted as are repugnant to the Rights and Privileges contained in this Charter; and that the inestimable Right of Trial by Jury shall remain confirmed, as a Part of the Law of this Colony without Repeal for ever.

23. That every Person, who shall be elected as aforesaid to be a Member of the Legislative Council or House of Assembly, shall, previous to his taking his Seat in Council or Assembly, take the following Oath or Affirmation, viz't. I, A. B. do solemnly declare, that, as a Member of the Legislative Council, (or Assembly, as the Case may be,) of the Colony of New Jersey, I will not assent to any Law, Vote, or Proceeding, which shall appear to me injurious to the publick Welfare of said Colony, nor that shall annul or repeal that Part of the third Section in the Charter of this Colony, which establishes that the Elections of Members of the Legislative Council and Assembly shall be annual, nor that Part of the twenty second Section in said Charter respecting the Trial by Jury, nor that shall annul, repeal, or alter any Part or Parts of the eighteenth or nineteenth Sections of the same. And any Person or Persons, who shall be elected as aforesaid, is hereby empowered to administer to the said Members the said Oath or Affirmation.

Provided always, and it is the true Intent and Meaning of this Congress, that if a Reconciliation between Great

Britain and these Colonies should take Place, and the latter be again taken under the Protection and Government of the Crown of Great Britain, this Charter shall be null and void, otherwise to remain firm and inviolable.

In Provincial Congress, New
Jersey, Burlington, July 2d., 1776.

By Order of Congress
SAML. TUCKER President

Extract from the Minutes
  WM. PATERSON, Secry.

VIII

THE CONSTITUTION OF THE STATE OF NEW JERSEY JUNE 29, 1844 (AS AMENDED)

[Text from the engrossed and signed original manuscript formerly in the office of the Secretary of State and now in the New Jersey Bureau of Archives and History. The texts of the various amendments of 1875, 1897, 1929, and 1939, as indicated in the footnotes, are taken from the official texts of statutes in the office of the Secretary of State.]

Constitution of the State of New Jersey
A Constitution agreed upon by the delegates of the people of New Jersey, in Convention, begun at Trenton on the fourteenth day of May, and continued to the twenty-ninth day of June in the year of our Lord one thousand eight hundred and forty four.

We, the people of the State of New Jersey, grateful to Almighty God for the civil and religious liberty which He hath so long permitted us to enjoy, and looking to Him for a blessing upon our endeavours to secure and transmit the same unimpaired to succeeding generations, do ordain and establish this constitution

Article I. *Rights and Privileges.*

1. All men are by nature free and independent, and have certain natural and unalienable rights, among which are those of enjoying and defending life and liberty, acquiring, possessing, and protecting property, and of pursuing and obtaining safety and happiness.

2. All political power is inherent in the people. Government is instituted for the protection, security, and benefit of the people, and they have the right at all times to alter or reform the same, whenever the public good may require it.

3. No person shall be deprived of the inestimable privilege of worshipping Almighty God in a manner agree-

able to the dictates of his own conscience; nor under any pretence whatever be compelled to attend any place of worship contrary to his faith and judgment; nor shall any person be obliged to pay tithes, taxes, or other rates for building or repairing any church or churches, place or places of worship, or for the maintenance of any minister or ministry, contrary to what he believes to be right, or has deliberately or voluntarily engaged to perform.

4. There shall be no establishment of one religious sect in preference to another; no religious test shall be required as a qualification for any office or public trust; and no person shall be denied the enjoyment of any civil right merely on account of his religious principles.

5. Every person may freely speak, write, and publish his sentiments on all subjects, being responsible for the abuse of that right. No law shall be passed to restrain or abridge the liberty of speech or of the press. In all prosecutions or indictments for libel, the truth may be given in evidence to the jury; and if it shall appear to the jury that the matter charged as libellous is true, and was published with good motives and for justifiable ends, the party shall be acquitted; and the jury shall have the right to determine the law and the fact.

6. The right of the people to be secure in their persons, houses, papers, and effects, against unreasonable searches and seizures, shall not be violated; and no warrant shall issue but upon probable cause, supported by oath or affirmation, and particularly describing the place to be searched and the papers and things to be seized.

7. The right of trial by jury shall remain inviolate: but the Legislature may authorize the trial of civil suits, when the matter in dispute does not exceed fifty dollars, by a jury of six men.

8. In all criminal prosecutions the accused shall have the right to a speedy and public trial by an impartial jury; to be informed of the nature and cause of the accusation; to be confronted with the witnesses against him; to have compulsory process for obtaining witnesses in his

favour, and to have the assistance of Counsel in his defense.

9. No person shall be held to answer for a Criminal offence, unless on the presentment or indictment of a grand jury, except in cases of impeachment, or in cases cognizable by Justices of the peace, or arising in the army or navy: or in the militia, when in actual service in time of war or public danger.

10. No person shall after acquittal, be tried for the same offence. All persons shall, before conviction, be bailable by sufficient sureties, except for capital offences, when the proof is evident or presumption great.

11. The privilege of the writ of Habeas Corpus shall not be suspended, unless in case of rebellion or invasion the public safety may require it.

12. The military shall be in strict subordination to the Civil power.

13. No soldier shall, in time of peace, be quartered in any house without the consent of the owner; nor in time of war except in a manner prescribed by law.

14. Treason against the State shall consist only in levying war against it, or in adhering to its enemies, giving them aid and comfort. No person shall be convicted of treason, unless on the testimony of two witnesses to the same overt act, or on confession in open court.

15. Excessive bail shall not be required, excessive fines shall not be imposed, and cruel and unusual punishments shall not be inflicted.

16. Private property shall not be taken for public use without just compensation; but land may be taken for public highways as heretofore until the legislature shall direct compensation to be made.

17. No person shall be imprisoned for debt in any action, or on any judgment founded upon contract, unless in cases of fraud: nor shall any person be imprisoned for a militia fine in time of peace.

18. The people have the right freely to assemble together, to consult for the common good, to make known

their opinions to their representatives, and to petition for redress of grievances.*

19. This enumeration of rights and privileges shall not be construed to impair or deny others retained by the people.

Article II. *Right of Suffrage.*

1. Every white male citizen of the United States, of the age of twenty-one years, who shall have been a resident of this State one year, and of the County in which he claims his vote five months, next before the election, shall be entitled to vote for all officers that now are, or hereafter may be elective by the people; *provided,* that no person in the military, naval, or marine service of the United States shall be considered a resident in this state, by being stationed in any garrison, barrack, or military or naval place or station within this State, and no pauper idiot, insane person, or person convicted of a crime which now excludes him from being a witness unless pardoned or restored by law to the right of suffrage, shall enjoy the right of an elector.*

* The following two paragraphs were inserted at this point and the number of paragraph 19 changed to 21 by an amendment effective September 28, 1875: "19. No county, city, borough, town, township or village shall hereafter give any money or property, or loan its money or credit, to or in aid of any individual association or corporation, or become security for, or be directly or indirectly the owner of any stock or bonds of any association or corporation."

"20. No donation of land of appropriation of money shall be made by the state or any municipal corporation to or for the use of any society, association or corporation whatever."

* This paragraph amended effective September 28, 1875 by the deletion of the word "white" in the first line and by the addition of the following: *"And provided further,* that in time of war no elector in the actual military service of the State, or of the United States, in the army or navy thereof, shall be deprived of his vote by reason of his absence from such election district; and the legislature shall have power to provide the manner in which, and the time and place at which, such absent electors may vote, and for the return and canvass of their votes in the election districts in which they respectively reside."

2. The legislature may pass laws to deprive persons of the right of suffrage who shall be convicted of bribery at elections.*

Article III. *Distribution of the powers of Government.*

1. The powers of the government shall be divided into three distinct departments—the Legislative, Executive, and Judicial: and no person or persons belonging to, or constitutioning one of these departments, shall exercise any of the powers properly belonging to either of the others, except as herein expressly provided.

Article IV. *Legislative.*
Section I.

1. The legislative power shall be vested in a Senate and General Assembly.
2. No person shall be a member of the Senate who shall not have attained the age of thirty years, and have been a citizen and inhabitant of the state for four years, and of the county for which he shall be chosen one year, next before his election; and no person shall be a member of the General Assembly who shall not have attained the age of twenty-one years, and have been a citizen and inhabitant of the state for two years, and of the county for which he shall be chosen one year next before his election; provided that no person shall be eligible as a member of either house of the legislature, who shall not be entitled to the right of Suffrage.
3. Members of the Senate and General Assembly shall be elected yearly and every year, on the second Tuesday of October; ** and the two houses shall meet separately on the second Tuesday in January next after the said day

* This paragraph amended effective September 28, 1875 by deletion of the two final words "at elections."
** By amendment effective September 28, 1875 this paragraph was altered to read: ". . . on the first Tuesday after the first Monday in November,"

of election, at which time of meeting, the legislative year shall commence; but the time of holding such election may be altered by the legislature.

Section II.

1. The Senate shall be composed of one Senator from each County in the State, elected by the legal voters of the Counties, respectively, for three years.

2. As soon as the Senate shall meet after the first election to be held in pursuance of this Constitution, they shall be divided as equally as may be into three classes. The seats of the Senators of the first class shall be vacated at the expiration of the first year; Of the second class at the expiration of the second year; And of the third class at the expiration of the third year, so that one class may be elected every year: And if vacancies happen, by resignation or otherwise, the persons elected to supply such vacancies shall be elected for the unexpired terms only.

Section III.

1. The General Assembly shall be composed of members annually elected by the legal voters of the Counties, respectively, who shall be apportioned among the said Counties as nearly as may be according to the number of their inhabitants. The present apportionment shall continue until the next census of the United States shall have been taken, and an apportionment of members of the General Assembly shall be made by the legislature at its first session after the next and every subsequent enumeration or census, and when made shall remain unaltered until another enumeration shall have been taken; *provided,* that each County shall at all times be entitled to one member: And the whole number of members shall never exceed sixty.

Section IV.

1. Each house shall direct writs of election for supplying vacancies, occasioned by death, resignation, or otherwise; but if vacancies occur during the recess of the legislature, the writs may be issued by the Governor, under such regulations as may be prescribed by law.

2. Each house shall be the judge of the elections, returns, and qualifications of its own members, and a majority of each shall constitute a quorum to do business: but a smaller number may adjourn from day to day, and may be authorized to compel the attendance of absent members, in such manner, and under such penalties, as each house may provide.

3. Each house shall choose its own officers, determine the rules of its proceedings, punish its members for disorderly behaviour, and, with the concurrence of two-thirds, may expel a member.

4. Each house shall keep a journal of its proceedings, and from time to time publish the same; and the yeas and nays of the members of either house on any question shall, at the desire of one-fifth of those present, be entered on the journal.

5. Neither house, during the session of the legislature, shall, without the consent of the other, adjourn for more than three days, nor to any place than that in which the two houses shall be sitting.

6. All bills and joint resolutions shall be read three times in each house, before the final passage thereof; and no bill or joint resolution shall pass, unless there be a majority of all the members of each body personally present and agreeing thereto; and the yeas and nays of the members voting on such final passage shall be entered on the journal.

7. Members of the Senate and General Assembly shall receive a compensation for their services, to be ascertained by law, and paid out of the treasury of the State; which compensation shall not exceed the sum of three dollars per day for the period of forty days from the commencement of the session; and shall not exceed the

sum of one dollar and fifty cents per day for the remainder of the session. When convened in extra session by the Governor, they shall receive such sum as shall be fixed for the first forty days of the ordinary session. They shall also receive the sum of one dollar for every ten miles they shall travel, in going to and returning from their place of meeting, on the most usual route. The President of the Senate and the Speaker of the house of Assembly shall, in virtue of their offices, receive an additional compensation, equal to one-third of their per diem allowance as members.*

8. Members of the Senate and General Assembly shall, in all cases except treason, felony, and breach of the peace, be privileged from arrest during their attendance at the sitting of their respective houses, and in going to and returning from the same: and for any speech or debate, in either house, they shall not be questioned in any other place.

Section V.

1. No member of the Senate or General Assembly shall, during the time for which he was elected, be nominated or appointed by the Governor or by the legislature in joint meeting, to any civil office under the authority of this State, which shall have been created, or the emoluments whereof shall have been increased, during such time.

2. If any member of the Senate or General Assembly shall be elected to represent this State in the Senate or House of Representatives of the United States, and shall accept thereof, or shall accept of any office or ap-

---

* This paragraph was amended effective September 28, 1875 to read: "7. Members of the Senate and General Assembly shall receive annually the sum of five hundred dollars during the time for which they shall have been elected, and while they shall hold their office, and no other allowance or emolument, directly or indirectly, for any purpose whatever. The President of the Senate and the Speaker of the House of Assembly shall, in virtue of their offices, receive an additional compensation, equal to one third their allowance as members."

pointment under the Government of the United States, his seat in the legislature of this State shall thereby be vacated.

3. No Justice of the Supreme Court, nor Judge of any other Court, Sheriff, Justice of the Peace, nor any person or persons possessed of any office of profit under the government of this State shall be entitled to a seat either in the Senate or in the General Assembly; but on being elected and taking his seat, his office shall be considered vacant; And no person holding any office of profit under the Government of the United States shall be entitled to a seat in either house.

Section VI.

1. All bills for raising revenue shall originate in the House of Assembly; but the Senate may propose or concur with amendments, as on other bills.
2. No money shall be drawn from the treasury but for appropriations made by law.
3. The credit of the State shall not be directly or indirectly loaned in any case.
4. The legislature shall not, in any manner, create any debt or debts, liability or liabilities, of the State, which shall singly or in the aggregate with any previous debts or liabilities at any time exceed One hundred thousand dollars, except for purposes of war, or to repel invasion, or to suppress insurrection, unless the same shall be authorized by a law for some single object or work, to be distinctly specified therein; which law shall provide the ways and means, exclusive of loans, to pay the interest of such debt or liability as it falls due, and also to pay and discharge the principal of such debt or liability within thirty-five years from the time of the contracting thereof, and shall be irrepealable until such debt or liability, and the interest thereon, are fully paid and discharged: And no such law shall take effect until it shall, at a general election, have been submitted to the people, and have received the sanction of a majority of all the votes cast for and against it at such election: And all

money to be raised by the authority of such law shall be applied only to the specific object stated therein, and to the payment of the debt thereby created. This section shall not be construed to refer to any money that has been, or may be, deposited with this State by the Government of the United States.*

Section VII.

1. No divorce shall be granted by the legislature.
2. No lottery shall be authorized by this State; And no ticket in any lottery not authorized by a law of this State shall be bought or sold within the State.**

* The following paragraph was added by amendment effective October 18, 1927: "5. The Legislature may enact general laws under which municipalities, other than counties, may adopt zoning ordinances limiting and restricting to specified districts and regulating therein, buildings and structures, according to their construction, and the nature and extent of their use, and the exercise of such authority shall be deemed to be within the police power of the State. Such laws shall be subject to repeal or alteration by the Legislature."

** This paragraph was amended effective October 19, 1897 to read as follows: "2. No lottery shall be authorized by the legislature or otherwise in this State, and no ticket in any lottery shall be bought or sold within this State, nor shall pool-selling, book-making or gambling of any kind be authorized or allowed within this State, nor shall any gambling device, practice or game of chance now prohibited by law be legalized, or the remedy, penalty or punishment now provided therefor be in any way diminished."

By amendment effective July 11, 1939 this paragraph was again amended to read: "2. It shall be lawful to hold, carry on, and operate in this State race meetings whereat the trotting, running or steeple-chase racing of horses only may be conducted between the hours of sunrise and sunset on week days only and in duly legalized race tracks, at which the pari-mutuel system of betting shall be permitted. No lottery, roulette, or game of chance of any form shall be authorized by the Legislature in this State, and no ticket in any lottery shall be bought or sold within this State, or offered for sale; nor shall pool-selling, book-making, or gambling of any kind be authorized or allowed within this State, except pari-mutuel betting on the results of the racing of horses only, from which the State shall derive a reasonable revenue for the support of government; nor shall any gambling device, practice, or game of chance, or pari-mutuel betting thereon now prohibited

3. The legislature shall not pass any bill of attainder, ex post facto law, or law impairing the obligation of contracts, or depriving a party of any remedy for enforcing a contract which existed when the contract was made.

4. To avoid improper influences which may result from intermixing in one and the same act such things as have no proper relation to each other, every law shall embrace but one object, and that shall be expressed in the title.*

5. The laws of this State shall begin in the following style, "Be it enacted by the Senate and General Assembly of the State of New Jersey."

6. The fund for the support of free schools, and all money, Stock, and other property, which may hereafter be appropriated for that purpose, or received into the treasury under the provision of any law heretofore passed to augment the said fund, shall be securely invested, and remain a perpetual fund; and the income thereof, except so much as it may be judged expedient to apply to an increase of the capital, shall be annually appropriated to the support of public schools, for the equal benefit of all the people of the State; And it shall not be competent for the legislature to borrow, appropriate, or use the said fund or any part thereof, for any other purpose, under any pretence whatever.**

---

by law, except as herein stated or otherwise provided, be legalized, or the remedy, penalty, or punishment now provided therefor be in any way diminished."

*This paragraph amended effective September 28, 1875 by the addition of the following: "No law shall be revived or amended by reference to its title only, but the act revived, or the section or sections amended, shall be inserted at length. No general law shall embrace any provision of a private, special or local character. No act shall be passed which shall provide that any existing law, or any part thereof, shall be made or deemed a part of the act or which shall enact that any existing law, or any part thereof, shall be applicable, except by inserting it in such act."

**This paragraph amended effective September 28, 1875 by the insertion of the word "free" between "public" and "schools" and by the addition of the following: "The legislature shall provide for the maintenance and support of a thorough and efficient system of free public schools for the instruction of all the children in this State between the ages of five and eighteen years."

7. No private or special law shall be passed authorizing the sale of any lands belonging in whole or in part to a minor or minors or other persons who may at the time be under any legal disability to act for themselves.

8. The assent of three-fifths of the members elected to each house shall be requisite to the passage of any law for granting, continuing, altering, amending, or renewing charters for banks or money corporations; and all such charters shall be limited to a term not exceeding twenty years.*

9. Individuals or private corporations shall not be authorized to take private property for public use, without just compensation first made to the owners.**

10. The legislature may vest in the Circuit Courts, or Courts of Common Pleas within the several Counties of this State Chancery powers, so far as relates to the foreclosure of mortgages, and sale of mortgaged premises.***

* This paragraph deleted by amendment effective September 28, 1875.

** The number of this paragraph was altered by amendment to paragraph 8 and the following additional paragraph was inserted by amendment effective September 28, 1875: "9. No private, special, or local bill shall be passed, unless public notice of the intention to apply therefor, and of the general object thereof, shall have been previously given. The legislature, at the next session after the adoption thereof, and from time to time thereafter, shall prescribe the time and mode of giving such notice, the evidence thereof, and how such evidence shall be preserved."

*** The two following paragraphs were added to Article IV, Section VII by amendment effective September 28, 1875: "11. The legislature shall not pass private, local or special laws in any of the following enumerated cases, that is to say:

Laying out, opening, altering and working roads or highways.

Vacating any road, town plot, street, alley or public grounds.

Regulating the internal affairs of towns and counties; appointing local offices or commissions to regulate municipal affairs.

Selecting, drawing, summoning or empanelling grand or petit jurors.

Creating, increasing or decreasing the percentage or allowance of public officers during the term for which said officers were elected or appointed.

Changing the law of descent.

Granting to any corporation, association or individual any exclusive privilege, immunity or franchise whatever.

Section VIII.

1. Members of the legislature, shall, before they enter on the duties of their respective offices, take and subscribe the following oath or affirmation: "I do solemnly swear, (or affirm, as the case may be,) that I will support the Constitution of the United States and the Constitution of the State of New Jersey, and that I will faithfully discharge the duties of Senator (or member of the General Assembly, as the case may be) according to the best of my ability." And members elect of the Senate or General Assembly are hereby empowered to administer to each other the said oath or affirmation.*

Article V. *Executive.*

1. The Executive power shall be vested in a Governor.
2. The Governor shall be elected by the legal voters

Granting to any corporation, association or individual the right to lay down railroad tracks.

Providing for changes of venue in civil or criminal cases.

Providing for the management and support of free public schools.

The legislature shall pass general laws providing for the cases enumerated in this paragraph, and for all other cases which, in its judgment, may be provided for by general laws. The legislature shall pass no special act conferring corporate powers, but they shall pass general laws under which corporations may be organized and corporate powers of every nature obtained, subject, nevertheless, to repeal or alteration at the will of the legislature."

"12. Property shall be assessed for taxes under general laws, and by uniform rules, according to its true value."

* This section was amended effective September 28, 1875 by the addition of the following paragraph: "2. Every officer of the Legislature shall, before he enters upon his duties, take and subscribe the following oath or affirmation: "I do solemnly promise and swear (or affirm) that I will faithfully, impartially and justly perform all the duties of the office of . . . . to the best of my ability and understanding; that I will carefully preserve all records, papers, writings, or property entrusted to me for safekeeping by virtue of my office, and make such disposition of the same as may be required by law."

of this state. The person having the highest number of votes shall be the Governor: but if two or more shall be equal and highest in votes, one of them shall be chosen Governor by the vote of a majority of the members of both houses in joint meeting. Contested elections for the office of Governor shall be determined in such manner as the legislature shall direct by law. When a Governor is to be elected by the people, such election shall be held at the time when and at the places where the people shall respectively vote for members of the legislature.

3. The Governor shall hold his office for three years, to commence on the third Tuesday of January next ensuing the election for Governor by the people, and to end on the Monday preceding the third Tuesday of January, three years thereafter: and he shall be incapable of holding that office for three years next after his term of service shall have expired: And no appointment or nomination to office shall be made by the Governor during the last week of his said term.

4. The Governor shall not be less than thirty years of age, and shall have been for twenty years, at least, a citizen of the United States, and a resident of this State seven years next before his election, unless he shall have been absent during that time on the public business of the United States or of this state.

5. The Governor shall, at stated times, receive for his services a compensation which shall be neither increased nor diminished during the period for which he shall have been elected.

6. He shall be the Commander in Chief of all the military and naval forces of the State; he shall have power to convene the Legislature * whenever in his opinion public necessity requires it; he shall communicate by message to the legislature at the opening of each session, and at such other times as he may deem necessary, the condition of the State, and recommend such measures as he may deem expedient; he shall take care that the laws

* This paragraph amended at this point effective September 28, 1875 by the addition of the following words: ". . . or the Senate alone. . . ."

be faithfully executed, and grant, under the great seal of the State, commissions to all such officers as shall be required to be commissioned.

7. Every bill which shall have passed both houses shall be presented to the Governor: if he approve he shall sign it, but if not he shall return it, with his objections, to the house in which it shall have originated, who shall enter the objections at large on their journal, and proceed to reconsider it; if, after such reconsideration a majority of the whole number of that house shall agree to pass the bill, it shall be sent, together with the objections, to the other house, by which it shall likewise be reconsidered, and if approved by a majority of the whole number of that house, it shall become a law; but, in neither house shall the vote be taken on the same day on which the bill shall be returned to it: and in all such cases, the votes of both houses shall be determined, by yeas and nays, and the names of the persons voting for and against the bill shall be entered on the journal of each house respectively. If any bills shall not be returned by the Governor, within five days (Sunday excepted) after it shall have been presented to him, the same shall be a law in like manner as if he had signed it, unless the legislature, by their adjournment, prevent its return in which case it shall not be a law.*

8. No member of Congress, or person holding an office

---

* This paragraph amended effective September 28, 1875 by the addition of the following: "If any bill presented to the governor contains several items of appropriations of money, he may object to one or more of such items while approving of the other portions of the bill. In such case he shall append to the bill, at the time of signing it, a statement of the items to which he objects, and the appropriations so objected to shall not take effect. If the legislature be in session he shall transmit to the house in which the bill originated a copy of such statement, and the items objected to shall be separately reconsidered. If, on reconsideration, one or more of such items be approved by a majority of the members elected to each house, the same shall be a part of the law, notwithstanding the objections of the governor. All the provisions of this section in relation to bills not approved by the governor shall apply to cases in which he shall withhold his approval from any item or items contained in a bill appropriating money."

under the United States, or this State, shall exercise the office of Governor; and in case the Governor, or person administering the Government, shall accept any office under the United States, or this State, his office of Governor shall thereupon be vacant.*

9. The Governor, or person administering the government, shall have power to suspend the collection of fines and forfeitures, and to grant reprieves, to extend until the expiration of a time not exceeding ninety days after conviction; but this power shall not extend to cases of impeachment.

10. The Governor, or person administering the Government, the Chancellor, and the six Judges of the Court of Errors and Appeals, or a major part of them, of whom the Governor, or person administering the government, shall be one, may remit fines and forfeitures, and grant pardons, after conviction, in all cases except impeachment.

11. The Governor and all other civil officers under this State shall be liable to impeachment for misdemeanor in office during their continuance in office and for two years thereafter.

12. In case of the death, resignation, or removal from office of the Governor, the powers, duties, and emoluments of the office shall devolve upon the President of the Senate, and in case of his death, resignation or removal, then upon the Speaker of the House of Assembly, for the time being until another Governor shall be elected and qualified; but in such case another Governor shall be chosen at the next election for members of the Legislature, unless such death, resignation or removal shall occur within thirty days immediately preceding such next election, in which case a Governor shall be chosen at the second succeeding election for members of the legislature. When a vacancy happens, during the

* This paragraph amended effective September 28, 1875 by the addition of the following: "Nor shall he be elected by the legislature to any office under the government of this State or of the United States, during the term for which he shall have been elected governor."

recess of the legislature in any office which is to be filled by the Governor and Senate, or by the Legislature in joint meeting, the Governor shall fill such vacancy and the commission shall expire at the end of the next session of the Legislature, unless a successor shall be sooner appointed: When a vacancy happens in the office of Clerk or Surrogate of any County, the Governor shall fill such vacancy, and the Commission shall expire when a successor is elected and qualified.*

13. In case of the impeachment of the Governor, his absence from the State or inability to discharge the duties of his office, the powers, duties and immoluments of the office shall devolve upon the President of the Senate; and in case of his death, resignation or removal, then upon the Speaker of the house of Assembly for the time being, until the Governor absent, or impeached shall return or be acquitted, or until the disqualification or inability shall cease, or until a new Governor be elected and qualified.

14. In case of a vacancy in the office of Governor from any other cause than those herein enumerated, or in case of the death of the Governor elect before he is qualified into office, the powers, duties and emoluments of the office shall devolve upon the President of the Senate, or Speaker of the House of Assembly, as above provided for, until a new Governor be elected and qualified.

Article VI. *Judiciary.*

Section I.

1. The Judicial power shall be vested in a Court of Errors and Appeals in the last resort in all causes as

* This paragraph amended effective October 19, 1897 by the addition of the following: "No person who shall have been nominated to the Senate by the Governor for any office of trust or profit under the government of this State, and shall not have been confirmed before the recess of the legislature, shall be eligible for appointment to such office during the continuance of such recess."

heretofore; a Court for the trial of impeachments; a Court of Chancery; a Prerogative Court; a Supreme Court; Circuit Courts, and such inferior Courts as now exist, and as may be hereafter ordained and established by law; which Inferior Courts the Legislature may alter or abolish, as the public good shall require.

Section II.

1. The Court of Errors and Appeals shall consist of the Chancellor, the Justices of the Supreme Court, and six Judges, or a major part of them; which Judges are to be appointed for six years.

2. Immediately after the Court shall first assemble, the six Judges shall arrange themselves in such manner that the seat of one of them shall be vacated every year in order that thereafter one Judge may be annually appointed.

3. Such of the six Judges as shall attend the Court shall receive, respectively, a per diem compensation, to be provided by law.

4. The Secretary of State shall be the Clerk of this Court.

5. When an appeal from an Order or decree shall be heard the Chancellor shall inform the Court, in writing, of the reasons for his order or decree; but he shall not sit as a member, or have a voice in the hearing or final sentence.

6. When a writ of Error shall be brought, no Justice who has given a Judicial opinion in the cause in favor of or against any Error complained of, shall sit as a member, or have a voice on the hearing, or for its affirmance or reversal; but the reasons for such opinion shall be assigned to the Court in writing.

Section III.

1. The House of Assembly shall have the sole power of impeaching by a vote of a majority of all the members;

and all impeachments shall be tried by the Senate: The members, when sitting for that purpose, to be on oath or affirmation "truly and impartially to try and determine the charge in question according to evidence:" And no person shall be convicted without the concurrence of two-thirds of all the members of the Senate.

2. Any Judicial officer impeached shall be suspended from exercising his office until his acquittal.

3. Judgment in cases of impeachment shall not extend farther than to removal from office, and to disqualification to hold and enjoy any office of honor, profit or trust under this State: but the party convicted shall nevertheless be liable to indictment, trial and punishment according to law.

4. The Secretary of State shall be the Clerk of this Court.

Section IV.

1. The Court of Chancery shall consist of a Chancellor.

2. The Chancellor shall be the Ordinary or Surrogate General, and Judge of the Prerogative Court.

3. All persons aggrieved by any order, sentence, or decree of the Orphans Court, may appeal from the same, or from any part thereof to the Prerogative Court; but such order, sentence, or decree shall not be removed into the Supreme Court, or Circuit Court if the subject matter thereof be held within the jurisdiction of the Orphans Court.

4. The Secretary of State shall be the register of the Prerogative Court, and shall perform the duties required of him by law in that respect.

Section V.

1. The Supreme Court shall consist of a Chief Justice and four associate Justices. The number of Associate Justices may be increased or decreased by law, but shall never be less than two.

2. The Circuit Courts shall be held in every County of this State, by one or more of the Justices of the Supreme Court, or a Judge appointed for that purpose; and shall in all cases within the County, except in those of a Criminal nature, have common law jurisdiction, concurrent with the Supreme Court; and any final judgment of a Circuit Court may be docketed in the Supreme Court and shall operate as a Judgment obtained in the Supreme Court from the time of such docketing.

3. Final judgments in any Circuit Court may be brought by writ of Error into the Supreme Court, or directly into the Court of Errors and Appeals.

Section VI.

1. There shall be no more than five Judges of the Inferior Court of Common Pleas in each of the Counties in this State after the terms of the Judges of said Court now in office shall terminate. One Judge for each County shall be appointed every year, and no more, except to fill vacancies which shall be for the unexpired term only.

2. The Commissions for the first appointments of Judges of said Court shall bear date and take effect on the first day of April next; and all subsequent commissions for Judges of said Court shall bear date and take effect on the first day of April in every successive year, except commissions to fill vacancies which shall bear date and take effect when issued.

Section VII.

1. There may be elected under this Constitution, two, and not more than five, Justices of the Peace in each of the townships of the several Counties of this State, and in each of the Wards, in Cities that may vote in Wards. When a township or ward contains two thousand inhabitants or less, it may have two Justices: when it contains more than two thousand inhabitants, and not more than four thousand, it may have four Justices: and when it

contains more than four thousand inhabitants, it may have five Justices: *provided,* that whenever any township not voting in wards contains more than seven thousand inhabitants, such Township may have an additional Justice for each additional three thousand inhabitants above four thousand.

2. The population of the Townships in the several Counties of the State and of the several wards shall be ascertained by the last preceeding census of the United States, until the Legislature shall provide, by law, some other mode of ascertaining it.

Article VII.
Appointing power and tenure of Office

Section I.
Militia Officers

1. The Legislature shall provide by law for enrolling, organizing and arming the Militia.

2. Captains, Subalterns, and non-commissioned officers, shall be elected by the members of their respective Companies.

3. Field officers of regiments, independent battalions, and squadrons, shall be elected by the commissioned officers of their respective regiments, battalions or squadrons.

4. Brigadier Generals shall be elected by the Field officers of their respective brigades.

5. Major Generals * shall be nominated by the Governor and appointed by him, with the advice and consent of the Senate.

6. The Legislature shall provide, by law, the time and manner of electing Militia officers, and of certifying their elections to the Governor, who shall grant their Commissions, and determine their rank, when not determined by

* This paragraph amended effective September 28, 1875 by the addition of the following words at this point: ". . . the adjutant-general and quarter-master general. . . ."

law; And no Commissioned Officer shall be removed from office, but by the sentence of a Court Martial, pursuant to law.

7. In case the electors of Subalterns, Captains, or Field Officers, shall refuse or neglect to make such elections, the Governor shall have power to appoint such officers, and to fill all vacancies caused by such refusal or neglect.

8. Brigade Inspectors shall be chosen by the Field Officers, of their respective brigades.

9. The Governor shall appoint the Adjudant General, Quarter Master General, and all other Militia officers, whose appointment is not otherwise provided for in this Constitution.*

10. Major Generals, Brigadier Generals and Commanding officers of regiments, independent battalions, and Squadrons, shall appoint the Staff officers of their divisions, Brigades, regiments, independent battalions, and Squadrons respectively.

Section II.
Civil Officers

1. Justices of the Supreme Court, Chancellor, and Judges of the Court of Errors and Appeals,** shall be nominated by the Governor, and appointed by him, with the advice and consent of the Senate. The Justices of the Supreme Court and Chancellor, shall hold their offices for the term of seven years: shall at stated times receive for their services a compensation which shall not be diminished during the term of their appointments; and

---

* This paragraph amended effective September 28, 1875 to read as follows: "9. The Governor shall appoint all militia officers, whose appointment is not otherwise provided for in this Constitution."

** This paragraph amended effective September 28, 1875 to read as follows: "1. Justices of the Supreme Court, Chancellor, Judges of the Courts of Errors and Appeals, and judges of the inferior Court of Common Pleas" and so to the end of the paragraph as above.

they shall hold no other office under the Government of this State or of the United States.

2. Judges of the Courts of Common Pleas shall be appointed by the Senate and General Assembly, in joint meeting. They shall hold their offices for five years; but when appointed to fill vacancies they shall hold for the unexpired term only.

3. The State Treasurer, and the Keeper and Inspectors of the State Prison shall be appointed by the Senate and General Assembly in Joint meeting. They shall hold their offices for one year, and until their successors shall be qualified into office.*

4. The Attorney General, Prosecutors of the Pleas, Clerk of the Supreme Court, Clerk of the Court of Chancery, and Secretary of State,** shall be nominated by the Governor and appointed by him with the advice and consent of the Senate. They shall hold their offices for five years.

5. The law reporter shall be appointed by the Justices of the Supreme Court or a majority of them; and the Chancery reporter shall be appointed by the Chancellor. They shall hold their offices for five years.

6. Clerks and Surrogates of Counties shall be elected by the people of their respective Counties, at the annual elections for members of the General Assembly. They shall hold their offices for five years.

* This paragraph amended effective September 28, 1875 to read as follows: "2. The State Treasurer and Comptroller shall be appointed by the Senate and General Assembly in joint meeting. They shall hold their offices for three years, and until their successors shall be qualified into office." The amendments of 1875 altered the provision for appointing judges of the Courts of Common Pleas (see note to paragraph ** Art VII, Sect. 2, §1.) and consequently altered the numbers of subsequent paragraphs of this section but failed to provide for the deletion of the existing paragraph 2.

** This paragraph amended effective September 28, 1875 to read as follows: "3. The Attorney General, Prosecutors of the Pleas, Clerk of the Supreme Court, Clerk of the Court of Chancery, Secretary of State, and the Keeper of the State Prison" and so on to the end of the paragraph as above.

7. Sheriffs and Coroners shall be elected annually by the people of their respective Counties at the annual elections for members of the General Assembly. They may be re-elected until they shall have served three years but no longer; after which, three years must elapse, before they can be again capable of serving.*

8. Justices of the Peace shall be elected by ballot at the annual meetings of the Townships in the several Counties of the State, and of the Wards in Cities that may vote in Wards, in such manner and under such regulations as may be hereafter provided by law. They shall be Commissioned for the County, and their Commissions shall bear date and take effect on the first day of May next after their election. They shall hold their offices for five years; but when elected to fill vacancies, they shall hold for the unexpired term only; *provided,* that the commission of any Justice of the Peace shall become vacant upon his ceasing to reside in the township in which he was elected. The first election for Justices of the Peace shall take place at the next annual town-meetings of the townships in the several Counties of the State, and of the Wards in cities, that may vote in wards.

9. All other officers, whose appointments are not otherwise provided for by law, shall be nominated by the Governor and appointed by him with the advice and consent of the Senate; and shall hold their offices for the time prescribed by law.

10. All civil officers elected or appointed, pursuant to the provisions of this Constitution shall be Commissioned by the Governor.

11. The term of Office of all officers elected or appointed pursuant to the provisions of this Constitution, except when herein otherwise directed, shall commence

* This paragraph altered by amendment effective September 28, 1875 to read as follows: "6. Sheriffs and Coroners shall be elected by the people of their respective Counties at the elections for members of the General Assembly, and they shall hold their offices for three years; after which, three years must elapse, before they can be again capable of serving. Sheriffs shall annually renew their bonds."

on the day of the date of their respective commissions; but no Commission for any office shall bear date prior to the expiration of the term of the incumbent of said office.

Article VIII.
General Provisions.

1. The Secretary of State shall be ex officio an Auditor of the accounts of the Treasurer, and as such, it shall be his duty to assist the legislature in the annual examination and settlement of said accounts, until otherwise provided by law.

2. The Seal of the State shall be kept by the Governor or person administering the Government, and used by him officially, and shall be called the great Seal of the State of New Jersey.

3. All grants and Commissions shall be in the name and by the authority of the State of New Jersey, sealed with the great seal, signed by the Governor or person administering the government, and countersigned by the Secretary of State, and shall run thus: "The State of New Jersey, to —— ————, Greeting." All writs shall be in the name of the State; and all indictments shall conclude in the following manner, viz. "against the peace of this State the government and dignity of the same."

4. This Constitution shall take effect and go into operation on the second day of September in the year of our Lord, one thousand eight hundred and forty-four.

Article IX.
Amendments.

Any specific amendment or amendments, to the Constitution may be proposed in the Senate or General Assembly, and if the same shall be agreed to by a majority of the members elected to each of the two houses, such proposed amendment or amendments shall be entered on their Journals, with the yeas and nays taken thereon, and referred to the Legislature then next to be chosen, and shall be published for three months previous to making such choice, in at least one newspaper of each County, if any be published therein; and if in the Legislature next chosen, as aforesaid, such proposed amendment or amendments, or any of them, shall be agreed to by a majority of all the members elected to each House, then it shall be the duty of the Legislature to submit such proposed amendment or amendments, or such of them as may have been agreed to as aforesaid by the two legislatures, to the people, in such manner and at such time, at least four months after the adjournment of the Legislature, as the legislative shall prescribe; And if the people at a special election to be held for that purpose only, shall approve and ratify such amendment or amendments, or any of them by a majority of the electors qualified to vote for members of the legislature voting thereon, such amendment or amendments so approved and ratified shall become part of the Constitution: *provided* that if more than one amendment be submitted, they shall be submitted in such manner and form that the people may vote for, or against each amendment separately and distinctly; but no amendment or amendments shall be submitted to the people by the Legislature oftener than once in five years.

Article X.
Schedule.

That no inconvenience may arise from the change in the Constitution of this State, and in order to carry the same into complete operation, it is hereby declared and ordained, that

1. The common law and statute laws now in force not repugnant to this Constitution, shall remain in force until they expire by their own limitation, or be altered or repealed by the Legislature; and all writs, actions, causes of action, prosecutions, contracts, claims and rights of individuals and of bodies corporate, and of the State,

and all Charters of incorporation, shall continue, and all indictments, which shall have been found, or which may hereafter be found, for any crime or offence committed before the adoption of this Constitution, may be proceeded upon as if no change had taken place. The several Courts of Law and equity, except as herein otherwise provided, shall continue with the like powers and jurisdiction as if this Constitution had not been adopted.

2. All officers now filling any office or appointment, shall continue in the exercise of the duties thereof, according to their respective Commissions or appointments, unless by this Constitution it is otherwise directed.

3. The present Governor, Chancellor and Ordinary or Surrogate General, and Treasurer shall continue in office until successors elected or appointed under this Constitution shall be sworn or affirmed into office.

4. In case of the death, resignation, or disability of the present Governor, the person who may be Vice President of Council at the time of the adoption of this Constitution shall continue in office and administer the government until a Governor shall have been elected and sworn or affirmed into office under this Constitution.

5. The present Governor, or in case of his death or inability to act, the Vice President of Council, together with the present members of the Legislative Council and Secretary of State shall constitute a board of State canvassers, in the manner now provided by law, for the purpose of ascertaining and declaring the result of the next ensuing election for Governor, members of the House of Representatives, and electors of President and Vice President.

6. The returns of the votes for Governor, at the said next ensuing election shall be transmitted to the Secretary of State, the votes counted, and the election declared, in the manner now provided by law in the case of the Election of Electors of President and Vice President.

7. The Election of Clerks and Surrogates, in those Counties where the term of Office of the present incumbents shall expire previous to the general election of

eighteen hundred and forty five, shall be held at the general election next ensuing the adoption of this Constitution; the result of which election shall be ascertained in the manner now provided by law for the election of Sheriffs.

8. The elections for the year eighteen hundred and forty four shall take place as now provided by law.

9. It shall be the duty of the Governor to fill all vacancies in office happening between the adoption of this Constitution and the first session of the senate, and not otherwise provided for, and the Commissions shall expire at the end of the first session of the Senate or when successors shall be elected or appointed and qualified.

10. The restriction of the pay of members of the Legislature, after forty days from the commencement of the session, shall not be applied to the first legislature convened under this Constitution.

11. Clerks of Counties shall be Clerks of the inferior Courts of Common Pleas and Quarter Sessions of the several counties, and perform the duties, and be subject to the regulations now required of them by law until otherwise ordained by the Legislature.

12. The Legislature shall pass all laws necessary to carry into effect the provisions of this Constitution.

Done in Convention, at the State House in Trenton, on the twenty-ninth day of June, in the year of our Lord, one thousand eight hundred and forty-four, and of the Independence of the United Sttaes of America the sixty-eighth.

IX

THE CONSTITUTION OF THE STATE OF NEW JERSEY SEPTEMBER 10, 1947 (AS AMENDED TO NOVEMBER 1, 1961)

[Text from the printed and signed copy in the office of the Secretary of State. Paragraph 4 of Section VI, Article IV was added by amendment in 1961.]

A CONSTITUTION agreed upon by the delegates of the people of New Jersey, in Convention, begun at Rutgers university, the State University of New Jersey, in New Brunswick, on the twelfth day of June, and continued to the tenth day of September, in the year of our Lord one thousand nine hundred and forty-seven.

We, the people of the State of New Jersey, grateful to Almighty God for the civil and religious liberty which He hath so long permitted us to enjoy, and looking to Him for a blessing upon our endeavors to secure and transmit the same unimpaired to succeeding geenrations, do ordain and establish this Constitution.

ARTICLE I

RIGHTS AND PRIVILEGES

1. All persons are by nature free and independent, and have certain natural and unalienable rights, among which are those of enjoying and defending life and liberty, of acquiring, possessing, and protecting property, and of pursuing and obtaining safety and happiness.

2. All political power is inherent in the people. Government is instituted for the protection, security, and benefit of the people, and they have the right at all

times to alter or reform the same, whenever the public good may require it.

3. No person shall be deprived of the inestimable privilege of worshiping Almighty God in a manner agreeable to the dictates of his own conscience; nor under any pretense whatever be compelled to attend any place of worship contrary to his faith and judgment; nor shall any person be obliged to pay tithes, taxes, or other rates for building or repairing any church or churches, place or places of worship, or for the maintenance of any minister or ministry, contrary to what he believes to be right or has deliberately and voluntarily engaged to perform.

4. There shall be no establishment of one religious sect in preference to another; no religious or racial test shall be required as a qualification for any office or public trust.

5. No person shall be denied the enjoyment of any civil or military right, nor be discriminated against in the exercise of any civil or military right, nor be segregated in the militia or in the public schools, because of religious principles, race, color, ancestry or national origin.

6. Every person may freely speak, write and publish his sentiments on all subjects, being responsible for the abuse of that right. No law shall be passed to restrain or abridge the liberty of speech or of the press. In all prosecutions or indictments for libel, the truth may be given in evidence to the jury; and if it shall appear to the jury that the matter charged as libellous is true, and was published with good motives and for justifiable ends, the party shall be acquitted; and the jury shall have the right to determine the law and the fact.

7. The right of the people to be secure in their persons, houses, papers, and effects, against unreasonable searches and seizures, shall not be violated; and no warrant shall issue except upon probable cause, supported by oath or affirmation, and particularly describing the place to be searched and the papers and things to be seized.

8. No person shall be held to answer for a criminal

offense, unless on the presentment or indictment of a grand jury, except in cases of impeachment, or in cases now prosecuted without indictment, or arising in the army or navy or in the militia, when in actual service in time of war or public danger.

9. The right of trial by jury shall remain inviolate; but the Legislature may authorize the trial of civil causes by a jury of six persons when the matter in dispute does not exceed fifty dollars. The Legislature may provide that in any civil cause a verdict may be rendered by not less than five-sixths of the jury. The Legislature may authorize the trial of the issue of mental incompetency without a jury.

10. In all criminal prosecutions the accused shall have the right to a speedy and public trial by an impartial jury; to be informed of the nature and cause of the accusation; to be confronted with the witnesses against him; to have compulsory process for obtaining witnesses in his favor; and to have the assistance of counsel in his defense.

11. No person shall, after acquittal, be tried for the same offense. All persons shall, before conviction, be bailable by sufficient sureties, except for capital offenses when the proof is evident or presumption great.

12. Excessive bail shall not be required, excessive fines shall not be imposed, and cruel and unusual punishments shall not be inflicted.

13. No person shall be imprisoned for debt in any action, or on any judgment founded upon contract, unless in cases of fraud; nor shall any person be imprisoned for a militia fine in time of peace.

14. The privilege of the writ of habeas corpus shall not be suspended, unless in case of rebellion or invasion the public safety may require it.

15. The military shall be in strict subordination to the civil power.

16. No soldier shall, in time of peace, be quartered in any house, without the consent of the owner; nor in time of war, except in a manner prescribed by law.

17. Treason against the State shall consist only in levy-

ing war against it, or in adhering to its enemies, giving them aid and comfort. No person shall be convicted of treason, unless on the testimony of two witnesses to the same overt act, or on confession in open court.

18. The people have the right freely to assemble together, to consult for the common good, to make known their opinions to their representatives, and to petition for redress of grievances.

19. Persons in private employment shall have the right to organize and bargain collectively. Persons in public employment shall have the right to organize, present to and make known to the State, or any of its political subdivisions or agencies, their grievances and proposals through representatives of their own choosing.

20. Private property shall not be taken for public use without just compensation. Individuals or private corporations shall not be authorized to take private property for public use without just compensation first made to the owners.

21. This enumeration of rights and privileges shall not be construed to impair or deny others retained by the people.

Article II

ELECTIONS AND SUFFRAGE

1. General elections shall be held annually on the first Tuesday after the first Monday in November; but the time of holding such elections may be altered by law. The Governor and members of the Legislature shall be chosen at general elections. Local elective officers shall be chosen at general elections or at such other times as shall be provided by law.

2. All questions submitted to the people of the entire State shall be voted upon at general elections.

3. Every citizen of the United States, of the age of twenty-one years, who shall have been a resident of this State one year, and of the county in which he claims his

vote five months, next before the election, shall be entitled to vote for all officers that now are or hereafter may be elective by the people, and upon all questions which may be submitted to a vote of the people.

4. In time of war no elector in the military service of the State or in the armed forces of the United States shall be deprived of his vote by reason of absence from his election district. The Legislature may provide for absentee voting by members of the armed forces of the United States in time of peace. The Legislature may provide the manner in which and the time and place at which such absent electors may vote, and for the return and canvass of their votes in the election district in which they respectively reside.

5. No person in the military, naval or marine service of the United States shall be considered a resident of this State by being stationed in any garrison, barrack, or military or naval place or station within this State.

6. No idiot or insane person shall enjoy the right of suffrage.

7. The Legislature may pass laws to deprive persons of the right of suffrage who shall be convicted of such crimes as it may designate. Any person so deprived, when pardoned or otherwise restored by law to the right of suffrage, shall again enjoy that right.

Article III

DISTRIBUTION OF THE POWERS OF GOVERNMENT

1. The powers of the government shall be divided among three distinct branches, the legislative, executive, and judicial. No person or persons belonging to or constituting one branch shall exercise any of the powers properly belonging to either of the others, except as expressly provided in this Constitution.

Article IV

LEGISLATIVE

Section I

1. The legislative power shall be vested in a Senate and General Assembly.
2. No person shall be a member of the Senate who shall not have attained the age of thirty years, and have been a citizen and resident of the State for four years, and of the county for which he shall be elected one year, next before his election. No person shall be a member of the General Assembly who shall not have attained the age of twenty-one years, and have been a citizen and resident of the State for two years, and of the county for which he shall be elected one year, next before his election. No person shall be eligible for membership in the Legislature unless he be entitled to the right of suffrage.
3. The Senate and General Assembly shall meet and organize separately at noon on the second Tuesday in January of each year, at which time the legislative year shall commence.
4. Special sessions of the Legislature shall be called by the Governor upon petition of a majority of all the members of each house, and may be called by the Governor whenever in his opinion the public interest shall require.

Section II

1. The Senate shall be composed of one Senator from each county, elected by the legally qualified voters of the county, for a term beginning at noon of the second Tuesday in January next following his election and ending at noon of the second Tuesday in January four years thereafter.
2. The members of the Senate shall be elected in two classes so that, as nearly as may be, one-half of all the members shall be elected biennially.

Section III

1. The General Assembly shall be composed of members elected biennially by the legally qualified voters of the counties, respectively, for terms beginning at noon of the second Tuesday in January next following their election and ending at noon of the second Tuesday in January two years thereafter. The members of the General Assembly shall be apportioned among the several counties as nearly as may be according to the number of their inhabitants, but each county shall at all times be entitled to one member and the whole number of members shall never exceed sixty. The present apportionment shall continue until the next census of the United States shall have been taken. Apportionment of the members of the General Assembly shall be made by the Legislature at the first session after the next and every subsequent census, and each apportionment when made shall remain unaltered until the following census shall have been taken.

Section IV

1. Any vacancy in the Legislature occasioned by death, resignation or otherwise shall be filled by election for the unexpired term only, as may be provided by law. Each house shall direct a writ of election to fill any vacancy in its membership; but if the vacancy shall occur during a recess of the Legislature, the writ may be issued by the Governor, as may be provided by law.

2. Each house shall be the judge of the elections, returns and qualifications of its own members, and a majority of all its members shall constitute a quorum to do business; but a smaller number may adjourn from day to day, and may be authorized to compel the attendance of absent members, in such manner, and under such penalties, as each house may provide.

3. Each house shall choose its own officers, determine the rules of its proceedings, and punish its members for

disorderly behavior. It may expel a member with the concurrence of two-thirds of all its members.

4. Each house shall keep a journal of its proceedings, and from time to time publish the same. The yeas and nays of the members of either house on any question shall, on demand of one-fifth of those present, be entered on the journal.

5. Neither house, during the session of the Legislature, shall, without the consent of the other, adjourn for more than three days, or to any other place than that in which the two houses shall be sitting.

6. All bills and joint resolutions shall be read three times in each house before final passage. No bill or joint resolution shall be read a third time in either house until after the intervention of one full calendar day following the day of the second reading; but if either house shall resolve by vote of three-fourths of all its members, signified by yeas and nays entered on the journal, that a bill or joint resolution is an emergency measure, it may proceed forthwith from second to third reading. No bill or joint resolution shall pass, unless there shall be a majority of all the members of each body personally present and agreeing thereto, and the yeas and nays of the members voting on such final passage shall be entered on the journal.

7. Members of the Senate and General Assembly shall receive annually, during the term for which they shall have been elected and while they shall hold their office, such compensation as shall, from time to time, be fixed by law and no other allowance or emolument, directly or indirectly, for any purpose whatever. The President of the Senate and the Speaker of the General Assembly, each by virtue of his office, shall receive an additional allowance, equal to one-third of his compensation as a member.

8. The compensation of members of the Senate and General Assembly shall be fixed at the first session of the Legislature held after this Constitution takes effect, and may be increased or decreased by law from time to time

thereafter, but no increase or decrease shall be effective until the legislative year following the next general election for members of the General Assembly.

9. Members of the Senate and General Assembly shall, in all cases except treason and high misdemeanor, be privileged from arrest during their attendance at the sitting of their respective houses, and in going to and returning from the same; and for any statement, speech or debate in either house or at any meeting of a legislative committee, they shall not be questioned in any other place.

Section V

1. No member of the Senate or General Assembly, during the term for which he shall have been elected, shall be nominated, elected or appointed to any State civil office or position, of profit, which shall have been created by law, or the emoluments whereof shall have been increased by law, during such term. The provisions of this paragraph shall not prohibit the election of any person as Governor or as a member of the Senate or General Assembly.

2. The Legislature may appoint any commission, committee or other body whose main purpose is to aid or assist it in performing its functions. Members of the Legislature may be appointed to serve on any such body.

3. If any member of the Legislature shall become a member of Congress or shall accept any Federal or State office or position, of profit, his seat shall thereupon become vacant.

4. No member of Congress, no person holding any Federal or State office or position, of profit, and no judge of any court shall be entitled to a seat in the Legislature.

5. Neither the Legislature nor either house thereof shall elect or appoint any executive, administrative or judicial officer except the State Auditor.

Section VI

1. All bills for raising revenue shall originate in the General Assembly; but the Senate may propose or concur with amendments, as on other bills.

2. The Legislature may enact general laws under which municipalities, other than counties, may adopt zoning ordinances limiting and restricting to specified districts and regulating therein, buildings and structures, according to their construction, and the nature and extent of their use, and the nature and extent of the uses of land, and the exercise of such authority shall be deemed to be within the police power of the State. Such laws shall be subject to repeal or alteration by the Legislature.

3. Any agency or political subdivision of the State or any agency of a political subdivision thereof, which may be empowered to take or otherwise acquire private property for any public highway, parkway, airport, place, improvement, or use, may be authorized by law to take or otherwise acquire a fee simple absolute or any lesser interest, and may be authorized by law to take or otherwise acquire a fee simple absolute in, easements upon, or the benefit of restrictions upon, abutting property to preserve and protect the public highway, parkway, airport, place, improvement, or use; but such taking shall be with just compensation.

4. The Legislature, in order to insure continuity of State, county and local governmental operations in periods of emergency resulting from disasters caused by enemy attack, shall have the power and the immediate and continuing duty by legislation (1) to provide, prior to the occurrence of the emergency, for prompt and temporary succession to the powers and duties of public offices, of whatever nature and whether filled by election or appointment, the incumbents of which may become unavailable for carrying on the powers and duties of such offices, and (2) to adopt such other measures as may be necessary and proper for insuring the continuity of governmental operations. In the exercise of the powers

hereby conferred the Legislature shall in all respects conform to the requirements of this Constitution except to the extent that in the judgment of the Legislature to do so would be impracticable or would admit of undue delay.

Section VII

1. No divorce shall be granted by the Legislature.

2. No gambling of any kind shall be authorized by the Legislature unless the specific kind, restrictions and control thereof have been heretofore submitted to, and authorized by a majority of the votes cast by, the people at a special election or shall hereafter be submitted to, and authorized by a majority of the votes cast thereon by, the legally qualified voters of the State voting at a general election.

3. The Legislature shall not pass any bill of attainder, ex post facto law, or law impairing the obligation of contracts, or depriving a party of any remedy for enforcing a contract which existed when the contract was made.

4. To avoid improper influences which may result from intermixing in one and the same act such things as have no proper relation to each other, every law shall embrace but one object, and that shall be expressed in the title. This paragraph shall not invalidate any law adopting or enacting a compilation, consolidation, revision, or rearrangement of all or parts of the statutory law.

5. No law shall be revived or amended by reference to its title only, but the act revived, or the section or sections amended, shall be inserted at length. No act shall be passed which shall provide that any existing law, or any part thereof, shall be made or deemed a part of the act or which shall enact that any existing law, or any part thereof, shall be applicable, except by inserting it in such act.

6. The laws of this State shall begin in the following style: "Be it enacted by the Senate and General Assembly of the State of New Jersey".

7. No general law shall embrace any provision of a private, special or local character.

8. No private, special or local law shall be passed unless public notice of the intention to apply therefor, and of the general object thereof, shall have been previously given. Such notice shall be given at such time and in such manner and shall be so evidenced and the evidence thereof shall be so preserved as may be provided by law.

9. The Legislature shall not pass any private, special or local laws:

(1) Authorizing the sale of any lands belonging in whole or in part to a minor or minors or other persons who may at the time be under any legal disability to act for themselves.

(2) Changing the law of descent.

(3) Providing for change of venue in civil or criminal cases.

(4) Selecting, drawing, summoning or empaneling grand or petit jurors.

(5) Creating, increasing or decreasing the emoluments, term or tenure rights of any public officers or employees.

(6) Relating to taxation or exemption therefrom.

(7) Providing for the management and control of free public schools.

(8) Granting to any corporation, association or individual any exclusive privilege, immunity or franchise whatever.

(9) Granting to any corporation, association or individual the right to lay down railroad tracks.

(10) Laying out, opening, altering, constructing, maintaining and repairing roads or highways.

(11) Vacating any road, town plot, street, alley or public grounds.

(12) Appointing local officers or commissions to regulate municipal affairs.

(13 Regulating the internal affairs of municipalities formed for local government and counties, except as otherwise in this Constitution provided.

The Legislature shall pass general laws providing for the cases enumerated in this paragraph, and for all other cases which, in its judgment, may be provided for by general laws. The Legislature shall pass no special act conferring corporate powers, but shall pass general laws under which corporations may be organized and corporate powers of every nature obtained, subject, nevertheless, to repeal or alteration at the will of the Legislature.

10. Upon petition by the governing body of any municipal corporation formed for local government, or of any county, and by vote of two-thirds of all the members of each house, the Legislature may pass private, special or local laws regulating the internal affairs of the municipality or county. The petition shall be authorized in a manner to be prescribed by general law and shall specify the general nature of the law sought to be passed. Such law shall become operative only if it is adopted by ordinance of the governing body of the municipality or county or by vote of the legally qualified voters thereof. The Legislature shall prescribe in such law or by general law the method of adopting such law, and the manner in which the ordinance of adoption may be enacted or the vote taken, as the case may be.

11. The provisions of this Constitution and of any law concerning municipal corporations formed for local government, or concerning counties, shall be liberally construed in their favor. The powers of counties and such municipal corporations shall include not only those granted in express terms but also those of necessary or fair implication, or incident to the powers expressly conferred, or essential thereto, and not inconsistent with or prohibited by this Constitution or by law.

Section VIII

1. Members of the Legislature shall, before they enter on the duties of their respective offices, take and subscribe the following oath or affirmation: "I do solemnly swear (or affirm) that I will support the Constitution of the United States and the Constitution of the State of New Jersey, and that I will faithfully discharge the duties of Senator (or member of the General Assembly) accord-

ing to the best of my ability". Members-elect of the Senate or General Assembly are empowered to administer said oath or affirmation to each other.

2. Every officer of the Legislature shall, before he enters upon his duties, take and subscribe the following oath or affirmation: "I do solemnly promise and swear (or affirm) that I will faithfully, impartially and justly perform all the duties of the office of .... , to the best of my ability and understanding; that I will carefully preserve all records, papers, writings, or property entrusted to me for safe-keeping by virtue of my office, and make such disposition of the same as may be required by law".

Article V

EXECUTIVE

Section I

1. The executive power shall be vested in a Governor.

2. The Governor shall be not less than thirty years of age, and shall have been for at least twenty years a citizen of the United States, and a resident of this State seven years next before his election, unless he shall have been absent during that time on the public business of the United States or of this State.

3. No member of Congress or person holding any office or position, of profit, under this State or the United States shall be Governor. If the Governor or person administering the office of Governor shall accept any other office or position, of profit, under this State or the United States, his office of Governor shall thereby be vacated. No Governor shall be elected by the Legislature to any office during the term for which he shall have been elected Governor.

4. The Governor shall be elected by the legally qualified voters of this State. The person receiving the greatest number of votes shall be the Governor; but if two or

more shall be equal and greatest in votes, one of them shall be elected Governor by the vote of a majority of all the members of both houses in joint meeting at the regular legislative session next following the election for Governor by the people. Contested elections for the office of Governor shall be determined in such manner as may be provided by law.

5. The term of office of the Governor shall be four years, beginning at noon of the third Tuesday in January next following his election, and ending at noon of the third Tuesday in January four years thereafter. No person who has been elected Governor for two successive terms, including an unexpired term, shall again be eligible for that office until the third Tuesday in January of the fourth year following the expiration of his second successive term.

6. In the event of a vacancy in the office of Governor resulting from the death, resignation or removal of a Governor in office, or the death of a Governor-elect, or from any other cause, the functions, powers, duties and emoluments of the office shall devolve upon the President of the Senate, for the time being; and in the event of his death, resignation or removal, then upon the Speaker of the General Assembly, for the time being; and in the event of his death, resignation or removal, then upon such officers and in such order of succession as may be provided by law; until a new Governor shall be elected and qualify.

7. In the event of the failure of the Governor-elect to qualify, or of the absence from the State of a Governor in office, or his inability to discharge the duties of his office, or his impeachment, the functions, powers, duties and emoluments of the office shall devolve upon the President of the Senate, for the time being; and in the event of his death, resignation, removal, absence, inability or impeachment, then upon the Speaker of the General Assembly, for the time being; and in the event of his death, resignation, removal, absence, inability or impeachment, then upon such officers and in such order of

succession as may be provided by law; until the Governor-elect shall qualify, or the Governor in office shall return to the State, or shall no longer be unable to discharge the duties of the office, or shall be acquitted, as the case may be, or until a new Governor shall be elected and qualify.

8. Whenever a Governor-elect shall have failed to qualify within six months after the beginning of his term of office, or whenever for a period of six months a Governor in office, or person administering the office, shall have remained continuously absent from the State, or shall have been continuously unable to discharge the duties of his office by reason of mental or physical disability, the office shall be deemed vacant. Such vacancy shall be determined by the Supreme Court upon presentment to it of a concurrent resolution declaring the ground of the vacancy, adopted by a vote of two-thirds of all the members of each house of the Legislature, and upon notice, hearing before the Court and proof of the existence of the vacancy.

9. In the event of a vacancy in the office of Governor, a Governor shall be elected to fill the unexpired term at the general election next succeeding the vacancy, unless the vacancy shall occur within sixty days immediately preceding a general election, in which case he shall be elected at the second succeeding general election; but no election to fill an unexpired term shall be held in any year in which a Governor is to be elected for a full term. A Governor elected for an unexpired term shall assume his office immediately upon his election.

10. The Governor shall receive for his services a salary, which shall be neither increased nor diminished during the period for which he shall have been elected.

11. The Governor shall take care that the laws be faithfully executed. To this end he shall have power, by appropriate action or proceeding in the courts brought in the name of the State, to enforce compliance with any constitutional or legislative mandate, or to restrain violation of any constitutional or legislative power or duty,

by any officer, department or agency of the State; but this power shall not be construed to authorize any action or proceeding against the Legislature.

12. The Governor shall communicate to the Legislature, by message at the opening of each regular session and at such other times as he may deem necessary, the condition of the State, and shall in like manner recommend such measures as he may deem desirable. He may convene the Legislature, or the Senate alone, whenever in his opinion the public interest shall require. He shall be the Commander-in-Chief of all the military and naval forces of the State. He shall grant commissions to all officers elected or appointed pursuant to this Constitution. He shall nominate and appoint, with the advice and consent of the Senate, all officers for whose election or appointment provision is not otherwise made by this Constitution or by law.

13. The Governor may fill any vacancy occurring in any office during a recess of the Legislature, appointment to which may be made by the Governor with the advice and consent of the Senate, or by the Legislature in joint meeting. An ad interim appointment so made shall expire at the end of the next regular session of the Senate, unless a successor shall be sooner appointed and qualify; and after the end of the session no ad interim appointment to the same office shall be made unless the Governor shall have submitted to the Senate a nomination to the office during the session and the Senate shall have adjourned without confirming or rejecting it. No person nominated for any office shall be eligible for an ad interim appointment to such office if the nomination shall have failed of confirmation by the Senate.

14. (a) Every bill which shall have passed both houses shall be presented to the Governor. If he approves he shall sign it, but if not he shall return it, with his objections, to the house in which it shall have originated, which shall enter the objections at large on its journal and proceed to reconsider it. If upon reconsideration, on or after the third day following the return of the bill,

two-thirds of all the members of the house of origin shall agree to pass the bill, it shall be sent, together with the objections of the Governor, to the other house, by which it shall be reconsidered and if approved by two-thirds of all the members of that house, it shall become a law; and in all such cases the votes of each house shall be determined by yeas and nays, and the names of the persons voting for and against the bill shall be entered on the journal of each house respectively. If a bill shall not be returned by the Governor within ten days, Sundays excepted, after it shall have been presented to him, the same shall become a law on the tenth day, unless the house of origin shall on that day be in adjourment. If on the tenth day the house of origin shall be in temporary adjournment in the course of a regular or special session, the bill shall become a law on the day on which the house of origin shall reconvene, unless the Governor shall on that day return the bill to that house.

(b) If on the tenth day the Legislature is in adjournment sine die, the bill shall become a law if the Governor shall sign it within forty-five days, Sundays excepted, after such adjournment. On the said forty-fifth day the bill shall become a law, notwithstanding the failure of the Governor to sign it within the period last stated, unless at or before noon of that day he shall return it with his objections to the house of origin at a special session of the Legislature which shall convene on that day, without petition or call, for the sole purpose of acting pursuant to this paragraph upon bills returned by the Governor. At such special session a bill may be reconsidered beginning on the first day, in the manner provided in this paragraph for the reconsideration of bills, and if approved upon reconsideration by two-thirds of all the members of each house, it shall become a law. The Governor, in returning with his objections a bill for reconsideration at any general or special session of the Legislature, may recommend that an amendment or amendments specified by him be made in the bill, and in such case the Legislature may amend and re-enact the bill.

If a bill be so amended and re-enacted, it shall be presented again to the Governor, but shall become a law only if he shall sign it within ten days after presentation; and no bill shall be returned by the Governor a second time. A special session of the Legislature shall not be convened pursuant to this paragraph whenever the forty-fifth day, Sundays excepted, after adjourment sine die of a regular or special session shall fall on or after the last day of the legislative year in which such adjournment shall have been taken; in which event any bill not signed by the Governor within such forty-five-day period shall not become a law.

15. If any bill presented to the Governor shall contain one or more items of appropriation of money, he may object in whole or in part to any such item or items while approving the other portions of the bill. In such case he shall append to the bill, at the time of signing it, a statement of each item or part thereof to which he objects, and each item or part so objected to shall not take effect. A copy of such statement shall be transmitted by him to the house in which the bill originated, and each item or part thereof objected to shall be separately reconsidered. If upon reconsideration, on or after the third day following said transmittal, one or more of such items or parts thereof be approved by two-thirds of all the members of each house, the same shall become a part of the law, notwithstanding the objections of the Governor. All the provisions of the preceding paragraph in relation to bills not approved by the Governor shall apply to cases in which he shall withhold his approval from any item or items or parts thereof contained in a bill appropriating money.

Section II

1. The Governor may grant pardons and reprieves in all cases other than impeachment and treason, and may suspend and remit fines and forfeitures. A commission or other body may be established by law to aid and advise the Governor in the exercise of executive clemency.

2. A system for the granting of parole shall be provided by law.

Section III

1. Provision for organizing, inducting, training, arming, disciplining and regulating a militia shall be made by law, which shall conform to applicable standards established for the armed forces of the United States.
2. The Governor shall nominate and appoint all general and flag officers of the militia, with the advice and consent of the Senate. All other commissioned officers of the militia shall be appointed and commissioned by the Governor according to law.

Section IV

1. All executive and administrative offices, departments, and instrumentalities of the State government, including the offices of Secretary of State and Attorney General, and their respective functions, powers and duties, shall be allocated by law among and within not more than twenty principal departments, in such manner as to group the same according to major purposes so far as practicable. Temporary commissions for special purposes may, however, be established by law and such commissions need not be allocated within a principal department.
2. Each principal department shall be under the supervision of the Governor. The head of each principal department shall be a single executive unless otherwise provided by law. Such single executives shall be nominated and appointed by the Governor, with the advice and consent of the Senate, to serve at the pleasure of the Governor during his term of office and until the appointment and qualification of their successors, except as herein otherwise provided with respect to the Secretary of State and the Attorney General.
3. The Secretary of State and the Attorney General shall be nominated and appointed by the Governor with

the advice and consent of the Senate to serve during the term of office of the Governor.

4. Whenever a board, commission or other body shall be the head of a principal department, the members thereof shall be nominated and appointed by the Governor with the advice and consent of the Senate, and may be removed in the manner provided by law. Such a board, commission or other body may appoint a principal executive officer when authorized by law, but the appointment shall be subject to the approval of the Governor. Any principal executive officer so appointed shall be removable by the Governor, upon notice and an opportunity to be heard.

5. The Governor may cause an investigation to be made of the conduct in office of any officer or employee who receives his compensation from the State of New Jersey, except a member, officer or employee of the Legislature or an officer elected by the Senate and General Assmbly in joint meeting, or a judicial officer. He may require such officers or employees to submit to him a written statement or statements, under oath, of such information as he may call for relating to the conduct of their respective offices or employments. After notice, the service of charges and an opportunity to be heard at public hearing the Governor may remove any such officer or employee for cause. Such officer or employee shall have the right of judicial review, on both the law and the facts, in such manner as shall be provided by law.

6. No rule or regulation made by any department, officer, agency or authority of this State, except such as relates to the organization or internal management of the State government or a part thereof, shall take effect until it is filed either with the Secretary of State or in such other manner as may be provided by law. The Legislature shall provide for the prompt publication of such rules and regulations.

Article VI

JUDICIAL

Section I

1. The judicial power shall be vested in a Supreme Court, a Superior Court, County Courts and inferior courts of limited jurisdiction. The inferior courts and their jurisdiction may from time to time be established, altered or abolished by law.

Section II

1. The Supreme Court shall consist of a Chief Justice and six Associate Justices. Five members of the court shall constitute a quorum. When necessary, the Chief Justice shall assign the Judge or Judges of the Superior Court, senior in service, as provided by rules of the Supreme Court, to serve temporarily in the Supreme Court. In case the Chief Justice is absent or unable to serve, a presiding Justice designated in accordance with rules of the Supreme Court shall serve temporarily in his stead.
2. The Supreme Court shall exercise appellate jurisdiction in the last resort in all causes provided in this Constitution.
3. The Supreme Court shall make rules governing the administration of all courts in the State and, subject to law, the practice and procedure in all such courts. The Supreme Court shall have jurisdiction over the admission to the practice of law and the discipline of persons admitted.

Section III

1. The Superior Court shall consist of such number of Judges as may be authorized by law, but not less than twenty-four, each of whom shall exercise the powers of the court subject to rules of the Supreme Court.

2. The Superior Court shall have original general jurisdiction throughout the State in all causes.

3. The Superior Court shall be divided into an Appellate Division, a Law Division, and a Chancery Division. Each such division shall have such Parts, consist of such number of Judges, and hear such causes, as may be provided by rules of the Supreme Court.

4. Subject to rules of the Supreme Court, the Law Division and the Chancery Division shall each exercise the powers and functions of the other division when the ends of justice so require, and legal and equitable relief shall be granted in any cause so that all matters in controversy between the parties may be completely determined.

Section IV

1. There shall be a County Court in each county, which shall have all the jurisdiction heretofore exercised by the Court of Common Pleas, Orphans' Court, Court of Oyer and Terminer, Court of Quarter Sessions, Court of Special Sessions and such other jurisdiction consistent with this Constitution as may be conferred by law.

2. There shall be a Judge of each County Court and such additional Judges as provided by law, and they shall be appointed in the same manner as heretofore provided for Judges of the Court of Common Pleas.

3. Each Judge of the County Court may exercise the jurisdiction of the County Court.

4. The jurisdiction, powers and functions of the County Courts and of the Judges of the County Courts may be altered by law as the public good may require.

5. The County Courts, in civil causes including probate causes, within their jurisdiction, and subject to law, may grant legal and equitable relief so that all matters in controversy between the parties may be completely determined.

Section V

1. Appeals may be taken to the Supreme Court:
    (a) In causes determined by the Appellate Division of the Superior Court involving a question arising under the Constitution of the United States or this State;
    (b) In causes where there is a dissent in the Appellate Division of the Superior Court;
    (c) In capital causes;
    (d) On certification by the Supreme Court to the Superior Court and, where provided by rules of the Supreme Court, to the County Courts and the inferior courts; and
    (e) In such causes as may be provided by law.
2. Appeals may be taken to the Appellate Division of the Superior Court from the Law and Chancery Divisions of the Superior Court, the County Courts and in such other causes as may be provided by law.
3. The Supreme Court and the Appellate Division of the Superior Court may exercise such original jurisdiction as may be necessary to the complete determination of any cause on review.
4. Prerogative writs are superseded and, in lieu thereof, review, hearing and relief shall be afforded in the Superior Court, on terms and in the manner provided by rules of the Supreme Court, as of right, except in criminal causes where such review shall be discretionary.

Section VI

1. The Governor shall nominate and appoint, with the advice and consent of the Senate, the Chief Justice and Associate Justices of the Supreme Court, the Judges of the Superior Court, the Judges of the County Courts and the judges of the inferior courts with jurisdiction extending to more than one municipality. No nomination to such an office shall be sent to the Senate for confirma-

tion until after seven days' public notice by the Governor.

2. The Justices of the Supreme Court, the Judges of the Superior Court and the Judges of the County Courts shall each prior to his appointment have been admitted to the practice of the law in this State for at least ten years.

3. The Justices of the Supreme Court and the Judges of the Superior Court shall hold their offices for initial terms of seven years and upon reappointment shall hold their offices during good behavior. Such Justices and Judges shall be retired upon attaining the age of seventy years. Provisions for the pensioning of the Justices of the Supreme Court and the Judges of the Superior Court shall be made by law.

4. The Justices of the Supreme Court, the Judges of the Superior Court and the Judges of the County Courts shall be subject to impeachment, and any judicial officer impeached shall not exercise his office until acquitted. The Judges of the Superior Court and the Judges of the County Courts shall also be subject to removal from office by the Supreme Court for such causes and in such manner as shall be provided by law.

5. Whenever the Supreme Court shall certify to the Governor that it appears that any Justice of the Supreme Court, Judge of the Superior Court or Judge of the County Court is so incapacitated as substantially to prevent him from performing his judicial duties, the Governor shall appoint a commission of three persons to inquire into the circumstances; and, on their recommendation, the Governor may retire the Justice or Judge from office, on pension as may be provided by law.

6. The Justices of the Supreme Court and the Judges of the Superior Court shall receive for their services such salaries as may be provided by law, which shall not be diminished during the term of their appointment. They shall not, while in office, engage in the practice of law or other gainful pursuit.

7. The Justices of the Supreme Court, the Judges of the Superior Court and the Judges of the County Courts

shall hold no other office or position, of profit, under this State or the United States. Any such Justice or Judge who shall become a candidate for an elective public office shall thereby forfeit his judicial office.

Section VII

1. The Chief Justice of the Supreme Court shall be the administrative head of all the courts in the State. He shall appoint an Administrative Director to serve at his pleasure.
2. The Chief Justice of the Supreme Court shall assign Judges of the Superior Court to the Divisions and Parts of the Superior Court, and may from time to time transfer Judges from one assignment to another, as need appears. Assignments to the Appellate Division shall be for terms fixed by rules of the Supreme Court.
3. The Clerk of the Supreme Court and the Clerk of the Superior Court shall be appointed by the Supreme Court for such terms and at such compensation as shall be provided by law.

Article VII

PUBLIC OFFICERS AND EMPLOYEES

Section I

1. Every State officer, before entering upon the duties of his office, shall take and subscribe an oath or affirmation to support the Constitution of this State and of the United States and to perform the duties of his office faithfully, impartially and justly to the best of his ability.
2. Appointments and promotions in the civil service of the State, and of such political subdivisions as may be provided by law, shall be made according to merit and fitness to be ascertained, as far as practicable, by examination, which, as far as practicable, shall be competitive; except that preference in appointments by reason of

active service in any branch of the military or naval forces of the United States in time of war may be provided by law.

3. Any compensation for services or any fees received by any person by virtue of an appointive State office or position, in addition to the usual salary provided for the office or position, shall immediately upon receipt be paid into the treasury of the State, unless the compensation or fees shall be allowed or appropriated to him by law.

4. Any person before or after entering upon the duties of any public office, position or employment in this State may be required to give bond as may be provided by law.

5. The term of office of all officers elected or appointed pursuant to the provisions of this Constitution, except as herein otherwise provided, shall commence on the day of the date of their respective commissions; but no commission for any office shall bear date prior to the expiration of the term of the incumbent of said office.

6. The State Auditor shall be appointed by the Senate and General Assembly in joint meeting for a term of five years and until his successor shall be appointed and qualify. It shall be his duty to conduct post-audits of all transactions and accounts kept by or for all departments, offices and agencies of the State government, to report to the Legislature or to any committee thereof as shall be required by law, and to perform such other similar or related duties as shall, from time to time, be required of him by law.

Section II

1. County prosecutors shall be nominated and appointed by the Governor with the advice and consent of the Senate. Their term of office shall be five years, and they shall serve until the appointment and qualification of their respective successors.

2. County clerks, surrogates and sheriffs shall be elected by the people of their respective counties at general elec-

tions. The term of office of county clerks and surrogates shall be five years, and of sheriffs three years. Whenever a vacancy shall occur in any such office it shall be filled in the manner to be provided by law.

Section III

1. The Governor and all other State officers, while in office and for two years thereafter, shall be liable to impeachment for misdemeanor committed during their respective continuance in office.

2. The General Assembly shall have the sole power of impeachment by vote of a majority of all the members. All impeachments shall be tried by the Senate, and members, when sitting for that purpose, shall be on oath or affirmation "truly and impartially to try and determine the charge in question according to the evidence". No person shall be convicted without the concurrence of two-thirds of all the members of the Senate. When the Governor is tried, the Chief Justice of the Supreme Court shall preside and the President of the Senate shall not participate in the trial.

3. Judgment in cases of impeachment shall not extend further than to removal from office, and to disqualification to hold and enjoy any public office of honor, profit or trust in this State; but the person convicted shall nevertheless be liable to indictment, trial and punishment according to law.

Article VIII

TAXATION AND FINANCE

Section I

1. Property shall be assessed for taxation under general laws and by uniform rules. All real property assessed and taxed locally or by the State for allotment and payment to taxing districts shall be assessed according to the same

standard of value; and such real property shall be taxed at the general tax rate of the taxing district in which the property is situated, for the use of such taxing district.

2. Exemption from taxation may be granted only by general laws. Until otherwise provided by law all exemptions from taxation validly granted and now in existence shall be continued. Exemptions from taxation may be altered or repealed, except those exempting real and personal property used exclusively for religious, educational, charitable or cemetery purposes, as defined by law, and owned by any corporation or association organized and conducted exclusively for one or more of such purposes and not operating for profit.

3. Any citizen and resident of this State now or hereafter honorably discharged or released under honorable circumstances from active service in time of war in any branch of the armed forces of the United States, shall be exempt from taxation on real and personal property to an aggregate assessed valuation not exceeding five hundred dollars, which exemption shall not be altered or repealed. Any person hereinabove described who has been or shall be declared by the United States Veterans Administration, or its successor, to have a service-connected disability, shall be entitled to such further exemption from taxation as from time to time may be provided by law. The widow of any citizen and resident of this State who has met or shall meet his death on active duty in time of war in any such service shall be entitled, during her widowhood, to the exemption in this paragraph provided for honorably discharged veterans and to such further exemption as from time to time may be provided by law.

Section II

1. The credit of the State shall not be directly or indirectly loaned in any case.

2. No money shall be drawn from the State treasury but for appropriations made by law. All moneys for the

support of the State government and for all other State purposes as far as can be ascertained or reasonably foreseen, shall be provided for in one general appropriation law covering one and the same fiscal year; except that when a change in the fiscal year is made, necessary provision may be made to effect the transition. No general appropriation law or other law appropriating money for any State purpose shall be enacted if the appropriation contained therein, together with all prior appropriations made for the same fiscal period, shall exceed the total amount of revenue on hand and anticipated which will be available to meet such appropriations during such fiscal period, as certified by the Governor.

3. The Legislature shall not, in any manner, create in any fiscal year a debt or debts, liability or liabilities of the State, which together with any previous debts or liabilities shall exceed at any time one per centum of the total amount appropriated by the general appropriation law for that fiscal year, unless the same shall be authorized by a law for some single object or work distinctly specified therein. Regardless of any limitation relating to taxation in this Constitution, such law shall provide the ways and means, exclusive of loans, to pay the interest of such debt or liability as it falls due, and also to pay and discharge the principal thereof within thirty-five years from the time it is contracted; and the law shall not be repealed until such debt or liability and the interest thereon are fully paid and discharged. No such law shall take effect until it shall have been submitted to the people at a general election and approved by a majority of the legally qualified voters of the State voting thereon. All money to be raised by the authority of such law shall be applied only to the specific object stated therein, and to the payment of the debt thereby created. This paragraph shall not be construed to refer to any money that has been or may be deposited with this State by the government of the United States. Nor shall anything in this paragraph contained apply to the creation of any debts or liabilities for purposes of war, or to repel invasion, or

to suppress insurrection or to meet an emergency caused by disaster or act of God.

Section III

1. The clearance, replanning, development or redevelopment of blighted areas shall be a public purpose and public use, for which private property may be taken or acquired. Municipal, public or private corporations may be authorized by law to undertake such clearance, replanning, development or redevelopment; and improvements made for these purposes and uses, or for any of them, may be exempted from taxation, in whole or in part, for a limited period of time during which the profits of and dividends payable by any private corporation enjoying such tax exemption shall be limited by law. The conditions of use, ownership, management and control of such improvements shall be regulated by law.

2. No county, city, borough, town, township or village shall hereafter give any money or property, or loan its money or credit, to or in aid of any individual, association or corporation, or become security for, or be directly or indirectly the owner of, any stock or bonds of any association or corporation.

3. No donation of land or appropriation of money shall be made by the State or any county or municipal corporation to or for the use of any society, association or corporation whatever.

Section IV

1. The Legislature shall provide for the maintenance and support of a thorough and efficient system of free public schools for the instruction of all the children in the State between the ages of five and eighteen years.

2. The fund for the support of free public schools, and all money, stock and other property, which may hereafter be appropriated for that purpose, or received into the treasury under the provision of any law heretofore passed

to augment the said fund, shall be securely invested, and remain a perpetual fund; and the income thereof, except so much as it may be judged expedient to apply to an increase of the capital, shall be annually appropriated to the support of free public schools, for the equal benefit of all the people of the State; and it shall not be competent for the Legislature to borrow, appropriate or use the said fund or any part thereof for any other purpose, under any pretense whatever.

3. The Legislature may, within reasonable limitations as to distance to be prescribed, provide for the transportation of children within the ages of five to eighteen years inclusive to and from any school.

Article IX

AMENDMENTS

1. Any specific amendment or amendments to this Constitution may be proposed in the Senate or General Assembly. At least twenty calendar days prior to the first vote thereon in the house in which such amendment or amendments are first introduced, the same shall be printed and placed on the desks of the members of each house. Thereafter and prior to such vote a public hearing shall be held thereon. If the proposed amendment or amendments or any of them shall be agreed to by three-fifths of all the members of each of the respective houses, the same shall be submitted to the people. If the same or any of them shall be agreed to by less than three-fifths but nevertheless by a majority of all the members of each of the respective houses, such proposed amendment or amendments shall be referred to the Legislature in the next legislative year; and if in that year the same or any of them shall be agreed to by a majority of all the members of each of the respective houses, then such amendment or amendments shall be submitted to the people.

2. The proposed amendment or amendments shall be

entered on the journal of each house with the yeas and nays of the members voting thereon.

3. The Legislature shall cause the proposed amendment or amendments to be published at least once in one or more newspapers of each county, if any be published therein, not less than three months prior to submission to the people.

4. The proposed amendment or amendments shall then be submitted to the people at the next general election in the manner and form provided by the Legislature.

5. If more than one amendment be submitted, they shall be submitted in such manner and form that the people may vote for or against each amendment separately and distinctly.

6. If the proposed amendment or amendments or any of them shall be approved by a majority of the legally qualified voters of the State voting thereon, the same shall become part of the Constitution on the thirtieth day after the election, unless otherwise provided in the amendment or amendments.

7. If at the election a proposed amendment shall not be approved, neither such proposed amendment nor one to effect the same or substantially the same change in the Constitution shall be submitted to the people before the third general election thereafter.

Article X

GENERAL PROVISIONS

1. The seal of the State shall be kept by the Governor, or person administering the office of Governor, and used by him officially, and shall be called the Great Seal of the State of New Jersey.

2. All grants and commissions shall be in the name and by the authority of the State of New Jersey, sealed with the Great Seal, signed by the Governor, or person administering the office of Governor, and countersigned by the Secretary of State, and shall run thus: "The State of

New Jersey, to ...., Greeting".

3. All writs shall be in the name of the State. All indictments shall conclude: "against the peace of this State, the government and dignity of the same".

4. Wherever in this Constitution the term "person", "persons", "people" or any personal pronoun is used, the same shall be taken to include both sexes.

5. Except as herein otherwise provided, this Constitution shall take effect on the first day of January in the year of our Lord one thousand nine hundred and forty-eight.

Article XI

SCHEDULE

Section I

1. This Constitution shall supersede the Constitution of one thousand eight hundred and forty-four as amended.

2. The Legislature shall enact all laws necessary to make this Constitution fully effective.

3. All law, statutory and otherwise, all rules and regulations of administrative bodies and all rules of courts in force at the time this Constitution or any Article thereof takes effect shall remain in full force until they expire or are superseded, altered or repealed by this Constitution or otherwise.

4. Except as otherwise provided by this Constitution, all writs, actions, judgments, decrees, causes of action, prosecutions, contracts, claims and rights of individuals and of bodies corporate, and of the State, and all charters and franchises shall continue unaffected notwithstanding the taking effect of any Article of this Constitution.

5. All indictments found before the taking effect of this Constitution or any Article may be proceeded upon. After the taking effect thereof, indictments for crime and complaints for offenses committed prior thereto may be

found, made and proceeded upon in the courts having jurisdiction thereof.

Section II

1. The first Legislature under this Constitution shall meet on the second Tuesday in January, in the year one thousand nine hundred and forty-eight.
2. Each member of the General Assembly, elected at the election in the year one thousand nine hundred and forty-seven, shall hold office for a term beginning at noon of the second Tuesday in January in the year one thousand nine hundred and forty-eight and ending at noon of the second Tuesday in January in the year one thousand nine hundred and fifty. Each member of the General Assembly elected thereafter shall hold office for the term provided by this Constitution.
3. Each member of the Senate elected in the years one thousand nine hundred and forty-five and one thousand nine hundred and forty-six shall hold office for the term for which he was elected. Each member of the Senate elected in the year one thousand nine hundred and forty-seven shall hold office for a term of four years beginning at noon of the second Tuesday in January following his election. The seats in the Senate which would have been filled in the years hereinafter designated had this Constitution not been adopted shall be filled by election as follows: of those seats which would have been filled by election in the year one thousand nine hundred and forty-eight, three seats, as chosen by the Senate in the year one thousand nine hundred and forty-eight, shall be filled by election in that year for terms of five years and three, as so chosen, shall be filled by election in that year for terms of three years, and those seats which would have been filled by election in the year one thousand nine hundred and forty-nine shall be filled by election in that year for terms of four years, so that eleven seats in the Senate shall be filled by election in the year one thousand nine hundred and fifty-one and every

fourth year thereafter for terms of four years, and the members of the Senate so elected and their successors shall constitute one class to be elected as prescribed in paragraph 2 of Section II of Article IV of this Constitution, and ten seats shall be filled by election in the year one thousand nine hundred and fifty-three and every fourth year thereafter for terms of four years, and the members of the Senate so elected and their successors shall constitute the other class to be elected as prescribed in said paragraph of this Constitution.

4. The provisions of Paragraph 1 of Section V of Article IV of this Constitution shall not prohibit the nomination, election or appointment of any member of the Senate or General Assembly first organized under this Constitution, to any State civil office or position created by this Constitution or created during his first term as such member.

Section III

1. A Governor shall be elected for a full term at the general election to be held in the year one thousand nine hundred and forty-nine and every fourth year thereafter.

2. The taking effect of this Constitution or any provision thereof shall not of itself affect the tenure, term, status or compensation of any person then holding any public office, position or employment in this State, except as provided in this Constitution. Unless otherwise specifically provided in this Constitution, all constitutional officers in office at the time of its adoption shall continue to exercise the authority of their respective offices during the term for which they shall have been elected or appointed and until the qualification of their successors respectively. Upon the taking effect of this Constitution all officers of the militia shall retain their commissions subject to the provisions of Article V, Section III.

3. The Legislature, in compliance with the provisions of this Constitution, shall prior to the first day of July, one thousand nine hundred and forty-nine, and may

from time to time thereafter, allocate by law the executive and administrative offices, departments and instrumentalities of the State government among and within the principal departments. If such allocation shall not have been completed within the time limited, the Governor shall call a special session of the Legislature to which he shall submit a plan or plans for consideration to complete such allocation; and no other matters shall be considered at such session.

Section IV

1. Subsequent to the adoption of this Constitution the Governor shall nominate and appoint, with the advice and consent of the Senate, a Chief Justice and six Associate Justices of the new Supreme Court from among the persons then being the Chancellor, the Chief Justice and Associate Justices of the old Supreme Court, the Vice Chancellors and Circuit Court Judges. The remaining judicial officers enumerated and such Judges of the Court of Errors and Appeals as have been admitted to the practice of law in this State for at least ten years, and are in office on the adoption of the Constitution, shall constitute the Judges of the Superior Court. The Justices of the new Supreme Court and the Judges of the Superior Court so designated shall hold office each for the period of his term which remained unexpired at the time the Constitution is adopted; and if reappointed he shall hold office during good behavior. No Justice of the new Supreme Court or Judge of the Superior Court shall hold his office after attaining the age of seventy years, except, however, that such Justice or Judge may complete the period of his term which remains unexpired at the time the Constitution is adopted.

2. The Judges of the Courts of Common Pleas shall constitute the Judges of the County Courts, each for the period of his term which remains unexpired at the time the Judicial Article of this Constitution takes effect.

3. The Court of Errors and Appeals, the present Su-

preme Court, the Court of Chancery, the Prerogative Court and the Circuit Courts shall be abolished when the Judicial Article of this Constitution takes effect; and all their jurisdiction, functions, powers and duties shall be transferred to and divided between the new Supreme Court and the Superior Court according as jurisdiction is vested in each of them under this Constitution.

4. Except as otherwise provided in this Constitution and until otherwise provided by law, all courts now existing in this State, other than those abolished in paragraph 3 hereof, shall continue as if this Constitution had not been adopted, provided, however, that when the Judicial Article of this Constitution takes effect, the jurisdiction, powers and functions of the Court of Common Pleas, Orphans' Court, Court of Oyer and Terminer, Court of Quarter Sessions and Court of Special Sessions of each county, the judicial officers, clerks and employees thereof, and the causes pending therein and their files, shall be transferred to the County Court of the county. All statutory provisions relating to the county courts aforementioned of each county and to the Judge or Judges thereof shall apply to the new County Court of the county and the Judge or Judges thereof, unless otherwise provided by law. Until otherwise provided by law and except as aforestated, the judicial officers, surrogates and clerks of all courts now existing, other than those abolished in paragraph 3 hereof, and the employees of said officers, clerks, surrogates and courts shall continue in the exercise of their duties, as if this Constitution had not been adopted.

5. The Supreme Court shall make rules governing the administration and practice and procedure of the County Courts; and the Chief Justice of the Supreme Court shall be the administrative head of these courts with power to assign any Judge thereof of any county to sit temporarily in the Superior Court or to sit temporarily without the county in a County Court.

6. The Advisory Masters appointed to hear matrimonial proceedings and in office on the adoption of this

Constitution shall, each for the period of his term which remains unexpired at the time the Constitution is adopted, continue so to do as Advisory Masters to the Chancery Division of the Superior Court, unless otherwise provided by law.

7. All Special Masters in Chancery, Masters in Chancery, Supreme Court Commissioners and Supreme Court Examiners shall, until otherwise provided by rules of the Supreme Court, continue respectively as Special Masters, Masters, Commissioners and Examiners of the Superior Court, with appropriate similar functions and powers as if this Constitution had not been adopted.

8. When the Judicial Article of this Constitution takes effect:

(a) All causes and proceedings of whatever character pending in the Court of Errors and Appeals shall be transferred to the new Supreme Court;

(b) All causes and proceedings of whatever character pending on appeal or writ of error in the present Supreme Court and in the Prerogative Court and all pending causes involving the prerogative writs shall be transferred to the Appellate Division of the Superior Court;

(c) All causes and proceedings of whatever character pending in the Supreme Court other than those stated shall be transferred to the Superior Court;

(d) All causes and proceedings of whatever character pending in the Prerogative Court other than those stated shall be transferred to the Chancery Division of the Superior Court;

(e) All causes and proceedings of whatever character pending in all other courts which are abolished shall be transferred to the Superior Court.

For the purposes of this paragraph, paragraph 4 and paragraph 9, a cause shall be deemed to be pending notwithstanding that an adjudication has been entered therein, provided the time limited for review has not expired or the adjudication reserves to any party the right to apply for further relief.

9. The files of all causes pending in the Court of Errors and Appeals shall be delivered to the Clerk of the new Supreme Court; and the files of all causes pending in the present Supreme Court, the Court of Chancery and the Prerogative Court shall be delivered to the Clerk of the Superior Court. All other files, books, papers, records and documents and all property of the Court of Errors and Appeals, the present Supreme Court, the Prerogative Court, the Chancellor and the Court of Chancery, or in their custody, shall be disposed of as shall be provided by law.

10. Upon the taking effect of the Judicial Article of this Constitution, all the functions, powers and duties conferred by statute, rules or otherwise upon the Chancellor, the Ordinary, and the Justices and Judges of the courts abolished by this Constitution, to the extent that such functions, powers and duties are not inconsistent with this Constitution, shall be transferred to and may be exercised by Judges of the Superior Court until otherwise provided by law or rules of the new Supreme Court; excepting that such statutory powers not related to the administration of justice as are then vested in any such judicial officers shall, after the Judicial Article of this Constitution takes effect and until otherwise provided by law, be transferred to and exercised by the Chief Justice of the new Supreme Court.

11. Upon the taking effect of the Judicial Article of this Constitution, the Clerk of the Supreme Court shall become the Clerk of the new Supreme Court and shall serve as such Clerk until the expiration of the term for which he was appointed as Clerk of the Supreme Court, and all employees of the Supreme Court as previously constituted, of the Clerk thereof and of the Chief Justice and the Justices thereof, of the Circuit Courts and the Judges thereof and of the Court of Errors and Appeals shall be transferred to appropriate similar positions with similar compensation and civil service status under the Clerk of the new Supreme Court or the new Supreme Court, or the Clerk of the Superior Court or the Superior Court, which shall be provided by law.

12. Upon the taking effect of the Judicial Article of this Constitution, the Clerk in Chancery shall become the Clerk of the Superior Court and shall serve as such Clerk until the expiration of the term for which he was appointed as Clerk in Chancery, and all employees of the Clerk in Chancery, the Court of Chancery, the Chancellor and the several Vice Chancellors shall be transferred to appropriate similar positions with similar compensation and civil service status under the Clerk of the Superior Court or the Superior Court, which shall be provided by law.

13. Appropriations made by law for judicial expenditures during the fiscal year one thousand nine hundred and forty-eight—one thousand nine hundred and forty-nine may be transferred to similar objects and purposes required by the Judicial Article.

14. The Judicial Article of this Constitution shall take effect on the fifteenth day of September, one thousand nine hundred and forty-eight, except that the Governor, with the advice and consent of the Senate, shall have the power to fill vacancies arising prior thereto in the new Supreme Court and the Superior Court; and except further that any provision of this Constitution which may require any act to be done prior thereto or in preparation therefor shall take effect immediately upon the adoption of this Constitution.

Done in Convention, at Rutgers University, the State University of New Jersey, in New Brunswick, on the tenth day of September, in the year of our Lord one thousand nine hundred and forty-seven, and of the independence of the United States of America the one hundred and seventy-second.

BIBLIOGRAPHICAL NOTE

There is no history of the fundamental laws and constitutions of New Jersey from the beginning to the present save Robert A. Petito's "A Constitutional History of New Jersey," an unpublished thesis written just after the adoption of the Constitution of 1947 (Department of Politics, Princeton University, 1948). This comprehensive survey, based on extensive research in both primary and secondary sources, is competently executed and very useful both for its facts and for its conclusions. The standard authority on the general history of the period from 1664 to 1702 is John E. Pomfret, whose two works, *The Province of West New Jersey 1609-1702* (Princeton, 1956) and *The Province of East New Jersey 1609-1702* (Princeton, 1962) are the product of impeccable scholarship. These volumes trace the general history of the province, including of course the history of its fundamental laws. The basic collection of documents is to be found in *New Jersey Archives,* 1st ser., Vols I, II (Newark, 1880-1881), and in that still indispensable compilation by Aaron Leaming and Jacob Spicer, *The Grants, Concessions and Original Constitutions of the Province of New-Jersey* (Philadelphia [1756]). Richard P. McCormick, "The Revolution of 1681 in East Jersey: A Document," *Proceedings of The New Jersey Historical Society,* LXXI (Apr. 1953), 111-124, presents, with illuminating commentary, an important document never theretofore published relating to the rebellion of that year. Edwin Tanner, *The Province of New Jersey, 1664-1738* (New York, 1908); Edgar J. Fisher, *New Jersey as a Royal Province, 1738-*

1776 (New York, 1911), and Donald L. Kemmerer, *Path to Freedom; The Struggle for Self-Government in Colonial New Jersey, 1703-1776* (Princeton, 1940), are the standard works for the political history of the province during the period covered, but two older works are still useful: Lucius Q. C. Elmer, *The Constitution and Government of the Province and State of New Jersey* (Newark, 1872) and John Whitehead, *The Judicial and Civil History of New Jersey* (Boston, 1897). Two excellent volumes in The New Jersey Historical Series should of course be consulted: Wesley Frank Craven, *New Jersey and the English Colonization of North America* and Richard P. McCormick, *New Jersey from Colony to State 1609-1789*.

Charles R. Erdman, Jr., *The New Jersey Constitution of 1776* (Princeton, 1929) is the definitive work on its subject, but again Lucius Q. C. Elmer, "History of the Constitution of New Jersey, Adopted in 1776, and of the Government Under It," *Proceedings of The New Jersey Historical Society*, 2d series, II 133-153, is not wholly obsolete. The principal issue of constitutional revision after 1776—that over the definition and extension of the franchise requirements—has been authoritatively discussed by Richard P. McCormick in *The History of Voting in New Jersey: A Study of the Development of Election Machinery, 1664-1911* (New Brunswick, 1953). Chilton Williamson's *American Suffrage from Property to Democracy, 1760-1860* (Princeton, 1960) traces the complex movement for the elimination of the freehold qualification both in its general and in its localized aspects. E. R. Turner, "Women's Suffrage in New Jersey, 1790-1807," in *Smith College Studies in History*, I, 167-187, is in reality a collaborative work with Annie H. Abel. It shows that sporadic exercise of the suffrage by women was not the result of anything like a feminist movement. J. R. Pole, "The Suffrage in New Jersey, 1790-1807," in *Proceedings of The New Jersey Historical Society*, LXXI (Jan. 1953), 39-61, confirms this judgment and adds some details to voting procedures in the confused period under review, but is less attentive to the influence of Joseph Cooper, a West Jersey Quaker, who argued with tenacity and serious purpose that women had the right to vote and who was no doubt responsible for the wording of the Act of 1790 that obviously intended to extend the franchise to women.

The Proceedings of the New Jersey State Constitutional Convention of 1844, compiled by the New Jersey Writers' Project of the Works Progress Administration (Trenton, 1942) is a documentary record made up of the journal of the Convention, together with extensive reports of the debates and proceedings gathered from two daily newspapers of Newark and Trenton. The editing is uncritical and the official journals and newspaper reports are intermingled, but the compilation is nevertheless a valuable and, indeed, indispensable source. It is made more useful by a lengthy and discerning introduction by John E. Bebout, who was active in the move for constitutional revision in the 1930's and 1940's. Mr. Bebout's introduction was issued separately under the title *The Making of the New Jersey Constitution* (Trenton, 1945).

The literature on the Constitution of 1947 is considerable. The proceedings of the drafting Convention are set forth in a five-volume compilation entitled *Constitutional Convention of 1947, held at Rutgers University* (Trenton, 1949-1953). Other sources useful for tracing the movement leading up to the adoption of the Constitution are Charles R. Erdman, Jr., *The New Jersey Constitution —A Barrier to Governmental Efficiency and Economy* (Princeton, 1934); Charles DeF. Besoré, *A New Constitution for the State, Constitution of 1844, As Amended, Arranged for Comparison* (Law Revision and Bill Drafting Commission, 1947); and various pamphlets issued by the Committee for Constitutional Revision, the New Jersey Constitutional Foundation, the New Jersey Taxpayers' Association, and other groups. Appraisals of the

Constitution of 1947 are to be found in Bennett M. Rich's "A New Constitution for New Jersey," *American Political Science Review,* LXI, 1126-1129; Leon S. Milmed's *Constitution of the State of New Jersey, with Comentary* (Newark, 1954); and Richard N. Baisden, *Charter for New Jersey: The New Jersey Constitutional Convention of 1947* (Trenton, 1952).

INDEX

By Mrs. Edwin C. Hutter

Absentee voting, 168, 198
Accused, rights of, 12, 85-89, 121-122, 161, 166-167, 195-196. *See also* Trial.
Acts of N. J. Legislature, of *1807* on suffrage, 31, 33; of *1943*, for referendum on *1944* Legislature as constituent assembly, 43. *See also* Laws.
Acts of Parliament, on frauds and abuses, in the plantation trade, 153; of *1698*, on rights and privileges of inhabitants, 19; of Trade and Navigation, 146
Adams, John, on government, 23-25
Admiral, High (Br.), 143-145
Affirmations. *See* Oaths or affirmations
Agriculture, 137-138, 149. *See also* Plantations.
Aldricks, Evert, 103
Algus, Markas, 103
Allen, Matthew, 104
Allinson's edition of laws, 162
Ambassadors, 108
Amendments, constitutional, 98, 124, 189-190, 225-226; prohibited, 14, 16, 83-84, 98, 106; to laws, form of, 98, 175, 204. *See also* Appropriations; Bills; Money bills; Legislation.
American Revolution, period of, 2, 4, 22-26

Andros, Sir Edmund, 17
Anne, Queen, instructions to N. J. Governor, 20, 126-154
Appeals, of Court decisions, 69, 117-118, 122-123, 149-150, 159, 180, 182-183, 215-217; of tax assessments, 160. *See also* Courts; Judiciary.
Appropriations, legislative bills for, 179, 212; of money, 168, 173, 222-224; for Judiciary, 234; for public education, 175, 224-225. *See also* Bills; Money.
Arms, right to bear, 34, 114-117
Arrest, protection against, 12, 85-86; Legislative immunity from, 172, 202. *See also* Accused; Imprisonment.
Assault, 92-93
Assembly, right of, 33, 167-168, 197
Assessments, property, 38, 56, 177; appeals from, 160; rules for, 49, 221-222. *See also* Taxation.
Atheists, 18, 120-121. *See also* Religious freedom.
Attainder, bills of, 175, 204
Attorney-General, 159-160, 213-214
Attorneys, practicing, 215, 230
Auditor, State, 189, 202, 220

Bagley, Charles, 102
Bail, right to, 167, 196
Ballot, secret, 14, 75, 96

Bankrupts, debts of, 151
Banks, charters for, 35, 176. *See also* Corporations.
Barclay, Robert, 110, 111
Baron, Machgyel, 102
Bartleson, Andrew, 104
Barton, Thomas, 104
Benson, Thomas, 104
Berkeley, Lord John, 9, 11, 15, 66, 70, 114
Beswick, Francis, 105
Biddle, William, 101
Bill of Rights (N. J. Constitutions), 27, 33-34, 43, 46, 48
Bills, passage of, 18, 35, 46, 97, 113, 157-158, 171-173, 176 179, 201, 203-206, 210-212, 225-226; ratification of, 56, 70, 107, 173, 190, 204, 223, 225-226. *See also* Appropriations; Money bills; Legislation; Veto power.
Bisbee, Henry H., 71
Bishop of London, 147-148
Black, William, 105
Board of Trade (Br.), 20, 126
Bond, required of officeholders, 220
Bonds, legality of, 90.
Borton, John, 105
Bowne, Andrew, 127
Bradway, Edward, 102
Braithwaite, W. C., 6
Bribery, in elections, 95-96, 112, 169; of justice, 121
Budd, Thomas, 13, 102
Buffington, Richard, 104
Burlington, 71, 155; delegates to Assembly from, 131; seat of Assembly, 20, 106, 130; seat of Provincial Congress, 23, 162
Business transactions, legality of, 89-90, 121
Butcher, John, 104
Byllynge, Edward, 11-13, 15-16, 101

Cantwell, William, 102
Canvassers, Board of, 191
Carolina, Charter of *1665*, 5; Fundamental Constitution of, *1669*, 13
Carteret, Sir George, 9, 11, 17, 66, 70, 114
Carteret, Philip, 17
Cases of law, against Proprietors, 119; change of venue in, 177, 205; proceedings in, 85-89, 121-123; after new Constitution takes effect, 190-191, 227-228, 232
  Civil, 89, 184; juries in, 166, 196; proceedings in, 85-88;
  Criminal, of impeached persons, 183; proceedings in, 59-60, 82, 87-88; rights of parties in, 161, 166-167, 195-196. *See also* Appeals; Trials.
Census, of N. J., 142; U. S., 170, 185, 200
Chance, games of, *see* Gambling.
Chancellor, Gov. as, 159; powers of, 180; of Courts, 182-183, 187
Chancery, powers of, 176
Charges, legal, 122, 166, 196
Charles I, 9
Charles II, 9, 128, 136
Checks and balances, 30, 36
Chief Justice of Supreme Court, administrative head of courts, 219, 231; presiding in impeachments, 221. *See also* Appeals; Judicial officer.
Christianity, conversions to, 148, 151
Christians, 61-62, 120, 142-143
Church, in political decisions, 37
Church of England, preference to, 20-21, 147-148. *See also*

Separation of Church and State.
Churches, 65, 147; taxes prohibited for, 161-162, 166, 195. *See also* Ministers.
Civil authority, over military, 167, 196
Civil service (N. J.), 219-220. *See also* Office, public.
Clemency, executive, 212
Clerks of courts, 192, 219, 233-234. *See also* Courts; Judicial officers.
Cloture, 14, 97
Collective bargaining, 4-5, 197
College of New Jersey, 24
Collins, Francis, 101
Collins, Isaac, 155
Colonies, 147, 156-157, 162; mutual aid of, 151-152; trade, 133-134, 153-154
Colonization, promotion of, 9-11, 61-66, 72-73, 75-79
Color, segregation by, 195
Commission on Revision of N. J. Constitution, 41, 43, 46
Commissioners of courts, 232
Commissioners of Province *(1677)*, 14-15; powers of, 72-75, 78-83, 87, 89-94; for interim government, 97
Commissions to public office, force of, 180-181, 192; form, 160, 188-189, 226-227; to judges, 184; militia officers, 185-186
Committee for the Preservation of the Publick Peace, 115-116
Committee on Preparatory Research for N. J. Constitutional Convention, 45-46
Committees, of Correspondence, 22, 26; of Council *(1683)*, 113-114; of Legislature, 202
Compromise, in framing constitutions, 2-4, 6, 47

Condemnation of property, for public use, 167, 176, 197, 203; for urban redevelopment, 224
Connecticut, trials of pirates in, 139-140
Conscience, freedom of, 12-14, 16, 18, 33. *See also* Bill of Rights; Religious freedom; Rights of individual.
Conscientious objectors, rights of, 115-117. *See also* Quakers.
Constables, 58, 82, 160. *See also* County officers.
Constitutions of New Jersey:
Concessions and Agreement of Proprietors of N. J., 1665, background of, 5, 9-11, 13-14, 17-18; effects of, 19, 21-22, 28, 114, 125; text, 51-66;
Declaration of . . . Intent . . . of Concessions, 1672, background of, 11, 17-18; text, 67-70;
Concessions and Agreements of Proprietors, Freeholders, and Inhabitants of West N. J., 1677, background of, 5-7, 11-16; effects, 3, 28, 48; inviolability, 83-84; text, 71-100; mentioned, 49, 105;
Fundamental Agreements of the Governor, Proprietors, Freeholders, and Inhabitants . . . of N. J., 1681, background, 15-16; not to be altered, 3, 106; text, 105-108;
Fundamental Constitutions for . . . East New-Jersey, 1683, background, 5, 18-20; conditions of repeal, 124; text, 109-125;
Instructions from Queen . . . to Governor of . . . N. J.,

1702, background, 20-22; text, 126-154;
Constitution of . . . N. J., *July 2, 1776*, background, 22-27; analysis, 13, 27-28, 31-33; public acceptance, 28-29; legislative construction and amendment of, 29-31; text, 155-162;
Constitution of . . . N. J., *1844* (as amended), background and analysis of, 21, 31-37; amendments to, and need for revision, 37-45; remnants in *1947* Const., 49; text, 164-192; amending, effect, and transition clauses, 189-192; text of amendments *(1875)*, 168, 169, 172, 175-180, 186, 187; *(1897)* 174, 181; *(1927* and *1939)* 174;
Constitution of . . . N. J., *1947* (as amended to Nov., *1961)*, background, 36-46; analysis, 4-5, 46-50; drafts, 41-44; text, 193-233; amending clause, 225-226; transition clauses, 227-234. *See also* Amendments; Bill of Rights; Fundamental Law.
Constitutional Conventions, question of authority for, 40-41; of *1844*, 34-35, 44, 165; of *1944*, 43-44; of *1947*, 20, 45-46, 48, 194
Constitutional Reform Act, *1947*, 45, 48
Constitutions of states, 23-24; regular revision of, 49
Continental Congress, 23, 25, 26, 156
Contracts, laws on, 175, 204
Conveyances, property, 52-53, 89-90, 121
Convoys, shipping, 146
Cornbury, Lord Edward, 126
Cornelious, Lause, 104

Cornelise, John, 102
Coroners, 58-59, 160. *See also* County officers.
Corporate rights, 35, 37-38
Corporations, 168, 190-191; legislation on, 176-177, 197, 205-206, 222, 224
Corruption of public office, 83, 161-162
Council of Proprietors of Western N. J., archives, xii, 70
Council. *See also* Executive.
  Under proprietors: *(1665)*, 52, 53, 57, 63-66; powers, 54, 55, 58-60; restraints on, 60-61, 66; *(1672)*, 68-70; *(1681)*, 106-108; *(1677), see* Commissioners of Province; *(1683)*, proposed Common Council of Eastern N. J., 18, 112, 117, 118, 120, 124; constituted, 113-114; committees of, 113, 115-116
  Under royal governor *(1702)*: 20, 127-131, 133; advice and consent of, 128, 130, 135, 138, 140, 143, 148, 153; powers, 149-152
Counsel, legal, no fees for, 88, 122; right to, 161, 167, 196
Counties, representation of, *see* Representation
County governments, 38, 74, 117, 176; corporations for, 38, 206; financial aid to corporations, 168, 224
County offices, appointments to, 181, 220, elections and terms for, 160, 187-188, 191-192, 220-221. *See also* Constables; Coroners; Officeholders; Sheriffs; Surrogates.
Courts (specific), Martial, 186; of Appeals, 117-118, 122-123, 159; of Common Pleas, 176, 192; of Common Right, 19-20; of Errors and Appeals,

242

180; of Exchequer, 140; Supreme, to determine a vacancy of Governship, 209. *See also* Appeals; Chief Justice; Judiciary.

Courts (general), circuit, 176; county, 176; inferior, clerks of, 192; of law and equity, 191; abolished and jurisdiction transferred from, 46, 216-217, 230-233; employees of, 233-234; rules and administration of, 215-219, 227. *See also* Appeals; Cases of Law; Trials.

Coxe, Daniel, 16

Creditors, relief of, 151

Crimes, capital, 88, 119, 123, 167, 196. *See also* Appeals; Cases of law; Impeachment; Murder; Penalties; Treason.

Criminals, denial of suffrage to, 168, 198

Cromwell, Oliver, 2

Daniel, Richard, 104
Daniel, William, 104
Davenport, Francis, 127
Deacon, George, 102, 127
Debtors, imprisonment of, 12, 167, 196
Debts, state, limitations on, 35, 37, 173-174, 223-224
Defense, of N. J., 18, 115-117, 145, 152; mutual, of colonies, 151-152. *See also* Fortifications; Militia.
Delaware River, 881
Democratic Party, 34, 44-45
Denna, John, 104
Deodands, prohibited, 94, 161
Descent, laws of, 176, 205
Devenish, Barnard, 104
Dickson, Anthony, 104
Discrimination, 195
Dissenters, religious, 10
Districting of province, 55-57,
95, 99, 111, 119. *See also* Proprieties.
Divorce, 174, 204
Doequet, Paul, 103
Driscoll, Gov. Alfred E., 45
Duties, customs, 146, 154; N. J.'s to equal N. Y.'s, 133-134; on wines, 135

Edge, Gov. Walter E., 43, 44
Edison, Gov. Charles, 40, 43, 44
Education, public, system of, 36, 38, 224-225; funds for, 175; legislation for, 177, 205; discrimination prohibited in, 195

Election, *1940* (N. J.), 40
Elections, annual, 23, 28, 55, 95-96, 157-158; bribery in, 95-96, 112, 169; and corporations for local government, 206; of Commissioners *(1677)*, 75; county officers, 160, 187-188, 191-192, 220-221; delegates to Legislature, 28, 55, 95-96, 111-113, 130-131, 157-158, 162, 169-171, 197-200, 228-229; Governor, 27, 158, 177-178, 180-181, 191, 207-209, 229; jurors, 119, 121-122; justices of the peace, 188; militia officers, 185-186; Proprietors, 119. *See also* Absentee voting; Ballot; Referendum; Suffrage.

Elizabeth I, Queen, 9
Emergency, national, 203-204
Eminent domain, right of, 197, 203
Emley, William, 101
Equal representation, in upper house, 20, 28, 36, 40, 43, 48-49, 157, 170, 199. *See also* Proportional representation.

Escheats and forfeitures, 94, 136,

161; redemption of, 123-124

Estates, attachment of, 86, 92; securing, 93-94; transfers, 89-90. See also Forfeitures; Property.

Eumenes (pseudonym of William Griffith) 30

Everson, Hendrick, 103

Eves, Thomas, 105

Examiners, court, 232

Exchange, rate of, 135

Executive branch, comparative authority of, 9-12, 14-20, 23, 27-30, 36, 37, 39, 41-43, 46; departments, administration and organization of, 37, 39, 41-43, 46, 213-214; their allocation, 229-230. See also Commissioners of Province; Council; Government; Governor.

Farrington, John, 101

Fees, 121, 140; to prison officers, 88

Felony, 88, 159, 172

Fenimore, Richard, 105

Fenton, Eliazer, 105

Fenwick, John, 11

Finance, state, 173-174, 221-224; for public education, 175, 224-225. See also Appropriations; Debts; Money; Revenue; Taxation; Treasury.

Fines, 132, 167, 196; appeals of, 150; powers concerning, 136, 180, 212

Fishing, 81

Forfeiture, of estates, 94, 123-124, 161; powers concerning, 136, 180, 212; of proprietorships, 119.

Forgery, 123

Forrist, John, 103

Fortifications, 57, 65, 114-115

Franchises, granting of, 176

Franklin, William, 26

Fraud, 14, 89, 153-154; in elections, 95-96, 112; penalty for, 167, 196

Freeholders, rights of, 9, 14, 55, 59, 69, 75, 160; property requirements for, 18, 68, 112, 131; and residency requirements, 157-158; relations with Indians, 90-91. See also Constitutions; Land Tenure, Property.

French, Thomas, 104

French-Indian Wars, 146

Fundamental law in N. J., evolution of, 2-51; question of altering, 3-4, 8, 14-16, 29-30, 40, 47-50, 165, 194-195; asserted inviolate, 83-84, 106; confusion with legislative acts, 4-8, 29-31, 47, 49-50; laws of 1665-1702, background of, 9-22, 26. See also Amendments; Bill of Rights; Constitutions; Rights of individual.

Gambling, 39, 174-175, 204

Gardner, Thomas, 105

General Assembly: for joint provisions for both houses, *see* Legislature.

(1665), 55-58; advice and consent of, 59, 60; delegates to, 55, 60; obligations, 53-54, 63; powers, 54-58, 63;

(1672), powers limited by Executive, 68-70;

(1677), under Quakers, 83, 94-99; delegates to, 75, 95-96, 97; obligations, 84, 96; powers of, 74, 78, 81-83, 87, 89, 94, 97-99; restraints, 83-84; voting, 96, 97;

(1681), restraining Executive, 106-108;

(1683), see Great Council;

(1702), under royal governor, 130-133; delegates to, 130-131, 133; including Quakers, 142; powers of, 131-137, 142, 143, 148, 150-152; obligations, 135, 141; restraints on, 134-137;
(1776), 157-159, 161-162;
(1844), delegates, 169-173; reapportionment of, 170; special powers, 173, 182-183;
(1947), members, 199-202; special powers of, 203, 221. *See also* Officeholders; Representation.
General Assembly, session of *1890*, and special legislation, 39
General Assembly, Speaker of, 102, 158, 172, 180, 201, 208
George III, 156
Georgia, constitution of, 29
Glebes, 147
Gold mines, 65, 124
Goldmann, Sidney, 45
Gosling, John, 105
Government, compromise in framing, 2-4, 6; and innovation in, 7-8, 47, 49-50; concern with purposes of, 30, 32, 35-36; John Adams' plan for, 24. *See also* Fundamental law; Officeholders.
Government (N. J.):
background of, proprietary, 9-20; provincial, 20-22, 26; state, 22-50;
financial aid to corporations, 168;
in national emergency, 203-204;
powers of, concentrated in Legislature, 27-28; separation of, 36, 169, 198; limited, rather than granted, 41;
question of altering, 8, 14-16, 47-50, 106, 165, 194-195;

support of, 99, 132-133, 222-223. *See also* Constitutions; County government; Executive; Judiciary; Legislature; Municipal governments.
Governor:
(1665) consent of, 57, 58; obligations, 53, 56, 63-66; powers, 52-55, 58-59; restraints on, 60-61, 66; support of, 58;
(1672) powers of, 68-70;
(1681) restraints on, 106-108;
(1683) proposals for, 110-111, 114, 117-118, 122, 124;
(1702) Queen's instructions to, 126-154;
(1776) limited powers of, 157-160;
(1844) 177-181, 189, 191; powers of appointment, 171, 172, 185-189;
(1947) 207-214, 223, 226-227; action on bills, 210-212; administration of Executive Departments, 213-214, 229-230; election and terms of, 197, 202, 207-209, 229; impeachment, 221; powers, 199, 200, 209-210, 212; especially, of appointment, 210, 217-218, 220, 234. *See also* Commissioners of Province; Executive; Veto power.
Great Britain, 22, 156, 162
Great Council *(1683)*, delegates to, 111-113, 120, 121; powers, 113-117, 119, 121, 124; voting in, 113-114, 118-120, 124
Griffith, William, 30
Grubb, John, 104
Guy, Richard, 102

Habeas corpus, 33, 167, 196
Hague, Frank, 44, 45
Haig, William, 101
Hancock, Godfrey, 104

245

Harding, Thomas, 104
Harris, John, 101
Hartshorne, Richard, 12
Haselwood, George, 103
Hedge, Samuel, 104
Helmsley, Joseph, 73, 74
Henry VIII, 140
Heretics, 120
Herman, Casper, 102
Heulings, Abraham, 104
Heulings, William, 102
Hooton, Thomas, 102
Horse racing, 39, 174-175
Hudson County, 44
Hughes, William, 103
Hunlock, Edward, 127
Hunting, 81
Hutchinson, George, 73, 74, 104
Hutchinson, Thomas, 73, 74
Hyde, Edward, 20

Immunity, legislative, 172, 202
Impeachment, 167, 195-196; of civil officers, 160, 180-181, 221; powers of, 182-183, 221
Impressment of seamen, 143-144
Imprisonment, protection against, 85-86, 121; for debts, 12, 167, 196. *See also* Accused; Arrest.
Indemnity, 167, 196
Indians, dealings with, for land, 72, 137; Quakers' fairness in, 90-92; under royal governor, 147, 150-152; war against, 57, 153
Indictments, form of, 158, 189; required, 167, 195-196; effective under new Constitutions, 191, 227-228
Industrial Revolution, 31
Investigations of Executive Departments, 214

Jacksonian era, 2-3, 31-36
Jacobson, Gruna, 105
James I, 9

James II, 20
Jansen, Aert, 102
Jansen, Claas, 103
Jefferson, Thomas, 23, 25; on altering constitutions, 2, 8, 35-36; on rights of man, 50
Jenings, Henry, 103
Jennings, Samuel, 13, 15, 102, 108, 127
Jersey City, 37-38, 44
Johnson, William, 102
Jonson, William Gill, 103
Journals, of Queen's Council, *(1702)*, 130, 136; of General Assembly, 136; of both houses of Legislature, 171, 179, 189-190, 201, 210, 225-226
Judges and Justices, *see* Judicial officers
Judicial officers, 217-219, 230-234; Commissioners serving as, 14, 87; of Court of Appeals, 117-118, 122-123, 159; of Court of Errors and Appeals, 180; appointment, elections, and terms of, 28, 98, 159-160, 184-189; conduct of office, 81-82, 160; impeachment of, 183, 218; ineligible for Legislature, 202; powers of, 149-150, 180; powers to appoint and regulate, 58-59, 81-82, 202; to remove, 138; protected from Executive review, 214; to hold no other office, 161, 173. *See also* Appeals; Chief Justice; Courts; Judiciary; Justices of the Peace; Officeholders.
Judiciary, disallowing special legislation, 38-39; power to constitute, 56-57, 68-69, 98, 140; provisions of *1665* for, retained, 125; weakness of, in *1776* Constitution, 28, 30;

provisions of *1844* for, 169, 181-185; need to simplify, 42, 43; of *1947* Constitution, 46-47, 198, 215-217; to effect changes of, 5, 230-234. *See also* Appeals; Chief Justice; Courts; Government, powers; Judicial officers.

Juries, and care of orphans, 94; eligibility for, 150; in law cases, 85-88, 92-93, 121-122, 166-167, 195, 196; when Indians involved, 91; when Proprietors, 119; special legislation on, 176, 205. *See also* Trial.

Justices of the Peace, 138, 159, 167; eligible for Assembly, 161-162; proportional to population, 184-185, 188. *See also* Judicial officers; Officeholders.

Kemble, Robert, 102
Kent, Thomas, 103
Kent, William, 101
King of England, allegiance to, 53-54, 124; right of appeal to, 69

Labor, 37, 44; right to organize, 4-5, 197
Lackerouse, Michael, 103
Lambert, John, 102
Lambert, Thomas, 102
Land:
  Conveyances of, recording, 52-53, 89, 121;
  Gifts of, by governing bodies to corporations, 168, 234;
  Grants of,
    for public use, 65-66, 80 vacating, 176, 205; for settlement, 52-53, 58, 61-66, 72-73, 75-80; allocation of, 61-64, 69, 76-79; certifying, 52-53, 59, 64-65, 69, 74, 79, 80; subdividing, 66, 69, 72, 74, 79-80;
  Tenure of, stipulations, 62-63, 65, 77-79; protected, 10, 60, 81, 123; qualifying Proprietors for government, 118-120.
  See also Freeholders; Plantations; Property; Proprieties; Surveys.

Lands, grazing by cattle on, 60-61; purchases of Indian, 72, 91-92, 137; Proprietors' shares of, 118-120; sale of minors', 176, 205; securing titles to, 125, 135-136; unprofitable, 137

Laswall, William, 105
Laurie (Lawry), Gawen, 74, 101
Laws, existing, compilation and revision of, 131, 162, 204; execution of, 153-154, 209-210; force of, 83, 162, 190-191, 227. *See also* Acts; Bills; Constitutions; Fundamental law; Legislation.

Leaming, Aaron, and Jacob Spicer, *Grants, Concessions, and . . . Constitutions of . . . N. J.*, cited, ix, x, xi, 21, 22, 51, 67, 105, 109, 126
Leeds, Daniel, 105, 127
Lefever, Hipolitas, 103
Legal documents, 89, 121
Legislation:
  Action, by Governor and Legislature, *see* Bills
  Confused with fundamental law, 4-8, 29, 47, 49;
  Prescribed, 55-58, 83, 98-99, 119-120, 131, 133, 136-137, 141-143, 148, 150-152, 169, 173-177, 185-186, 192, 198, 203-206, 213-214, 218, 222-225, 227, 229-230; force of, 56, 124, 135, 176; form and

unity of subject, 114, 131-134, 160, 175, 204;
Prohibited, 83-84; 106-107, 113, 135-137, 162, 166, 173-175, 195-196, 198, 204, 223; or alteration or repeal of, 124, 173, 222; special, 4-5, 37-38, 175-177, 204-206. *See also* Amendments; Appropriations; Money bills; Legislature, powers of.
Legislative construction, 14, 29-31
Legislative Council *(1776)*, 157-160, 162; Vice-President of, 191
Legislature, session of *1944*, as Constitutional Convention, 43-44; of *1947*, barring reapportionment, 48
Legislature:
 Under proprietary government *(1665)* 9-10, 21; *(1672)* in conflict with Executive, 17-18; under Quaker trusteeship *(1677)*, 12-16; *(1681)* limiting power of Executive, 15-16; *(1683)* proposals for, 18-19;
 Under royal governor *(1702)*, 20-21;
 Of state government
 (1776) broad powers of, 27-30, 157-162;
 (1844) certain powers circumscribed, 35-36; abuses by, 37-39; proposed revisions of, 39-41; question of, as constituent assembly, 40, 41; constituted, 169-177; delegates to, 169-173, 177, 192; powers of, 166-169, 173-178, 185-187, 189-190; restraints on, 166, 172-177, 179;
 (1947) provisions for, 46, 198-207; delegates to, 197, 199-202, 206-208, 210-212, 214, 228-229; obligations of, 200, 203-204, 206, 214, 223-224; powers, 196, 198, 202-210, 213, 220, 222-226, 229-230; protected from Executive, 209-210, 214; restraints on, 195-196, 202, 204-208, 222-224, 226.
 See also General Assembly; Government, powers; Great Council; Legislative Council; Provincial Congress; Senate; Voting.
Leonard, Samuel, 127
Libel, 166, 195
Lieber, Francis, 32
Livingston, Gov. William, 29, 30
Locke, John, 13
London, Bishop of, 147-148
Lotteries, 174-175. *See also* Gambling.
Lovet, Samuel, 104
Lucas, Nicholas, 74, 101

Maddocks, John, 103
Maiming, 150-151
Malfeasance. *See* Officeholders
Map of N. J., 138
Marcks, Thomas, 103
Marketplaces, 99
Marque, commissions of, 149
Marriages, 123, 148
Marriot, Isaac, 104
Martial law, 143
Mason, George, 25
Master, William, 104
Masters, Advisory, 231-232
Masters, mistreatment by, 150-151
Matthews, Richard, 101
Mental incompetence, legal determination of, 196
Merchants (Br.), 146
Mew, Richard, 101
Meyor, E., 104
Military authority, subordinate to civil, 167, 196

Military forces, civil service preference to, 219-220; criminal offenses in, 167, 195; quartering of, 167, 196; voting by, 168, 198
Military forces (N. J.), command of, 178, 210; raising, 69, 107, 114-116, 152. *See also* Defense; Militia.
Militia, fines, 167, 196; fitness for service in, 142; powers concerning, 9, 15, 57, 59, 185-186, 213; officers, 159, 229; segregation in, 195; training of, 114-116, 152-153. *See also* Defense.
Mills, Daniel, 101
Mines, profits from, 65, 124
Ministers, appointments of, 54-55, 68; preference to Anglican, 147-148; lands for, 65; taxes for support of, 161-162, 166, 195. *See also* Separation of church and state.
Minors, lands of, 176, 205
Money bills, 56, 99, 113, 133, 158, 173, 203. *See also* Amendments.
Money, public, grants of, 133-134; accounts of, 135; for sectarian uses, 38. *See also* Appropriations; Finance; Revenue; Treasury.
Monmouth County, 34
Monopolies, 35, 148
Morgan, Richard, 103
Morris, Lewis, 127
Mortgages, 89-90, 176
Municipal governments, corporations for, 38, 206; aid to corporations, 168, 224; party control of, 44; provisions for, 38, 74, 117, 176. *See also* Justices of the Peace; Officeholders.
Municipalities, and urban redevelopment, 224; zoning ordinances of, 174, 203. *See also* Townships; Wards.
Murder, 88, 121; penalty for, 94, 150-151

Naturalization, 58
Navy, British, 143-145
Negroes, 148-151; and suffrage, 31, 168
Nelthorp, Edward, 101
Nevill, James, 102
New Brunswick, 194, 234
N. J. Bureau of Archives and History, 67, 105, 155, 164
N. J. Committee for Constitutional Convention, 41, 43-45
N. J. Constitutional Foundation, 42-43
New Jersey, development of fundamental law in, 2-8; under proprietary government, 9-11, 51-66, 67-70; divided, 11; western division, 11-16, 71-100, 105-108; eastern, 16-20, 109-125; under royal governor, 20, 126-154; divisions, in opposition, 128, 130; their representatives in government, 129-131; in transition to independence, 22-29; as state, 155-163; impulses for stronger Executive, 29-31; imbalance of powers redressed, 164-192; economy of, in Jacksonian era, 35-36; under legislative abuses during Industrial Revolution, 37-39; moves in, for revision of old Constitution, 40-51; under present Constitution, 193-233
New York, and N. J.'s trade exemptions, 133-134; defense of, 151-152; trial of pirates in, 139-140
Newbold, John, 104
Nicholson, Samuel, 103

Oaths or affirmations, of office, 53-54, 83, 96, 124-125, 128, 137-138, 161-162, 177, 206-207, 219; special law for Quakers, 141-142; on search warrants, 166, 195; of Senate in impeachments, 183

Offices, public, constituted *(1844)*, 186-189; *(1947)*, 219-221, 229; eligibility for, 129; of Quakers, 21, 142; persons excluded from, 11, 17, 68, 87, 88, 95-96, 112-113, 120, 148, 172, 202, 218; religion no bar to, 108, 166, 195; religious test for, 18, 120, 161; rotation of, 111, 113; vacancies in, 138-139, 180-181, 191, 192, 203-204; power of appointment, diffused, 36; by Legislature, 21, 98, 108, 159-160, 187, 220; by Executive, 69, 117, 138-139, 178; and Senate, 180-181, 186-187, 210; by Civil Service, 219-220

Officeholders, 82, 121, 220; elections, 98, 158, 197-198; power to remove, 138-139; salaries, terms, and perquisites, 132-133, 159-160, 176, 205, 220, 229; subject to Executive authority, 58-59, 213-214; to hold no other office, 121, 138, 161-162, 169, 173, 179-180, 198, 202, 207; misconduct of, 53-54, 58-59, 83, 114, 117, 121, 138-139, 183; of Judges, 81-82, 98; of Legislators, 96, 172, 200-201, 202; impeachment for, 160, 180, 183, 221; investigations of Executive Department for, 214. *See also* Executive; Freeholders; Judicial officers; Legislature; County officers; Justices of the Peace; Municipal governments; Property qualification.

Oldale, Samuel, 105
Ollive, Thomas, 101, 108
Ordinances, local, 206. *See also* Zoning ordinances.
Orphans, 93-94
Outhout, Foppe, 102
Overseers, mistreatment by, 150-151

Page, Anthony, 104
Paine, John, 104, 105
Paine, Thomas, 8, 23, 24
Pancoast, John, 105
Pardon, power of, 60, 82, 88, 117, 159, 180, 198, 212
Pari-mutuel betting, 39, 174-175
Parker, Joel, 38
Parliament (Br.), 153-154; Acts of, 133, 176
Parole system, 213
Paterson, William, 24-25, 155, 162
Peachee, William, 101
Pearce, James, 102
Pearson, Thomas, 73, 74
Pedrick, Rodger, 103
Peirce, Thomas, 103
Peiterson, Walter, 104
Penalties, for crimes, 12, 59, 87-88, 107, 123-124, 141, 150, 168, 198; "cruel and unusual," 167, 196. *See also* Fines; Forfeitures; Impeachment; Maiming.
Penford, John, 101
Penn, William, 2, 12, 17; and Quakers' government for western N. J., 3, 5, 6, 11-15, 34, 74, 101
Pennsylvania, constitutions of, 5, 29
Pension plans, 218
Penton, William, 104
Perjury, 87-88, 123
Perth Amboy, 20, 130-131

Petition, right of, 33, 66, 167-168, 197
Petty, John, 104
Pinhorne, William, 127
Pirates, 139-140
Plaintiffs, in law cases, 85-86, 88, 122
Plantations, Council's committee on, 18, 113; settling of, promoted, 61-65, 72-73, 75-79; cultivation and profits of, 136-138, 149. *See also* Colonization; Land grants.
Pledger, John, 102
Plese, Turrse, 102
Plowden, Sir Edmund, 9
Police power (N. J.), 174, 203
Political parties, 34-35, 37, 43-45
Pomfret, John, 13
Poor, workhouses for, 151
Ports, establishment of, 57, 99
Powell, Robert, 104
Presidential electors, 191
Press, freedom of, 33, 166, 195; limited, 153
Prince George of Denmark, 143-145
Princeton, N. J., 24-25, 155
Prison inspectors, 187
Prisoners, 86, 88, 123
Property:
 Condemnation of, 167, 176, 197, 203, 224;
 Qualification, for office and suffrage, 9, 11, 17, 18, 31, 68, 112-113, 131, 157-158; for jurors, 150; Rights, 10, 32; protection of, 85, 94, 107, 121, 125, 136-137, 141, 161;
 Theft of, 92;
 Transfers, 52-53, 89-90, 121
 See also Estates; Freeholders; Land Tenure.
Proportional representation, 158, 170, 200
Proprieties, 72-73, 75, 95, 118-119

Proprietors of West New Jersey, records of, 105
Proprietors, 119, 122; powers of, 56, 89, 90, 117-118; proxies, 111-119, 124; rents due to, 58, 76-79, 82, 137;
 Lands of, 56, 60-61, 137; grants of, to, them, 73, 78-79; rights to, 66, 136-137;
 Rights of, 53, 54, 56, 70, 115-117, 124; of government, 110, 111, 113-114, 124; shares of, 118-120, 125; surrendered to people, 11-15, 49, 71-100; to crown, 20.
 See also Constitutions; Land Grants.
Prosecutors, 161. *See also* County officers; Officeholders.
Protestants, 161-162. *See also* Religious freedom; Separation of Church and State.
Provincial Congresses, of colonies, 22; of N. J., 23-29, 155-157, 162
Public Records Office, 126
Public welfare, taxation for, 99
Punishments, *see* Penalties
Puritans, 16, 19, 120-121

Quakers, frame of government, 5-8, 11-16, 34, 71-100; their influence on religious freedom, 6; in eastern N. J., 18; rights of, 21, 115-117, 120, 141-142. *See also* Oaths or affirmations; Religious freedom.
Quary, Robert, 127

Railroads, 35, 177, 205
Raleigh, Sir Walter, 9
Ratification, *see* Amendments; Bills; Referendum
Reapportionment, legislative, *see* Representation

Rebellion, of *1672* (eastern N. J.), 11, 17, 18
Reeve, Mark, 103
Referendum Act, 43
Referendum, on state debts, 173-174, 223; on constitutional amendments, 190, 225-226; gambling, 204, on revision of *1844* Constitution, 43, 45, 48-49; times of holding, 197
Register, recording land and property conveyances, 52-53, 64-65, 74, 79-80, 91-92, 137; and business transactions, 89-90, 121; marriages, 123; fees of, 80. *See also* Secretary.
Religious freedom, in colonies, 5; in N. J., guarantees of, under proprietors, 10, 54-56, 68; under Quakers, 6-7, 11-15, 84-85, 108; atheists excluded from, 18, 120; Catholics excluded from, 20, 21, 141-142; to all, 27, 161-162, 165-166, 195. *See also* Church of England; Quakers; Separation of Church and State.
Religious test for office, 18, 120, 161-162; prohibited, 108, 165-166, 195
Rents due to Proprietors, 58, 65-66, 76-79, 80, 82, 137
Representation in Legislature, equal in upper house, 20, 28, 36, 40, 43, 48-49, 157, 170, 199; equal in lower house, 95, 111, 130-131; proportional, 158, 170, 200
Reprieve, power of, 59-60, 82, 117, 180, 212
Reprisal, commissions of, 149
Republican Party, 43-44
Resolutions before Legislature, 171, 201
Revell, Thomas, 105, 127

Revenue, under royal governor, 133-136, 140-141; from horse racing, 174; power to raise, 9, 10, 22, 56, 60, 82, 99, 108, 113, 133-134, 158, 173, 203; Quakers' shares of, 117. *See also* Assessments; Duties; Finance; Taxation; Treasury.
Rhode Island, charter of, 5, 33
Riders, *see* Legislation
Rights of individual, fundamental laws for, 2-8; under proprietary government, 10, 17, 18, 54, 58, 66, 68; under Quakers, 11-16, 83-88, 97, 114-117, 121; royal governor, 140-142, 153; under state government, 33, 161-162, 165-169, 194-197; need for new safeguards of, 47-51; in law cases, 85-89, 121-123, 161. *See also* Bill of Rights; Fundamental law; Office; Religious freedom; Suffrage.
Roads, land for, 65, 80, 167; work on, and vacating of, 176, 205
Roberts, John, 105
Robison, Richard, 103
Roll calls, of voting in Legislature, 14, 97, 171, 201
Roman Catholics, 19, 20, 141, 161-162
Royal African Company of England, 148-149
Roydon, William, 101
Rudyard, George, 101
Rumsey, William, 103
Rutgers University, 45, 194, 234

Salaries, of Governor, 178, 209; of Judges, 182, 218; of Legislature, 171-172, 192, 201-202; of public officeholders, 133, 140, 176, 220
Sanders, Christopher, 102
Sandford, William, 127

Schooley, Thomas, 105
Scott, Benjamin, 101
Seal of N. J., 159, 189, 226
Seamen, impressment of, 143-144
Searches and seizures, 166, 195
Secretary (N. J.), 69, 114, 117, 136; Provincial, 159-160; of State, 164, 182, 183, 191, 193, 213-214, 226; as auditor of accounts, 189. *See also* Register.
Sectarianism in constitutional reform, 44
Sedgwick, Theodore, 32
Seizures, *see* Searches and seizures
Senate (constituted *1844* and *1947*), delegates to, 169-170, 178, 181, 199, 228; advice and consent of, in Executive appointments, 180-181, 185-188, 210, 213, 214, 217-218, 230, 234; special powers of, 173, 182-183, 203, 221; for joint provisions for both houses, *see* Legislature. *See also* Legislative Council; Representation.
Senate, President of, 172, 180-181, 201, 208, 221
Separation of church and state, 6, 20-21, 33, 38, 161-162, 166, 195. *See also* Religious freedom.
Separation of powers, 36, 169, 198
Sergeant, Jonathan Dickinson, 24, 25
Servants, 121, 142-143; size of land grants based on number held, 61-62, 65, 76-79; mistreatment of, 150-151
Seventeenth century, spirit of, 2
Shaftesbury, Earl of, 13
Shennek, Andrew, 103
Sheriffs, 88, 112, 122; elections and terms of, 160. *See also* County officers; Officeholders.
Shipping, in colonial trade, 145-146. *See also* Trade.
Ships, involuntary passengers of, 92; of British Navy, 143-145
Silver mines, 65, 124
Slavery, 148-151. *See also* Servants.
Slum clearance, 224
Smart, Isaac, 103
Smith, Daniel, 103
Smith, John, 102
Smith, Richard, 101
Smith, Thomas, 102
Smith, William, xi
Smuggling, 146
Snowden, John, 105
Society for Useful Manufactures, 35
Special legislation, 4-5, 37; laws controlling, 37-38, 175-177, 204-206
Speech, freedom of, 166, 195
Spicer, Jacob, *see* Leaming and Spicer
Stacy, Henry, 102
Stacy, Mahlon, 73, 74, 102
Stacy, Robert, 101
States, constitutions of, 23-24, 47
Stockton, Richard, 24, 25
Stokes, Thomas, 104
Stubbens, Henry, 103
Subpoena power, 166-167, 196. *See also* Witnesses.
Suffrage, under proprietary government, 9, 11, 17, 18; its extension, in N. J., 31; in other states, 33; constitutional provisions for, 68, 75, 95, 112-113, 131, 157-158, 168-169, 197-198. *See also* Ballot; Elections; Property qualification; Referendum.
Suicides, 94, 161

Summons, legal, 85-86, 122
Surege, John, 102
Surrogate General, 159, 183
Surrogates, county, 181. *See also* County officers; Officeholders.
Surveyor General, 53, 69, 74, 79-80, 137-138
Surveys, land, 58, 69; procedures in, 63-66; protection against review of, 10, 60, 81, 123. *See also* Land grants.

Taxation, for orphans, 94; for churches, prohibited, 161-162, 166, 195; exemptions from, 65-66, 80, 137, 221-222, 224; rates of, and assessments for, 49, 221-222; special legislation, 205; without representation, 22. *See also* Assessments; Money bills; Revenue.
Taxes, payment of, to Governor, 108; required for suffrage, 31
Theft, penalties for, 92-93
Thompson, Andrew, 103
Thompson, John, 102
Tomesen, Jillis, 103
Towle, Percival, 101
Towns, in western N. J., 73, 74, 99
Townships, elections of officers, 160, 188; of justices of the peace, 184-185. *See also* Constables; Coroners; Justices of the Peace; Municipal governments; Officeholders.
Trade and Plantations, Queen's Commissioners for, 129-130, 132, 135-136, 138-142, 145-146, 149, 153
Trade, committee of Council on, 18, 113-114
Trade, 145-146, 148-149; customs duties in N. Y. and N. J., 133-134; with Indians, 151; abuses in colonial, 153-154
Transportation, school, 225
Treason, 88, 212; by members of Legislature, 172, 202; forfeiture of estates for, 123-124; pardon of, 159; power to punish, 94; what constitutes, 14, 84, 107, 167, 196-197
Treasurer (Receiver), 133, 187, 189; Provincial, 159-160; High (Br.), 134-136
Treasury, Committee of Council on, 113-114; Queen's Commissioners of, 134-136, 145; accounts of, 98; receipts of, 123, 124, 220, 224; withdrawals from, 94, 171, 173, 222. *See also* Finance; Money; Revenue.
Treaties and alliances, 108
Trenton, 165, 192
Trial by jury, right of, 16, 27, 28, 33, 85, 121, 162, 166, 196
Trials, 107; involving Indians, 91; pirates, 139-140; proceedings in, 85-89, 121-123, 166-167, 196; Proprietors, 119; review of, 60, 82. *See also* Accused; Appeals, Cases of law; Impeachment.
Tucker, Samuel, 155, 162
Twentieth century, 3, 4; threats to individual freedom in, 7-8

U. S. Congress, members of, 179-180, 202, 207; N. J. delegates to, 172-173, 191; powers of, 41
U. S. *Constitution*, 29, 41, 48, 217
U. S. Constitutional Convention *(1787)*, 34
U. S. Government, funds on de-

posit with N. J., 173, 223; offices of, 172-173, 180, 202
U. S. Supreme Court, decision on legislative reapportionment, 48 n. *See also* Representation.
U. S. Veterans Administration, 222
Urban redevelopment, 224

Vanhighst, Abraham, 103
Vanhurst, Reneare, 102
Van Jumne, Gerret, 102
Venue, changes of, 177, 205
Veterans, tax exemptions for, 222
Vethake, Henry, 32
Veto power, 14, 36, 42, 46, 179, 211
Vicary, James, 103
Vice, discouragement of, 120-121, 148
Virginia Company, 9
Virginia, Constitution, 25; Constitutional Convention *(1831)*, 33
Voting in Legislature, 97, 113, 118, 124, 171, 201 *See also* Amendments; Bills

Wade, Samuel, 102
Walker, Samuel, 127
War, power to make, 15, 107, 115, 143, 153 185, 188
Wards, elections of officers, 184-185, 188

Warne, Joseph, 103
Warner, William, 103
Watson, Thomas, 103
Web, Edward, 102
Welfare, public, 32, 99
White, Christopher, 103
White, John, 105
Wilkinson, William, 103
Wilkison, Richard, 102
Willis, William, 103
Williams, Roger (of Rhode Island), 5
Wills, legal, 93-94, 148
Wilson, Woodrow, 39
Wines, duties on, 135
Witherspoon, John, 25
Witnesses, in law cases, 86-88, 123, 161, 166-167, 196
Women, 39, 227
Wood, John, 105
Woodhouse, Anthony, 105
Woodrofe, Thomas, 102
Woollison, Woolley, 104
Workhouses, for poor, 151
Worlidge, John, 104
Wright, Joshua, 101
Wright, R., 104
Writs, form of, 152, 160, 189, 227; of election, 200; of error, 182, 184; habeas corpus, 167, 196; prerogative, 217

York, Duke of, 9, 11, 13, 15, 17, 110, 136-137

Zane, Robert, 104
Zoning ordinances, 39, 174, 203

THE NEW JERSEY HISTORICAL SERIES
Published Under the Auspices of
STATE OF NEW JERSEY TERCENTENARY COMMISSION

Paul L. Troast, *Chairman*   Charles E. Farrington, *Vice-Chairman*
David S. Davies, *Executive Director* Roger H. McDonough, *Secretary*
      Kenneth Chorley   Marion West Higgins
      Mrs. A. R. Green   Clifford L. Lord
      Frederick H. Groel   John T. Soja
      Anthony J. Grossi   Richard R. Stout
           William A. Wachenfeld

Date Due

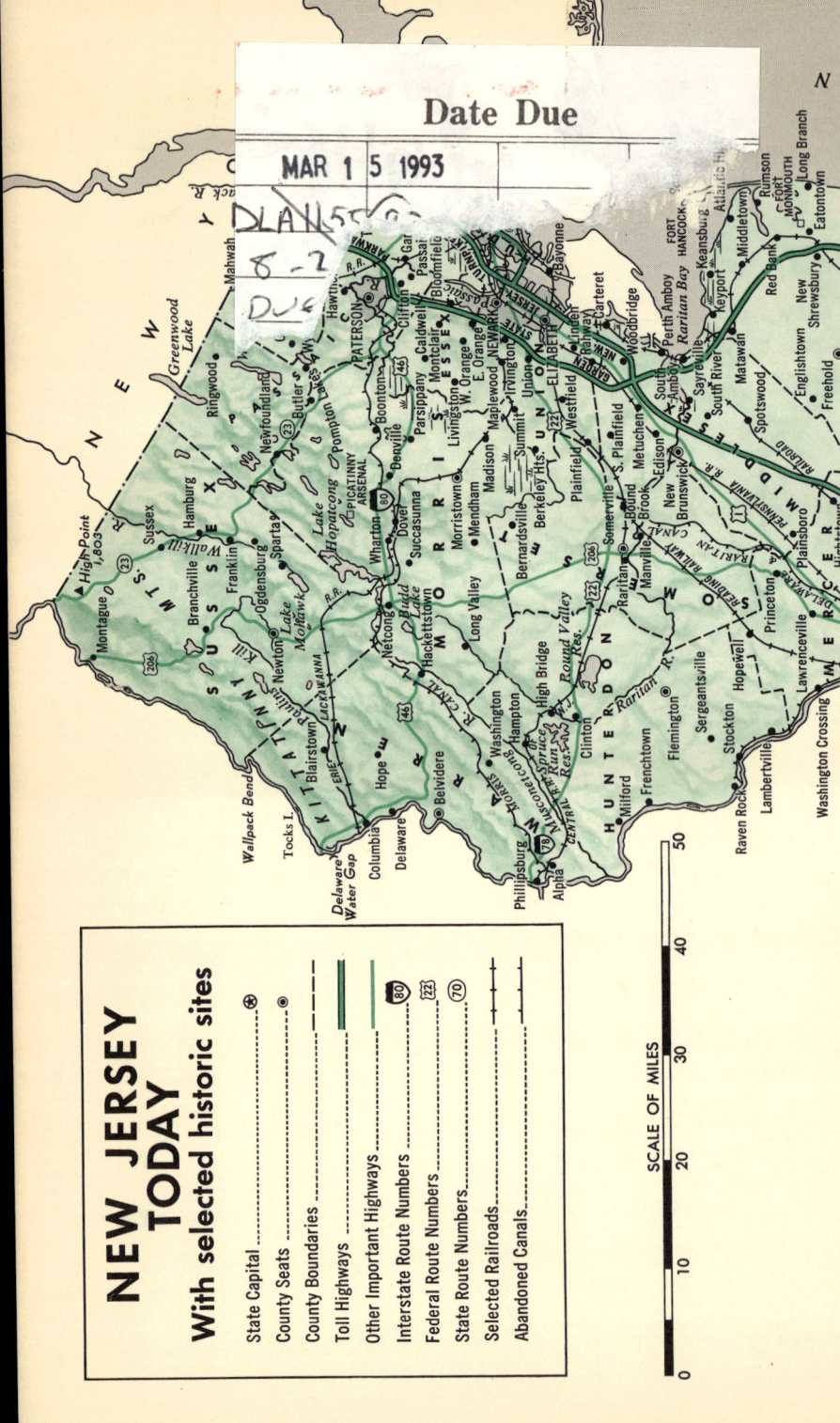

MAR 15 1993

NEW JERSEY TODAY
With selected historic sites

State Capital ⊛
County Seats ⊙
County Boundaries
Toll Highways
Other Important Highways
Interstate Route Numbers 🛡 80
Federal Route Numbers ⬡ 22
State Route Numbers ◯ 70
Selected Railroads
Abandoned Canals

SCALE OF MILES
0 10 20 30 40 50